ns Alexander Hamilton

Other books by Samantha Wilcoxson

Nonfiction
Women of the American Revolution

Historical Fiction
But One Life: The Story of Nathan Hale
Luminous: The Story of a Radium Girl
Plantagenet Princess, Tudor Queen: The Story of Elizabeth of York
Faithful Traitor: The Story of Margaret Pole
Queen of Martyrs: The Story of Mary I
The Last Lancastrian: A Story of Margaret Beaufort (novella)
Once a Queen: A Story of Elizabeth Woodville (novella)
Prince of York: A Story of Reginald Pole (novella)

James Alexander Hamilton

Son of the American Revolution

Samantha Wilcoxson

First published in Great Britain in 2025 by
Pen & Sword History
An imprint of Pen & Sword Books Limited
Yorkshire – Philadelphia

Copyright © Samantha Wilcoxson 2025

ISBN 978 1 39905 908 4

The right of Samantha Wilcoxson to be identified as
Author of this Work has been asserted by her in accordance
with the Copyright, Designs and Patents Act 1988.

A CIP catalogue record for this book is
available from the British Library

All rights reserved. No part of this book may be reproduced or
transmitted in any form or by any means, electronic or mechanical
including photocopying, recording or by any information storage and
retrieval system, without permission from the Publisher in writing.

Typeset by Mac Style
Printed in the UK by CPI Group (UK) Ltd, Croydon, CR0 4YY.

Pen & Sword Books Limited incorporates the imprints of After
the Battle, Atlas, Archaeology, Aviation, Discovery, Family History,
Fiction, History, Maritime, Military, Military Classics, Politics,
Select, Transport, True Crime, Air World, Frontline Publishing, Leo
Cooper, Remember When, Seaforth Publishing, The Praetorian Press,
Wharncliffe Local History, Wharncliffe Transport, Wharncliffe True
Crime and White Owl.

For a complete list of Pen & Sword titles please contact

PEN & SWORD BOOKS LIMITED
47 Church Street, Barnsley, South Yorkshire, S70 2AS, England
E-mail: enquiries@pen-and-sword.co.uk
Website: www.pen-and-sword.co.uk
or
PEN AND SWORD BOOKS
1950 Lawrence Road, Havertown, PA 19083, USA
E-mail: uspen-and-sword@casematepublishers.com
Website: www.penandswordbooks.com

For all those whose names have been forgotten but whose lives helped forge the world we are blessed to live in today.

Contents

Acknowledgments		ix
Chapter 1	Son of a Founding Father	1
Chapter 2	Coming of Age	11
Chapter 3	Washington's Farewell Address	19
Chapter 4	Secretary of State	25
Chapter 5	The Eaton Scandal	40
Chapter 6	District Attorney	45
Chapter 7	Defending Hamilton's Bank	50
Chapter 8	Nullification Crisis	59
Chapter 9	Family Life	63
Chapter 10	Nevis	67
Chapter 11	The Great Fire of 1835	71
Chapter 12	Hamilton in Europe	74
Chapter 13	Portents of War	84
Chapter 14	Hamilton in Russia	87
Chapter 15	Texas and Mexico	94
Chapter 16	Hamilton in Europe II	99

Chapter 17	America's Cup	106
Chapter 18	The 1853 Crystal Palace Exhibition	111
Chapter 19	Family Life II	113
Chapter 20	North and South	118
Chapter 21	The Private Side of James A. Hamilton	127
Chapter 22	Slavery and Secession	130
Chapter 23	Civil War	136
Chapter 24	Emancipation	148
Chapter 25	Election of 1864	159
Chapter 26	A Last Defense of Alexander Hamilton	164
Chapter 27	Hamilton Remembered	167

Notes 173
Bibliography 196
Index 198

Acknowledgments

I became fascinated with James Alexander Hamilton during my research for *Women of the American Revolution*. I had expected Eliza to be one of my favorite ladies to write about, but I was surprised to discover her son's memoir and even more shocked to learn how much of America's history he had been eyewitness to. The *Reminiscences of James A Hamilton; or, Men and Events, at Home and Abroad, During Three Quarters of a Century* is fascinating and full of history, but also full of gaps. He had recorded a sort of public diary of what he felt was important as he looked back on his life, lacking the amount of personal insight I wanted to see and not providing explanations for some of the complex historical events to which he referred. It was going to require a lot of digging, but I had found the subject of my next book.

Letters to and from James are found in numerous collections, and I thank the librarians at the University of Michigan, New York Public Library, the College of William and Mary, and Historic Hudson Valley for their assistance with accessing them. The boxes of correspondence made available for my perusal helped me see and share with my readers a more comprehensive picture of James than what is available through his *Reminiscences* alone. Discovering this personal side of James A. Hamilton was the most challenging aspect of this project, not least because, as he admits himself in one of his letters to daughter Eliza, his handwriting has been a constant challenge to decipher! It has been said that great minds produce bad penmanship. If this is true, James A. Hamilton was every bit the genius I have credited him with being.

I also thank William Seligman at Columbia University for sharing his photographs and passion for James A. Hamilton's history. Columbia University, as the current owners of James's Nevis, hold a treasure, and I thank Amy Garwood for my impromptu tour. The highlight of my research trip was standing in the home James had built and imagining him there with his shelves full of books and happy family gathered around. Every time I looked at the Hudson River, I wondered how similar my view was to what he had observed almost two centuries ago. With the western shore undeveloped over long stretches, I convinced myself that the view could very well be quite unchanged and took pleasure in this shared experience.

The enthusiastic staff at Hamilton Grange were also welcoming and helpful, offering a fantastic tour of the Hamilton homestead. Unlike Nevis, Hamilton Grange is maintained as a historic site and has priceless relics of the eighteenth century on display. It was possible to envision the Hamiltons gathered around the piano or the dinner table, but these happy thoughts are clouded by picturing Alexander at his writing desk issuing the fatal challenge to Aaron Burr. It is more difficult to imagine the family at the Grange without Alexander, even though they lived there for many more years without him than with. Visiting the places that were so important to James during his lifetime helped me feel close to him despite the years that have passed.

The support I receive from my fellow writers in the Historical Writers Forum is a blessing. I especially thank Stephanie Churchill, Sharon Bennett Connolly, Paula Lofting, Lynn Bryant, Cathie Dunn, and Virginia Crow for their constant encouragement and friendship. This book could not have been completed without the priceless help of early readers, especially Stacey Roberts, who has been an enthusiastic supporter of this project and helped me gather my thoughts and see my gaps, hopefully clearing up any confusion in my early drafts. He helped me see the many areas where it was meaningful to compare second-generation men like James A. Hamilton and John Quincy Adams to their larger-than-life fathers, and my fascination with John Quincy became almost as keen as that for James.

I also thank the editors at Pen & Sword for catching those tricky errors that are so easy to read over in one's own writing. Any remaining errors or lack of clarity are entirely *mea culpa*.

I could not put a single word to paper without the love and tireless support of my husband, Duane, who was the first person to encourage me to start writing. He and our three amazing children have traveled thousands of miles with me to visit libraries and historic sites through the years. They have endured hours of my recitation of Hamilton facts, my excitement over James's connections to influential people, and my complaints about his terrible penmanship. Thank you for believing in me and putting up with word count updates and other minutiae of writing life. As I watch each of my children launch into careers chosen with their own particular passions in mind, I reflect that they perhaps appreciated being constantly bombarded with mine for history.

No writer can succeed without dear readers, and I appreciate each and every one of mine. I read and value every book review and love interacting through social media. Whether you have been reading my novels since I started with the story of Elizabeth of York or are just meeting me due to our shared Hamilton passion, thank you, from the bottom of my heart.

Abridged Hamilton Family Tree

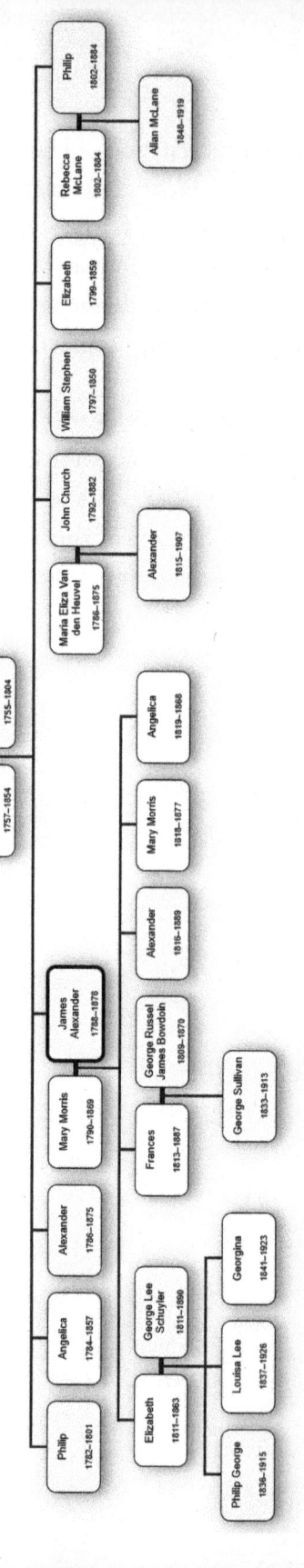

Chapter 1

Son of a Founding Father

A varied and somewhat eventful life.[1]

The first line of James A. Hamilton's *Reminiscences* reads, 'In my seventy-ninth year I have employed a winter's leisure in committing to paper these recollections of a varied and somewhat eventful life.' James was understating his experience as the son of America's first Secretary of the Treasury, the controversial Alexander Hamilton, and a life that spanned a country's coming of age, from the Constitutional Convention to the conclusion of the Civil War. Few people in the first half of the nineteenth century were in a position like James A. Hamilton to observe the formative politics and events that began the evolution of the United States into the country it is today. His *Reminiscences* and personal papers give modern readers a unique glimpse of that world.

During his lifetime, James observed the original thirteen states begin as a loosely connected confederation of separate governments and grow into thirty-eight states forming a unified nation. All this occurred under the leadership of nineteen different presidents, most of whom James knew personally. His mother danced with the first president on 7 May 1789 at George Washington's first inaugural ball. Eight of the original colonies ratified the Constitution and officially became states in 1788, the year James was born on 14 April, just a fortnight before Maryland became the seventh state. He watched US politics split into Republicans and Democrats and the Union split into North and South. He saw black men who had been enslaved become legal, voting citizens and women begin to strive toward their right to vote.

'Without having been a principal actor in any of those affairs of public interest to which I shall refer, I have had peculiar opportunities for understanding the purposes and appreciating the characters of many of the leaders in these transactions, and I indulge the hope that I may now and then be able to throw a valuable side-light upon events in our past history,'[2] James wrote with modesty that he must have inherited from his mother, Elizabeth Schuyler Hamilton. James described himself as a bystander to history, despite holding various positions, including District Attorney and Secretary of State, but his most important role was as a confidant and advisor to presidents and political leaders like Martin Van Buren, Andrew Jackson, and Salmon P. Chase. Why did these leaders seek James out? As Van Buren once wrote, 'I know that you cannot intentionally do wrong.'[3] As political leaders were often tempted to consider right from wrong, James was a dependable voice for what was morally good.

Perhaps observing what personal fame had done to his father discouraged James from seeking his own, or maybe he was simply a man of quieter character who enjoyed advising those whose names would go down in history. And what a history it was! While most Americans know at least a few facts about the American Revolution and remember names like Samuel Adams and Paul Revere, the United States was truly forged into a nation through the growing pains of the nineteenth century. The Founding Fathers had set the course, but the next generation had to journey into the wilderness and determine what it meant to live in a modern republic. Fewer people remember names like John Quincy Adams, Henry Clay, Daniel Webster, Andrew Jackson, John Marshall, and John C. Calhoun, but without them the American journey and resulting republic would have been quite different even before men like Abraham Lincoln and a bloody Civil War entirely revolutionized what it meant to be an American.

James A. Hamilton, who always signed his name with his middle initial to honor his father, did not grasp fame nor fortune for himself while living through this unprecedented time, and he did not record any regrets for not doing so. The same cannot be said of his father, though Alexander Hamilton did decline the opportunity to run for governor of New York and an offer of appointment to the Supreme Court.[4] Hamilton's name has become especially well known since the Broadway debut of the musical bearing his name and telling his story in 2015. That version of events is, of course, a blend of history and entertainment in which quiet young James does not appear.

Alexander was the ultimate self-made man. Born in obscurity in the West Indies on a tiny island called Nevis, Alexander was ambitious and intelligent, but also of little means and orphaned by age 14. He was employed as a clerk in the Beekman and Cruger mercantile house, which had New York connections and became his ticket to a new life.[5] During this time, Alexander learned valuable lessons that would serve him well when helping to form a new nation.

The experience of working in Caribbean trade may also have given him feelings against slavery from an early age. This, at least, is proposed by some biographers, though plenty of eighteenth-century men came of age surrounded by slavery without ever questioning its morality. Alexander likely grew up in a home with at least one or two slaves since two are listed in his mother's will,[6] but it is uncertain if he ever owned any himself. He left behind expense logbooks with slave purchases listed, but it is unknown if these were for himself, family members, or clients.[7]

During the American Revolution, Alexander reportedly said of black soldiers, 'The contempt we have been taught to entertain for the blacks, makes us fancy many things that are founded neither in reason nor in experience.'[8] His sons, James and John, would later quote their father's anti-slavery statements as they spoke out in favor of emancipation in the 1860s, but many men of Alexander's time spoke out against the evils of slavery even while owning slaves. It was a time when people confessed the evil of slavery while admitting that they did not know what to do about it. What better example can be given than Thomas Jefferson, who penned the famous phrase 'all men are created equal' while enslaving more people on his plantation than any other US president? Jefferson's contradictory statements on slavery and his relationship with Sally Hemmings, an enslaved half-sister of his late wife, demonstrate the national confusion on the topic.

Alexander Hamilton arrived in the American colonies on the eve of revolution and served as aide-de-camp to General George Washington, taking the next vital step toward his future. He would remain a confidante of Washington for the remainder of the general's life and receive vital support from the beloved first president.

His father's relationship with Washington may have set a precedent for James, who befriended and corresponded with many of the presidents who followed, not ever seeming to be intimidated by the power of their office. James often proudly mentioned the name of his illustrious father, even decades after Alexander's death in 1804. This habit he may have inherited from his mother. Elizabeth Hamilton dedicated much of her fifty years as a widow to solidifying Alexander's public reputation and seeing that he received the honor he deserved. As part of her quest, she convinced another of her sons, John Church Hamilton, to write a lengthy biography and collection of Alexander's writing.

Many men of this era understood that they were living through historic times and were careful to document their observations and actions. George Washington, throughout the Revolutionary War, kept impeccable records, even of spy activity that men such as Benjamin Tallmadge and Abraham Woodhull had instructed to have destroyed after reading to protect those working in secret against the British. John Adams also preserved thousands of pages of letters, diaries, and other documents, a habit he passed down through generations of diary keepers until his great-grandson Henry Adams wrote an extensive history and other works. Alexander Hamilton did not survive to see his own papers archived, but his wife made sure to see it done.

James was born to Alexander and Elizabeth (called Betsey or Eliza by friends and family) on 14 April 1788 and named for his paternal grandfather, James Hamilton of Scotland. Shortly following his birth, James was baptized at Trinity Church on 12 October 1788 alongside his siblings, Alexander and Angelica.[9] The Hamiltons rented pew ninety-two, and, later, Alexander, Eliza, and their eldest son, Philip, were buried in Trinity's churchyard.

In the year of James's birth, the United States elected its first Congress under the Constitution. Those gathered in New York included many names that remain familiar today, such as James Madison, Rufus King, Robert Morris, and James's grandfather, Philip Schuyler, who had been a general during the American Revolution. It was not only his father who left James with big shoes to fill. This Congress faced many challenges to unite the country they had made with the division between North and South already emerging but mollified with the horrific three-fifths compromise and plans to locate the nation's new capital on the Potomac. Little did New Englanders realize at the time that the three-fifths compromise, which gave Southern states representation based on a portion of their enslaved population, would ensure power of the slaveholding states over the nation's politics until tensions exploded in the Civil War. But that was far into the future, and those at the Constitutional Convention surely hoped their descendants would find a better solution.

In 1791, James was too young to be aware of the scandal of his father's affair with Maria Reynolds. He was 3 years old when his mother took him to her parents' home in Albany to avoid the miasma of illness that tended to hover over the city in the summer months. Despite this precaution, James did fall ill, and Alexander, who had remained in Philadelphia to work, encouraged Eliza to remain in Albany until the children's health was renewed. On 2 August, Alexander wrote to his wife, 'I thank you my beloved Betsey for your letter announcing your safe arrival; but my satisfaction at learning this has been greatly alloyed by the intelligence you give me of the indisposition of my darling James. Heaven protect and preserve him!' He sounds the loving father when he continues, 'I am myself in good health & will wait with all the patience I can the time for your return. But you must not precipitate it. I am so anxious for a perfect restoration of your health that I am willing to make a great sacrifice for it.'[10] His great sacrifice was sleeping with his mistress while his wife and children were away, but Eliza did not know this and James would not know the truth until many years later.

James recalled an early memory of his parents in his *Reminiscences*. As a 5-year-old when yellow fever struck Philadelphia in 1793, James remembered 'both my father and mother were attacked by the disease at the same time.'[11] Thankfully, both Alexander and Eliza recovered, or the history of the young United States might be remembered quite differently. It was the same illness that summer that caused the death of Dolley Payne Todd's husband and infant son. The next year, she married an older man many had believed to be a confirmed bachelor, James Madison.

While Alexander Hamilton was a controversial character, who tended to inspire strong feelings in both friends and enemies, the recollection of his son was of a devoted and loving father, who moved his family into the country in 1802. In an area of Harlem that is now crowded and urban, Alexander built the Grange for his family amid rolling fields and forests with the Hudson River in the distance. A yellow Federalist-style home that is modest compared to that of other Founding Fathers, the Grange was the first home owned by the Hamiltons. Alexander had thirteen gum trees planted in a circle, one for each state. However, his grandson later wrote that 'they were so closely set that they never attained a great size, and all eventually languished and died, their destruction being hastened by the depredations of the relic hunters.'[12]

James remembered his father 'drove back and forth in a two-wheeled carriage with a single horse' the eight miles to the city for work each day.[13] When home, Alexander's 'gentle nature rendered his house a most joyous one to his children and friends' and he 'was always affectionate and confiding, which excited in them a corresponding confidence and devotion.'[14]

His memories of his mother are no less idyllic. 'My dear mother, seated as was her wont at the head of the table with a napkin in her lap, cutting slices of bread and spreading them with butter for the younger boys, who, standing at her side, read in turn a chapter in the Bible or a portion of Goldsmith's Rome.'[15]

Perhaps time had healed old wounds by the time James was writing his memoir or he chose to focus on his happy memories, for he only mentions that his oldest brother, Philip, had died before the family moved to the Grange and does not record any reflection on how the family coped or reacted to the tragedy of losing the promising 19-year-old. For example, James does not mention that their sister, Angelica, suffered a mental collapse from which she never fully recovered.[16]

Philip had died on 24 November 1801 after challenging George Eacker to a duel in an effort to protect his father's honor. Alexander died under eerily similar circumstances less than three years later.

The only other mention of his oldest brother by James is the inclusion of a letter that Philip wrote to their father in April 1797. In it, Philip asks Alexander to express his thanks to Philip Schuyler, 'grandpapa,' for a gift of £100 and laments that a professor has struck what Philip thought the best line from a speech he prepared to give. 'Americans, you have fought the battles of mankind; you have enkindled that sacred fire of freedom which is now.'[17] Philip's letter is affectionate and eager to please, demonstrating the devotion that would lead to his death in his passion to defend his father.

The Hamiltons were crushed by the death of their firstborn son. A letter to Alexander from Benjamin Rush recognizes their grief. 'Permit a whole family to mingle their tears with yours upon the late distressing event that has taken place in your family,' he offers sympathetically, before sharing some memories of Philip's visit to Philadelphia. He then closed with, 'You do not weep alone. Many, many tears have been Shed in our city upon your Account. If afforded your friends a great Consolation to hear of the pious manner in which your son closed the last hours of his life.'[18]

James seems as eager in his old age to guard his father's reputation as Philip was in his youth. Dozens of pages of his *Reminiscences* are devoted to defenses of Alexander's actions and work on behalf of the government. Many notes from people sharing their own experiences with his father evince that his acquaintances knew that this was something of utmost importance to James.

A letter from Martin Van Buren, received 30 December 1826, reads, 'My Dear Hamilton ... You have certainly a right to use all lawful weapons to get at the means necessary to do justice to your father's memory,' before he goes on to request 'correspondence between General Washington and your father as relates to the power of the General Government over the subject of internal improvements.'[19] James insisted for years after the fact that, Burr 'under color [sic] of the duel, sought to and did assassinate Hamilton.'[20]

Alexander Hamilton's relationship with Aaron Burr may have been how James became acquainted with Washington Irving. Before he became a famous author, Irving begrudgingly studied law and was working in the office of Brockholst Livingston in 1799 when he was part of the defense team, alongside Alexander Hamilton and Aaron Burr, in the trial of Levi Weeks for the murder of Guliema Sands.[21] If the two young men did meet at this time, they may not have been fast friends.

Irving admired Burr, despite describing himself as a Federalist at this point[22] and continued to support him after the infamous duel. Irving admitted to thinking highly of both Hamilton and Burr, but the persecution of Burr after the duel 'made my blood boil in my veins.'[23] He was friends with James by the time they became neighbors in the 1830s. Irving seems to have decided whether he admired people regardless of their political affiliation, a rare quality he shared with James.

Albert Gallatin is another possible connection between James and Washington Irving. Irving spent time with Gallatin in Paris in 1820.[24] Gallatin later reassured James that he 'found the most perfect system ever formed' when Thomas Jefferson ordered him to examine the accounts of the Treasury Department after Alexander's departure from it. James 'rose, took Mr Gallatin's hand, and thanked him most heartily.'[25] This was in 1829, a quarter of a century after Alexander's death. Both James and Irving believed Gallatin to be an able and trustworthy statesman, rising above the politics of the day.

James remembered a caring father with a sense of humor. He recorded asking his father for a dissertation while away at Columbia for his education. Alexander, shortly before his death, sent his son a Thesis on Discretion, with a note: 'You may need it.'[26] And, indeed, James did grow into a man of quieter lifestyle and greater discretion than his father had ever been. James left it for his readers to decide, 'How far I have profited by the admonition this relation of the errors of my life may prove. The reader may perhaps say that in attempting to write these reminiscences I have shown that the admonition was thrown away.'[27]

The death of Alexander Hamilton, an event that some considered murder, changed the future of the nation and was a stunning personal blow to his family. Alexander knew when he met Aaron Burr in Weehawken, New Jersey, that his demise was a possible outcome, but perhaps he was overconfident due to situations that he had survived thus far. He had prepared a final message to his wife that could not have brought much comfort. 'This letter, my very dear Eliza, will not be delivered to you, unless I shall first have terminated my earthly career; to begin, as I humbly hope from redeeming grace and divine mercy, a happy immortality.' After explaining that the duel had been impossible to avoid, he closes, 'Adieu best of wives and best of Women. Embrace all my darling Children for me.'[28]

He did not die immediately after being shot. A memory that must have stayed with James for the rest of his long life was being lined up before his father's deathbed by their mother, her intention that they would all kiss him farewell. However, Alexander waved them away after having baby Philip (it was common at the time for younger children to be named for siblings who had passed before their birth) raised to his lips. In pain and sorrow at seeing his children for the last time, Alexander Hamilton could endure no more.[29]

The funeral, on 14 July 1804, was the grandest New York City had ever seen, and one must wonder how James felt as a grief-filled teenage boy. Perhaps this public display was one that made him wish to avoid them in the future. Family friend Gouverneur Morris gave the funeral oration while the Hamilton sons sat on the stage behind him. Eliza and Angelica did not attend, as was common at the time.[30] Morris began, 'Far from attempting to excite your emotions, I must try to repress my own, and yet I fear that instead of the language of a public speaker, you will hear only the lamentations of a bewailing friend. But I will struggle with my bursting heart, to portray that Heroic Spirit, which has flown to the mansions of bliss.'[31] Morris charged his fellow citizens to 'protect his fame – It is all he has left – all that these poor orphan children will inherit from their father.'[32] Hamilton's children, and his wife, took that duty to heart.

Alexander Hamilton died in debt, a truth not learned by his son until years later. A pact signed on 16 November 1804 includes a list of names and contributions for the support of the Hamilton family:

> Having in remembrance the exalted worth and pre-eminent services of the late General Hamilton – his extraordinary and truly patriotic exertions, which contributed so much to save our country from the greatest impending calamities ... especially recollecting that the devotion of his time & talents to these public interests has operated to deprive his family of a common share of those pecuniary advantages, which his labours if applied to them, would have easily made abundant, we therefore, where names are subscribed, to testify in some degree our sense of departed excellence and our gratitude for benefits conferred on our country, do engage that we will pay ... sums of money set against our respective names, to be by them applied to the benefit of the Children or Family of General Hamilton.[33]

Only due to this generosity was Eliza able to maintain her family at the Grange at that time.

Years later, upon realization that friends had pooled donations in order to save the Grange for the Hamilton family, James wrote to Major William Popham on 14 October 1824, 'I was this day for the first time informed ... that you advanced one hundred dollars to pay my father's debts. The gratitude that is due to you from every member of his family for this generous act can never be effaced.'[34] With this letter, James included a repayment of the $100.

Shortly after their father's death, the Hamilton children started forging their own way. Alexander Jr graduated from Columbia, and Eliza struggled with the fact that her life would never be the same as it had been when her husband was alive. She took her place in a new public sphere that women of her day were creating by participating in important charitable work. She helped found the first public orphanage in New York City and had a free public school built near Hamilton Grange.

James returned to Columbia in the autumn of 1804 to continue his studies, so it was a few years before he took his own place in society and politics. In the meantime, under President Jefferson, Americans waited for news of the Lewis and Clark expedition and debated the wisdom – and constitutionality – of the Louisiana Purchase. In 1808, they elected James Madison as the country's fourth president and were soon reading Washington Irving's *A Knickerbocker's History of New York*, a satirical commentary on America's history and early politics that was likely read by James A. Hamilton.

Chapter 2

Coming of Age

Experience teaches us sad but useful lessons.[1]

James A. Hamilton graduated from Columbia in 1805 and continued his study of law in the office of Judge Nathaniel Pendleton, who had been a friend of his father's and served as his second in the deadly duel.[2] James was following in his father's footsteps into law, just as his brother, Alexander, recently had. In May 1809, he was admitted to the bar the same year his younger brother, John, graduated from Columbia.[3] When practicing in Waterford, New York, the following year, he had one of many encounters in which his father's name came into play, or as James recorded it, 'a year was spent in Waterford without any other event worthy of note than the following act of folly, and perhaps wickedness, into which I was drawn by the folly of another.'[4]

At a Democratic meeting at The Borough near Waterford, a lawyer named John Cramer 'spoke disparagingly' of Alexander Hamilton, and a listener who had fought in the American Revolution, Captain Ten Broeck, spoke in Hamilton's defense.[5] In denouncing the attack, 'the gallant captain forthwith challenged him in my name; announcing at the same time that if I did not adopt the challenge he would.'[6]

Cramer refused a written challenge issued by Captain Ten Broeck, and James was safe from the prospect of a duel while his opponent was reported as a coward.[7]

The following year, James married Mary Morris on 17 October 1810, and the couple moved to Hudson, New York.[8] Mary was also born to a Founding Family, including her great-uncle, Gouverneur Morris, who had given the eulogy at Alexander Hamilton's funeral, and her grandfather, Richard Morris, Chief Justice for New Jersey. At 22, James was relatively young for a man to be married at that time, indicating a love match. 'Both I and my wife were without means – our parents not being in a situation to do much for us. This I have always considered the most fortunate event of my life. I realized the embarrassments of my situation, and met them with the determination to overcome them.' Like his father, James was driven toward success, and not with bitterness regarding his lowly financial position.

> Our poverty was so extreme that during our first year we boarded at four dollars per week for each. I now look back upon this event as not only the happiest but the most fortunate occurrence of my long and eventful life. My poverty, with its burdens and responsibilities, nerved me to exertion, and necessity taught me the value of economy and self-denial.[9]

James quickly became acquainted with other ambitious young men, among them Martin Van Buren, who James described as 'the leader of the Democratic party' in New York, despite his 'obscure parentage.'[10] James uses the familiar political party name in his memoir, though the term 'democrat' was not widely used in a positive way in the United States until the administration of Andrew Jackson. The country's founders had been proud to form a republic but equated democracy with mob rule. Later, democracy became the calling card of those politicians claiming to represent the common man.

While admiring Van Buren's political abilities, James also observed that, 'His knowledge of books outside of his profession was more limited than that of any other public man I ever knew.'[11] They would remain friends for decades before growing political differences and Van Buren's constant maneuvering put distance between them in later years.

James and Mary welcomed their first child almost precisely a year after their marriage on 8 October 1811. Elizabeth was named for her grandmother and would later marry George Lee Schuyler. Therefore, the older was Elizabeth Schuyler Hamilton and the younger became Elizabeth Hamilton Schuyler. This daughter was particularly close to her father, and they would exchange countless letters through the decades.

The same year, the charter for the First Bank of the United States, founded by Alexander Hamilton, was allowed to expire. James foresaw consequences that would plague the nation later when the Second Bank met a similar fate. James wrote:

One of the many evil consequences of the winding up of that bank was to induce a vast increase in numbers of State banks, particularly in the city of New York; and above all, the attempt by shameless intrigue, to establish the Bank of America in the city of New York, with a capital of six millions. This measure was earnestly supported by the Federal faction in the middle district as a party engine.[12]

Soon, the War of 1812, sometimes known as the Second War for Independence or Mr Madison's War, proved James right about the banking industry even as it threatened the very existence of the nation. President Madison had hoped to avoid war, but Great Britain put him in a difficult position. They impressed sailors on American ships, so boldly as to sometimes do so within view of US soil. Protestors argued that a state of war already existed and others pointed out that Britain continued to treat the independent states as colonies for them to plunder. When it could be avoided no longer, the US went to war, and the weakened banking system groaned under the strain.

The national struggle also invaded the peace of the young Hamilton family. In 1814, they moved from Hudson to New York City, where there was fear of a British attack.[13] On 22 July, James wrote to Governor Tompkins offering his services. 'I hold myself in readiness to perform the duties of any military station you shall please to assign to me,' calling it 'my duty, as well as the duty of every good citizen, to take part in the burden of a vigorous defence.'[14]

James records that 'the next day I was appointed a deputy Quartermaster of Col. Varian's Infantry Regiment, and was appointed Brigade Major and Inspector of Gen. Height's Brigade.' Therefore, he would have been responsible for the acquisition and organization of supplies and accommodations, similar to work his father had performed for General Washington. If James had any notable personal experience during the war, he does not record it, and only remarks that, 'At the close of the war I returned to my profession.'[15]

The most infamous event of the War of 1812 was the burning of Washington DC on 24 August 1814. James does not record his thoughts on this event that British troops felt was an appropriate retaliation for the burning of York in Canada by American troops during their failed invasion attempt. President Madison had fled in disgrace after US troops at Bladensburg, Maryland were routed by a much smaller number of British, but Dolley Madison inspired some by saving the Gilbert Stuart portrait of George Washington before leaving the White House. (She likely had an enslaved man see to the painting rather than taking it from the wall herself, but she is often credited for the act just the same.)

The United States had brighter moments during the war following this embarrassing defeat. British forces moved on from Washington toward Baltimore, where they anticipated taking Fort McHenry, but Major George Armistead was better prepared to defend Baltimore than the president had been to protect Washington DC. He even ordered a giant American flag to be flown over the sturdy brick fortress. When that flag was still visible after a spectacular British barrage, Francis Scott Key was inspired to write 'The Star Spangled Banner,' a poem that was later set to music and eventually made the US national anthem.

The victory at Fort McHenry reassured Americans, and especially President Madison, that all was not lost. It was soon followed by a shocking victory for the US Navy on Lake Champlain. By the time General Andrew Jackson obtained his legendary triumph at New Orleans, a peace treaty had already been signed in Ghent. The war ended with little changed or gained on either side, but the United States felt it had flexed and proven its independence.

Almost on their third anniversary and two years since the birth of their first child, on 2 October 1813, James and Mary welcomed their second daughter, Frances. She may have been named for Frances Antil, who had been raised alongside James as an adopted sister. Both women were called Fanny. The elder had married Arthur Tappan in 1810.

Tappan came from a family of abolitionists, and Arthur was heavily involved in and a principal donor to the American Anti-Slavery Society. His brother, Lewis, arranged for legal aid to the captives of the *Amistad* in 1839, eventually convincing former president John Quincy Adams to represent them before the Supreme Court. Another Tappan brother, Benjamin, attempted to be an anti-slavery voice within the heavily pro-slavery Democratic party as a senator for Ohio. The connection with the Tappans is evidence of Alexander Hamilton's possible abolitionist leanings, though the wedding occurred after his death and Fanny was living with her sister and brother-in-law rather than the Hamiltons by the time of her marriage.

In 1815, James took on the role as Master of Chancery for New York. He had turned down the position the year before; however, finding he was still appointed to it, changed his mind and accepted it. 'The office was of great value to me.'[16] He was grateful to those who remembered his father and sent legal business his way. Because of the welcomed increase in income, 'I was enabled to purchase a small house in Varick Street.'[17] The home he purchased stood at 64 Varick Street in what is now Lower Manhattan.

The Hamiltons' first year in their new home was one plagued by strange weather caused worldwide by a volcano eruption in Indonesia in April 1815. Volcanic gases released into the atmosphere resulted in summer snow in New England and crop-killing frosts in the Carolinas.[18] James did not record his observations on the chilly temperatures or increase in food prices that made it a challenging year for many families across the globe.

One of the jobs that came James's way was as agent for the estate of Gouverneur Morris, who had spoken so eloquently at Alexander Hamilton's funeral. Morris died on 6 November 1816, and his wife, Ann C. Morris, employed James to settle the estate and unravel her late husband's web of finances, which James proved his skill in accomplishing.[19]

James and Mary needed the extra income since they had added a third child, their first and only son, to the family on 26 January 1816. He was named for his grandfather and, therefore, had much to live up to with the name Alexander Hamilton.

The understandable tendency to name Hamilton sons Alexander leads to some confusion at times. James had a brother, son, and nephew all named Alexander, and they were each sometimes referred to as Alexander Hamilton Jr. James's brother and son were also both sometimes called Alexander Hamilton II. In addition, his son and nephew were born within months of one another. Though the difference was likely clear to family at the time, the modern reader must carefully consider any references in historical documents to an Alexander Hamilton.

In 1817, the state of New York, in which James lived his entire life, signed into law emancipation for all slaves in the state as of 4 July 1827 without compensation to their owners (besides the decade of work that was required before the law went into effect). Among many others, a woman who decided to call herself Sojourner Truth gained her freedom through this law.[20] While laws abolishing slavery in Northern states were a positive advance, they caused the divide to deepen between Northerners and Southerners as neutrality on the issue became impossible.

James A. Hamilton did not own slaves and was likely encouraged by what this step meant for the country as a whole. He did not record active involvement in the abolition movement or the Underground Railroad until he spoke in favor of emancipation during the Civil War. However, on several occasions, James expressed his dismay with the three-fifths compromise that enabled Southern slaveholders to maintain control of the federal government for much of the early republic era. Without it, Jefferson would not have defeated Adams in the election of 1800.[21]

James and Mary welcomed their third daughter, Mary, just under two years after the birth of their son on New Year's Day 1818. She would go on to join the Mount Vernon Ladies' Association, working to preserve the home and memory of George Washington, who had been such an important part of the life of her grandfather, whom she never had the chance to meet.

When his uncle, John Barker Church, died on 27 April 1818, James was called upon to settle his estate. Church had been married to his mother's sister, Angelica, who had died in 1814. James and Mary named their fifth child, a daughter born on 13 November 1819, after Angelica. Eliza had been closer to this sister than their other siblings and had named one of her own sons after John Church. With this brother, James would later speak out boldly against slavery in the United States.

With his own home filling with little ones, James must have felt pulled back in time when a friend of his father's brought a note to his office alleged to be written by himself. The message, carried by Colonel Troup, read: 'Aaron Burr – Sir: Please meet me with the weapon you choose, on the 15th May, where you murdered my father.'[22]

James promptly demonstrated to Troup that the writing did not match his own, and Troup agreed, 'I am satisfied it is a forgery.'[23] However, the incident stirred up anxiety and bad memories. 'I was very much excited and angered that Burr should dare to make any communication to me … and under the excitement I very foolishly replied, "Sir I am not satisfied – the note is, as you say, a forgery, but if you come here as the friend of Aaron Burr to accept the challenge if sent by me, I adopt it."'[24]

Thankfully, Troup did not wish for the incident to escalate and returned the note to Burr to inform him of its falsity without forwarding James's impetuous challenge. Although no duel resulted from this incident, James continued to be frustrated by related rumors. One was that Burr had replied to the forgery, saying, 'Boy I never injured you, nor wished to injure your father,' a statement that would have insulted James twofold – by disparaging his father's name and referring to him as a boy when 'I was then over thirty years of age.'[25]

James believed the note to have been forged by one 'devoted to the corrupt faction' that was targeted by the *New York American*.[26] James joined with friends, Charles King and Johnston Ver Planck, to establish the weekly newspaper with the purpose to 'expose the corrupt practices of a faction in the State of New York.'[27]

An editorial on 26 January 1820 accused William Van Ness, a New York District Court judge, with accepting bribes in return for advocating the charter of the Bank of America.[28] Martin Van Buren later wrote of the case, 'The fact that the Bank obtained its charter thro' the most daring and unscrupulous bribery practiced upon various persons, occupying different positions in the public service, is undeniable.'[29] William Van Ness had also served as second for Aaron Burr when Alexander Hamilton was killed,[30] so James was unlikely to have much sympathy for him and might have been eager to prove his corruption.

As a result of his outspokenness, James was removed from his position as Master in Chancery by Governor DeWitt Clinton, 'without any alleged cause; but evidently because I had made a charge against Judge Van Ness.'[31] It did not prevent James from acting as counsel for the *American* when Van Ness filed a lawsuit for libel in 1822.[32] The case was decided in favor of Van Ness; however, the judge resigned from the New York Supreme Court that year and died soon afterward.

James recorded a challenging experience with the Bank of America a few years later. He cashed a check for $5,200 but found he was $1,000 short. 'I advertised the loss in the *Evening Post* the day it occurred, and offered a reward.'[33] Years later, he was informed that a man had charges brought against him for the theft of the note. James finally received $500 after the bank won the suit, although he had still been forced to put pressure on them and remind the bank that the loss was actually his. The experience convinced him that 'Corporations have no souls.'[34]

When the dust settled, James was left figuring out how to replace the income that he had earned in his Chancery post. His legal work brought him in contact with legends of the era like John Quincy Adams, who, as Secretary of State was negotiating key treaties that would make the Monroe Doctrine a lasting American philosophy. The Adams–Onis Treaty ensured that James was successful in his work for clients who paid him generously for his work on claims in Florida, which was ceded to the US.

Though comfortable corresponding with men like Adams, James did not seem to see himself as their equal. At least as he remembered these events decades later in his memoir, James was skeptical when men like John C. Calhoun invited him to parties and 'expressed much pleasure at seeing me.'[35] Sending his thanks, James understood that Calhoun 'doubtless supposed I would communicate to my Federal friends' a favorable report.'[36]

Despite their previous profitable correspondence, James was not beholden to Adams in the election of 1824, when he supported William Crawford for president in the crowded candidate field that also included Andrew Jackson and Henry Clay.[37] The election was decided by the House of Representatives because none of the men received adequate electoral votes. When Clay indicated that his support should go to Adams, Jackson lost, despite having won the highest percentage of the popular vote. This is somewhat misleading, however, since not all states utilized popular vote in 1824. Of the twenty-four states that existed at that time, six of them did not determine electoral votes based on popular vote. Without the three-fifths compromise, Adams would have won without the need of a decision by the House of Representatives.[38]

James appreciated the intellect and patriotism of John Quincy Adams, even if he had preferred Crawford. Though he had not supported the candidacy of Andrew Jackson, it was that president that James would have the most impact on when he defeated Adams in their 1828 rematch.

Chapter 3

Washington's Farewell Address

Such of these papers as referred to the Farewell Address were held by me with my mother's permission.[1]

Today, it is understood that Alexander Hamilton assisted George Washington in drafting his Farewell Address when the first president had decided to make an unprecedented move. Washington planned to give up his office and set into motion a peaceful transfer of power. Modern readers do not, perhaps, realize what an unheard of idea it was for a popular head of state to quietly retire and allow another to take his place, but people of the late eighteenth century were astonished. Washington made it clear that the presidency was not a lifetime appointment and established the two-term precedent not broken until Franklin D. Roosevelt in the twentieth century.

In his Farewell Address, which was printed rather than given as a speech, Washington reassured his 'friends and fellow citizens' that the republic was strong enough to continue under new leadership.[2] He encouraged unity and support of the Constitution. He wrote of the 'sacred ties' that had created 'an indissoluble community of Interest as one Nation.'[3] Little did Washington know that, within a generation, many would challenge this idea of indissolubility, but he did his best to discourage it. He also warned against parties, ignoring the fact that he was considered the head of one. 'Cunning, ambitious and unprincipled men' would use party power 'to subvert the Power of the People and to usurp for themselves the reins of Government.'[4] Washington had been the unanimous choice for president because of his ability to put the country first and unite people through his own integrity and trustworthiness. He clearly hoped that others would rise up to do the same.

Washington attempted to point to the synergy between different regions of the country, stating that an 'essential advantage' was gained when northern commerce, southern agriculture, eastern maritime industry, and western expansion were viewed as varied but cooperative strengths. 'While then every part of our country thus feels an immediate and particular interest in union, all the parts combined cannot fail to find in the united mass of means and efforts greater strength, greater resource, proportionably greater security from external danger, a less frequent interruption of their peace by foreign nations; and, what is of inestimable value!'[5]

No one knew that Alexander Hamilton had assisted in the authorship of the Address until rumors began a few years after his death. Even then, many wished to protect Washington's reputation and denied Hamilton's involvement. However, since the collaboration had occurred through letters and written drafts, it was easy to prove, at least once the Hamilton family managed to obtain those papers.

At some point, James learned from Nathaniel Pendleton, who had served as second at the deadly duel and as one of the executors of Alexander's estate, that he had found drafts of the Address in Alexander's papers after his death. (James's *Reminiscences* place this conversation in 1824, but Pendleton died in 1821.) He told James, 'That he had placed the draft in my father's handwriting, with correspondence between him and General Washington, in the hands of Mr King for safe-keeping.'[6] Pendleton had believed that Eliza Hamilton would publicize the papers but that Rufus King would withhold them. He was correct.

Apparently, after two decades had passed, Pendleton felt Washington's reputation was beyond damage and that the Hamiltons deserved to know the truth, or he simply wished to clear his conscious before he died. He instructed James to go to King, saying, 'you ought to get those papers and you may ask for them in my name.'[7]

Both James and his mother were keen to repossess the documents, but he must have known that Rufus King would not be eager to give them up because James recorded attempts to obtain them through other channels. In a 4 December 1820 letter to Timothy Pickering, who had served as Secretary of State under Washington and John Adams, James wrote referencing a conversation between Pickering and Chief Justice Marshall 'respecting my father and particularly that part of it having reference to the various communications from the latter found among General Washington's papers.'[8]

In this letter, James admits that he has approached others for help. 'An application was some time ago made to Judge Washington for the original or copies of communications made by my father to the General.'[9] James is referring to Judge Bushrod Washington, inheritor of Mount Vernon and all that entailed and who gave access to the Washington papers to Justice Marshall when he was researching and writing a biography of the first president.

James was not alone in his efforts. The letter to Pickering also notes that his mother had 'went to Mount Vernon' after Justice Marshall had advised Judge Washington that 'he thought it right she should have copies.' However, 'to our very great astonishment the only papers she was permitted to see or to receive were some unimportant letters with a report on the subject of the military academy.'[10] It seemed Bushrod Washington was also willing to withhold information to protect his uncle's reputation and the support for Federalist ideals, which some thought might lose ground if Washington's authorship was questioned. In fact, though he was the one who held papers proving otherwise, Bushrod claimed that Hamilton's authorship was a rumor 'now slyly propagating.'[11] One Federalist felt so strongly about this topic that he proclaimed, 'If I had it in his [Hamilton's] hand-writing, I would burn it.'[12]

Eliza was also in communication with Pickering herself. In 1823, she requested assistance, because 'my youngest son has come of age,' and she asked him to write recommendations on young Philip's behalf.[13] But Pickering does not seem to have been able to help so far as the Washington estate was concerned. James did thank him for sharing what papers he had. 'Every paper which relates to the history of our country although not immediately connected with my father will be useful in writing his life and will be received with gratitude.'[14]

Pickering responded a month later, confirming his recollection of Chief Justice Marshall's support for the Hamiltons, adding the encouragement that Marshall's study of the Washington papers had settled in his mind the belief that General Hamilton 'the greatest man (or one of the greatest men) that had ever appeared in the United States.'[15] While this sentiment surely touched James, who was always happy to receive any positive word on his father, he still wished to obtain the papers relating to the Farewell Address.

Finally, since other efforts had failed, James went to Rufus King's home on 20 May 1825, 'at the earnest solicitation of my mother,' but King 'would not part with them.'[16] King insisted that he would never part with them and that, at his death, he would see them turned over to his own children rather than Eliza. One of his sons, Charles, was a friend of James with whom he had founded the *New York American*. James asked 'if he would permit me to see them … I told him my mother was extremely solicitous about the papers.'[17] He left dissatisfied but wrote to King again three days later:

> Since my last interview with you, its particular object has engrossed much of my attention, and I am confirmed in the opinion that it is not only reasonable but quite proper, that the draft of the farewell address, with the correspondence on that subject between my father and General Washington, deposited with you by my father's executors, should be returned.[18]

Failing that, James repeats his request to at least 'peruse those papers at your house.'[19]

James then recruited the assistance of his brother, John, who called upon the remaining surviving executor of their father's estate, Colonel Nicholas Fish. After reviewing the correspondence between James and King, Fish agreed to accompany John to repeat the request, but he was also denied.[20]

The Hamiltons finally resorted to filing legal suit for possession of the papers in 1825. Rufus King asked Bushrod Washington to join forces to fight the lawsuit, but Bushrod took Justice Marshall's advice not to get involved, insisting that doing so would blacken Washington's name more than the authorship rumors had.[21] Like the Hamilton sons, Bushrod considered his actions in the light of how they would impact the great name he had inherited. In October 1826, Rufus King delivered a bundle of correspondence to James that included letters written by Washington that alluded to Hamilton's assistance but not the supporting documents written by Hamilton.[22] The lawsuit was dropped, despite the Hamiltons' disappointment that the papers were incomplete.[23]

> Thus ended a proceeding of some importance, which gave me much pain; because my personal relations with Mr King were confidential

and affectionate. Nevertheless, believing, as I did, that he was wrong in withholding from their rightful owner papers which did not belong to him, I was satisfied that in doing so he was governed by considerations connected with public interest, which were highly commendable.[24]

The correspondence between Hamilton and Washington clearly established collaboration. A letter from Hamilton on 30 July 1796 encourages Washington to read an enclosed draft, 'and after perusing, and noting anything you wish changed, send it to me, I will with pleasure shape it as you desire.'[25] From Washington to Hamilton on 25 August 1796, 'I have given the paper herewtih enclosed, several serious & attentive readings; and prefer it greatly to the other draughts, being more copious on material points; more dignified on the whole; and with less egotism.'[26]

Debate over the authorship of Washington's Farewell Address continued for decades, with some of those arguing against Hamilton's involvement those close enough to know the falsehood of that stand. On 7 August 1840, Eliza Hamilton, just two days short of her 83rd birthday, released a statement regarding the Address. She testified that Washington requested that her husband write the Address and that

> Mr Hamilton did so, and the address was written, principally at such times as his office was seldom frequented by his clients and visitors, and during the absence of his students to avoid interruption; at which times he was in the habit of calling me to sit with him, that he might read to me as he wrote, in order, as he said, to discover how it sounded upon the ear and making the remark, 'My dear Eliza, you must be to me what Moliere's old nurse was to him.' The whole or nearly all the 'Address' was read to me by him as he wrote it and a greater part if not all was written by him in my presence.[27]

Eliza harbored no doubts regarding her husband's involvement and was 'desirous that my children should be fully acquainted with the services rendered by their Father to our country, and the assistance given by him to General Washington during his administration, for the one great object, the Independence and Stability of the Government of the United States.'[28]

The truth of the Washington–Hamilton collaboration was only widely accepted after Horace Binney's *An Inquiry into the Formation of Washington's Farewell Address* in 1859.[29] At this point, as the country skidded toward civil war, the fact that Hamilton had assisted the first president with his writing seemed much less important than it had previously.

The papers, so long sought after by James and his mother, were sold to the United States government as part of the Hamilton Papers.[30]

Chapter 4

Secretary of State

An enterprising man, and not a little disposed to be gallant.[1]

James A. Hamilton and Martin Van Buren began their careers in New York law at approximately the same time, but Van Buren's ambition far outpaced Hamilton's. Van Buren was a master politician, making connections and plans for his own future. He discerned that James was a valuable resource and one who could be trusted not to usurp power for himself, as he was more concerned with legacy and upholding the Constitution than personal advancement. They discussed law and politics at length, including the election of 1824.

This election was unique in the number of candidates. Gone were the days, idyllically called the Era of Good Feelings, when James Monroe had run practically unopposed. A single elector had defected, casting his vote for John Quincy Adams, keeping Monroe from repeating George Washington's unanimous election. In 1824, four men competed for the highest office, all nominally claiming to be Democratic-Republicans as it was the only major national party at the time. James supported William Crawford, Monroe's Treasury Secretary, and 'worked hard for his election.'[2] Crawford's is the least remembered name today compared to his opponents, Henry Clay, John Quincy Adams, and Andrew Jackson.

James felt that Crawford was 'intelligent, well informed, and scrupulously upright.'[3] He also noted Washington Irving's support of Crawford, indicating they had built a friendship by this time. James likely also appreciated Crawford's fiscal conservatism and support for the First Bank of the United States. Crawford was a slave owner from Georgia and firm believer in states' rights, but James makes no remark on this in his memoir. His support of Crawford possibly indicates that fiscal responsibility was more of a key issue to him at that time than the emancipation of the enslaved, though the rights of black Americans would become more important to James over time.

John Quincy Adams was Monroe's Secretary of State, a position considered heir apparent to the presidency in the early nineteenth century. That, combined with his father's legacy as the nation's second president, made Adams eager for the position. However, his outdated belief that candidates not promote themselves was dangerous to indulge in when facing opponents like Jackson and Clay.

Henry Clay was Speaker of the House of Representatives and a skilled politician who combined the charismatic ability to succeed in politics with a genuine concern for the future of the country, and he worked tirelessly on the compromises that kept the US from civil war until after his death. At the time of this election, the Missouri Compromise was fresh in voters' minds. Missouri had been accepted into the Union as a slave state with Maine accepted as a free state to maintain the delicate balance in power. When it became clear that Clay would not win the election himself, he gave Adams the vital support he needed, which gained the animosity of Jackson.

Andrew Jackson was a military general popular with the people, especially for his victory in New Orleans that became tied in the public mind to the end of the War of 1812, but he was feared by politicians who thought him unfit to lead. He had the popular vote in 1824, but not a majority, and he would maintain that the election was stolen from him and the American people. However, his claim had faults, including the fact that not all states decided electoral votes by popular vote in 1824. This election, and the chaotic, disputed results, would cause a movement in New York state to have electors selected by the people rather than state legislature.

After the election of 1824 was decided by the House of Representatives in favor of John Quincy Adams, he named Henry Clay as his Secretary of State, informally naming Clay his heir. Jackson was livid at this 'corrupt bargain,' but he would have his revenge in 1828 when he won by a large majority and had ample opportunity to make corrupt bargains of his own. Crawford declined to serve as Treasury Secretary under Adams, as he had under Madison and Monroe, but he could use his failing health as justification.

Adams began his presidency with high hopes that he would be more successful than his father had been. In his inaugural address, he promised that his 'first resort will be to that Constitution which I shall swear to the best of my ability to preserve, protect, and defend ... It is the work of our forefathers. Administered by some of the most eminent men who contributed to its formation, through a most eventful period in the annals of the world.'[4] Those men, of course, included both his own father and James's. John Quincy recognized the work of their fathers and those who had served since, noting that the population of the country had tripled in those years. Then he set forth his own lofty goals that included discharging the national debt, reducing the military, 'and to proceed in the great system of internal improvements'[5] that had long been promoted by Henry Clay but were becoming a more palatable idea to many Americans. Southerners, however, still feared this display of federal power.

While James continued in his law practice, his friend, Martin Van Buren, served in Congress and joined with others to block passage of legislation supported by President Adams. He continued writing frequently to James about his political maneuverings. How much the federal government should be involved in national infrastructure was a source of great debate. While New Yorkers celebrated the opening of the Erie Canal in 1825, many legislators were reluctant to give the federal government the power to make similar improvements elsewhere.

As Nathaniel Macon of North Carolina wrote, 'If Congress can make canals, they can with more propriety emancipate.'[6] States' rights advocates were primarily concerned with the singular right to own human property. It was a debate that would come to a head again and again in a way other disagreements between states had not until the ultimate showdown of the American Civil War of the 1860s. The largest nationwide responsibility of the federal government in the 1820s was the postal service, and even this would become a hotly debated topic when abolitionists began using the mail to distribute anti-slavery materials.

James recorded few of his own thoughts regarding the Adams presidency or Van Buren's scheming to thwart him. Instead, James began investing in New York real estate, a strategy that may have seemed risky at the time but earned him great financial returns. One large lot he purchased was on Broadway. After paying $52,000 and holding it for 'three or four years,' James was able to sell it 'in parcels at a very great advance.'[7]

John Quincy Adams recorded a 'somewhat extraordinary' conversation he had with James regarding property investment.

> He said among other things that I had made his fortune; by writing in 1822 a Letter to the Commissioners under the Florida Treaty with Spain, which had enabled clients of his to recover a large sum, of which he had received 24000 dollars. With these he had purchased 80 acres of land at 300 dollars an acre, in the vicinity of the City of New-York, which he had sold last year for 1600 dollars an acre.[8]

James needed these profits, not only to support his own large family, but to have the resources to help his aging mother.

Eliza Hamilton wrote to James on 11 May 1827 when she was months shy of her 70th birthday. 'Your unremitting kindness and attentions, and in this last instance of providing for my comfort, demands my most ardent and affectionate thanks … As all good acts are recorded in the habitation where your father now is, I have no doubt this one will be proclaimed to him, and have thus given him another motive to implore continued blessings upon you.'[9] Eliza remained at Hamilton Grange until 1833, but continued to struggle financially. Besides receiving back pay for her late husband's military service, she received support of family and friends even as her own focus was on philanthropic work.

James met Andrew Jackson when he was appointed in 1827 to represent the City of New York in New Orleans at the celebration of the anniversary of the General's most famous victory. The Battle of New Orleans may have technically taken place after the Treaty of Ghent was signed on Christmas Eve 1814, but it did not stop Americans from celebrating it as the triumph that had won the war. James wrote of his appointment, 'I accepted it with pleasure, because it afforded me an opportunity to see much of our country, and particularly one of those men who, by a brilliant military achievement, had rendered it a very important service.'[10] He left Washington on 13 December 1827 and arrived at Andrew Jackson's Hermitage in Tennessee on Christmas Eve, where 'the General received us most cordially.'[11]

The Hermitage was quite new when James saw it. Built between 1819 and 1821, it was designed in the Federal style similar to Hamilton Grange but on a grander scale. Even before renovations that would increase the size of the mansion to its modern appearance, it had soaring ceilings and four large rooms on each floor with the broad central hall common to southern homes to catch cool breezes in the summer.[12] James 'observed during all my visit that the table was loaded with food, and in all the spare rooms there were two beds. The General's house was the stopping-place for travellers going to Nashville. Here they ate and slept, not occasionally, but from day to day ... He kept a tavern, without the privilege of making a bill.'[13]

James, Jackson, and the rest of their party took the steamer *Pocahontas* to travel from Nashville to New Orleans.[14] This trip down the Mississippi was the farthest west that James would ever travel. During the journey, James became acquainted with Rachel Jackson as well and 'found her an amiable, sensible woman. It has frequently occurred to me that it was a very great misfortune that she did not live to exert her influence over the General, and guide him by her good sense and good feelings, when he was President.'[15] Since he was writing about events years later, James was almost certainly thinking of the embarrassing Eaton Affair when he made this remark. Rachel died of a heart attack after her husband's election but before he moved to Washington, and Jackson always believed the stress his critics put her under had killed her.

James was also able to observe the situation in the west and understand banking difficulties due to the remoteness of the area during this trip. Cash was shockingly scarce in the western settlements, where the barter system was extensively utilized. Bank notes were also more difficult for people living in the west to value, given their distance from issuing institutions. This is knowledge James would draw upon later as he advised Jackson during his presidency.

As the party continued toward New Orleans, stopping at towns along the Mississippi River, Rachel Jackson asked James to 'do me a great favor.' Hearing that other ladies on board the steamer had engaged him to get them bonnets at the next stop, Rachel requested 'a becoming one' for herself. Upon arrival in January 1828, James was quick to go 'to the most fashionable milliner in New Orleans' where he 'purchased for the ladies their several bonnets.'[16]

During the anniversary celebrations in New Orleans, James delivered an address on behalf of the Committee appointed by the Republicans of New

York City. He praised General Jackson's defense of New Orleans fourteen years earlier, an effort 'unparalleled in the annals of war.'[17] His 'Republican Fellow Citizens throughout the union' showed their appreciation of Jackson by electing him to 'the highest office in the gift of a Free People … The Republicans of New York look upon you as eminently qualified for the High Trust of the Chief magistracy because they believe you cherish with undiminished ardour that Republican Principle' that all authority comes from the will of the American people.[18]

Other addresses were also given in honor of Jackson. Afterwards, James was employed for the first time in a service that would become his habit when he wrote Jackson's response to the speech that James himself had given.[19]

When James accepted the appointment to go to Louisiana, he had wanted to see more of the world and have new experiences, but he was not anticipating one of the events to which he was invited. 'It was a Quadroon ball. There was an amphitheatre of seats where the black wenches sat, while the girls who were brought there for sale, and others, danced with white men.' James later wrote that it was a 'novel and disgusting scene.'[20] Custom of the country was further explained to him, that men often had 'Quadroon girls' as mistresses, and that 'unless the act of adultery was committed in the domicil of the husband, there could be no divorce.' Therefore, the mistresses were kept along the 'Yellow Bend' of the river where the women raised their mixed-race children.[21] James records that the families 'were well off, owning lands' despite the immoral arrangement.[22] Perhaps some of his observations on this trip nudged James toward greater consideration of the status of black people in the United States, though his greatest passion would always remain for loyalty to the Constitution.

James left New Orleans 'after a most interesting visit' to begin the long trek back to New York.[23] While in route, they encountered a slave trader in Virginia who had a young black boy in handcuffs. 'When we next stopped, we examined the boy, and found him in great distress, from being separated from his parents. We conferred together, and decided that the white miscreant should not ride in the stage with us, and told him so.'[24] The modern reader might fault James for not doing more for the young boy, but in 1828 Virginia, he likely felt he had made a strong stand by refusing to share a coach with the trader. Though the informal network of what would become known as the Underground Railroad was operating in some border regions between free and slave states, James does not record being involved in any such organization or activity. Few people in his position would have bothered to ask the unfortunate young boy about his predicament, but James was ever eager to learn and understand different points of view, as he would prove over the course of several trips to Europe and his relationships with those who did not share his political beliefs. One wonders if he later regretted not doing more for the boy or if he thought of him decades later when he passionately spoke in favor of emancipation.

Upon his return to New York, James and Martin Van Buren began their discussions of the upcoming elections, which they also laid bets on.[25] James wrote confidently, partly based upon his observations during recent travels, 'The election is much contested, and will result in the choice of General Jackson.'[26] Van Buren offered to help James 'obtain your father's title of "Colonel Hamilton" through an appointment' in Jackson's administration.[27] James declined this 'very flattering mark of your attention,' possibly not realizing, despite the closeness of their relationship, that every move Van Buren made was carefully calculated.[28]

The election of 1828 was closer to what we might recognize today with mudslinging, demagoguery, and motivated voter involvement. An expanded popular vote and media coverage resulted in the defeat of one of the greatest statesmen of the day, John Quincy Adams, by an uneducated authoritarian who appealed to the 'common man,' Andrew Jackson. It was a turning point that solidified the power of the slaveholding South for decades.

James A. Hamilton became highly involved in the Jackson administration, even if he had not originally supported his candidacy.

> The election of General Jackson was an event in our country of vast importance, because it violated a course of public policy which received the sanction of the wisest men of the country of all parties, from the adoption of the Constitution. He was elected only because he had been a successful soldier, not having that familiar acquaintance with public affairs which can alone form a statesman ... More than this, he was wholly uneducated and without talent; his intentions were upright, his integrity unquestionable, his will unyielding, and his devotion to his

friends so great as to induce him to use the patronage of his office to reward their services.[29]

In other words, Jackson was a common man who appealed to other common men, and he saw it as good and right to give positions and contracts to those who would continue to support him.

Alexander Hamilton had hoped for a meritocracy, but Jackson introduced American cronyism. James experienced the result of this while in Washington DC in 1829 when he served as temporary Secretary of State, a position he came into largely because of his own personal connections with Martin Van Buren and Andrew Jackson, even if he filled it competently.

> Men came, women came, to sustain the applications of their husbands and other relatives. The crowd was so great and the persistence so unreasonable, that an order was issued not to admit any person to the office of the secretary until a late hour of the day. This was necessary to give time to perform the public duties.[30]

Henry Clay, another prominent statesman of the era who failed to beat Jackson and was often credited for his pursuit compromise during the years between the Revolution and Civil War, also spoke against using public positions as rewards for party loyalty in his famous Fowler's Garden Speech on 16 May 1829.

> One of the worst consequences of the introduction of this tenure of public office will be, should it be permanently adopted, to substitute for a system of responsibility, founded upon the ability and integrity with which public officers discharge their duties to the community, a system of universal rapacity. Incumbents, feeling the instability of their situations, and knowing their liability to periodic removals, at short terms, without any regard to the manner in which they have executed their trusts, will be disposed to make the most of their uncertain offices, whilst they hold them. And hence we may expect innumerable cases of fraud, speculation, and corruption.[31]

Jackson had accused Clay of scheming with Adams for the 1824 election and position of Secretary of State, but Clay accused Jackson of much worse.

James would speak out more boldly regarding these issues in later years, but at the beginning of the Jackson administration, he seemed simply happy to serve and to try impact decisions made regarding the banking system. Contrary to what some historians have written about James supporting Jackson in his attack on the Bank of the United States, James worked hard to see the bank reformed or another compromise made. He foresaw the financial chaos that ensued when the bank was simply demolished.

Martin Van Buren had been named Jackson's Secretary of State, but his duties as governor of New York kept him from immediately leaving for Washington. In the meantime, James, who was trusted by Van Buren not to usurp the position and trusted by Jackson after their cross-country trek together, was selected to serve as Secretary of State ad interim. His activities to support and guide the Jackson administration eventually stretched far beyond this appointment.[32]

James's own reflection on this time was characteristically modest. 'I have this day received from the General, a letter appointing me acting Secretary of State ... Thus I will at least have the gratification of being connected with the history of our Government, and have had some slight influence upon its affairs.'[33] He also expressed doubts in his friend's ability to fill the post, though no evidence exists that Martin Van Buren had any qualms. 'Mr Van Buren was certainly not eminently fitted for the State Department, by his knowledge of public affairs, by his education, which was very limited, or his intellectual endowments.'[34]

John Quincy Adams recorded James's appointment in the diary he famously kept throughout most of his life. He wrote with surprising humility, 'This man is Aid de Camp to Governor Van Buren, and has taken charge of the Department of State ad interim till he comes, by a written order from President Jackson. And he took the first day of his instalment at the Department of State to write me this Letter.'[35] John Quincy was not only a former president himself, but his father, who had been the president to follow George Washington, had been part of a public rivalry with Alexander Hamilton that proved toxic enough to hasten the downfall of the Federalist party. The correspondence between their sons indicates that they did not share their fathers' animosity toward each other. James and John Quincy seemed to share a devotion to the country and Constitution that went beyond party politics. Both men came from Federalist roots but developed their own political stances.

One of the first duties with which James was tasked was assisting with the draft of Jackson's Inaugural Address. 'There was a paragraph which was absolute nonsense. I revised it, amended it, and made it proper ... Several other alterations had been made; some of them I considered quite important ... Had it gone forth as it at first stood, it would have been absolutely disgraceful.'[36] One can't help but wonder if James thought about his father editing President Washington's writing as he worked.

Even when James was recording the inauguration and cabinet selections of the Jackson administration, he reverted to memories of his father and the recommendation of Robert Morris that helped him gain the position of Washington's Treasury Secretary.[37] The cabinet being formed at the time by Jackson compared poorly to that carefully molded first cabinet. James demonstrated concern that 'no thought appeared to be given as to the fitness of the persons for their places. I am sure I never heard one word in relation thereto.'[38] Perhaps, he was disappointed that others did not decline positions for which they were not well-suited as he had the integrity to do.

The trust President Jackson had in James is clear in how frequently he asked for his advice or entrusted him with speaking to people on his behalf. James's *Reminiscences* includes several requests from Jackson like this one: 'he [Jackson] requested me to come to his lodgings early in the morning, that he might, as he said, confer with me uninterruptedly before other persons should call.'[39] This early morning meeting, however, was interrupted by a visit from Senator Calhoun of South Carolina. Jackson informed James, 'I know what he is about. He cannot succeed. I wish you to remain in this house until he leaves. Then return and you shall know all about it.'[40]

James may have been 'one of three who enjoy all the General's confidence'[41] but he did not inherit his father's passion for politics. He wrote on 17 February 1829, before his official appointment had even been made, 'I am most heartily sick of Washington, and not a little tired of the intrigue in which we all live.'[42] However, he was not able to leave. Jackson called upon him constantly and claimed, 'I cannot spare you.'[43]

Although kept busy by his duties as acting Secretary of State, James found several opportunities to discuss his father with those who remembered him. He wrote to John Quincy Adams on 9 March 1829 to request information on a meeting that had taken place during the winter of 1803–1804, when James was only a teenager. He, 'deeming it a sacred duty to preserve the memory of my father from all stain,' asked Adams if 'you are in possession of any evidence, or that you believe, that the late Alexander Hamilton consented to attend the alleged meeting of the leading Federalists at Boston, or that he was at any time concerned in a project to dissolve the Union and establish a Northern Confederacy.'[44]

The plot to which James referred was a secret project of disillusioned Federalists who had attempted to establish a 'Northern Confederacy' that would be friendly to Great Britain and free of President Jefferson's embargo. James certainly did not believe this was a project that his father would be involved in, knowing he had said, 'To break the Union would break my heart,'[45] but James saw it as his duty to squash any rumors that hinted at Hamilton's involvement.

He must have been pleased to receive a prompt reply from Adams recollecting that Alexander had 'entirely disapproved of it,' and any connection to his name was by those who had hoped to solicit his involvement but had failed. Hamilton had died before the proposed meeting was held, but Adams believed, 'your father's purpose was to dissuade the parties concerned from the undertaking, and to prevail upon them to abandon it.'[46]

James soon met with John Quincy in his role as Secretary of State and seems to have worked well with him. Perhaps he no longer regretted Crawford's loss to Adams in 1824. He wrote, 'Mr Adams was an honest man; but he was a man of strong feelings, perhaps I may justly say resentments.'[47] Adams also recorded the meeting in his diary of 11 March 1829, writing that he and James discussed some issues of state before, 'He spoke to me also of my Letter to him concerning his father, with which he appeared to be satisfied.'[48] He wrote more about the 'disunion project of 1804' a week later, admitting that it 'cannot be fully exposed without developing the causes of dissatisfaction with Mr Jefferson's administration by which it was instigated. Most of those were well founded. I felt them deeply myself … My present course is to write with the boldness of truth.'[49] He had received a letter that would 'rescue Hamilton's reputation from having participated in the disunion project,' which he passed on to James.[50] A few days later, James had this information published in the *New-York Evening Post*, and Adams recorded in his diary that it was republished in the *National Journal*.[51]

Preparing a report for President Jackson based on his discussions with Henry Clay, John Quincy Adams, and others, James proved he took his role seriously, regardless of it being temporary. Jackson approved of the summary on foreign relations and treaties and asked James to submit his report to the Senate. An understanding of and appreciation for foreign relations was something for which James had a talent, and he would continue to advise successive presidents and their cabinets in this capacity. He would also travel abroad several times, making important connections and collecting information wherever he went. It was a skill he passed down to his son, Alexander, who served as secretary of legation to Spain under Washington Irving in the 1840s.

In the course of his Secretary of State duties, James came into contact with Albert Gallatin, who had served as Treasury Secretary under President Jefferson and not been a particular friend of Alexander Hamilton. Gallatin recalled that Jefferson had instructed him,

> your most important duty will be to examine the accounts, all the letters and records of your Department, in order to discover the blunders and frauds of Hamilton, and to ascertain what changes may be required to reform the system – this is a most important duty; it will require all your industry and acuteness, and to do it thoroughly, you may employ whatever extra force may be required.

Gallatin told James that 'the work was performed most thoroughly, occupying much time,' but he had been forced to disappoint Jefferson. He had informed the president, 'I have found the most perfect system ever formed, and any change that should be made, would only injure it – Hamilton made no blunders, committed no frauds – he did nothing wrong.'[52] James was understandably pleased with this testimony and kept in touch with Gallatin. Their correspondence includes rich discussions of diplomacy and finance.

Before Van Buren's arrival in Washington, Jackson requested that James 'make a synopsis of our foreign relations as to commerce, navigation, and friendship' including 'names of our ministers of every grade; our consuls and commercial agents, and their places of residence.' This was 'a work of great labor,' but James was 'determined to finish before Van Buren should take office.' Where others may have left such an arduous task to the man who would receive the benefits of the office, James got to work. 'I worked night and day ... a copy now before me, comprises one hundred pages of cap.'[53]

Jackson recognized James for his hard work and appointed him to the post of District Attorney for Southern New York. Van Buren showed his lack of appreciation when he failed to support this decision. He later wrote in his autobiography, 'The President was well warranted in assuming that I was friendly to Mr Hamilton and took an interest in his welfare ... But he was mistaken in supposing that I wished Mr Hamilton to have or would have recommended him for the appointment conferred upon him. I could not have done so with justice to my political friends.'[54] While James had been glad to give positive testimony of his friend[55] despite his misgivings regarding his lack of talent, and he had worked tirelessly to fill Van Buren's post as long as necessary, this loyalty was rewarded with disdain because providing James with a lucrative office did not give Van Buren the political power for which he constantly strived. James reflected that, 'he called upon me to serve him, and that I did render him essential services, and he certainly never rendered me a service of any kind.'[56]

Van Buren had recommended James to the governor of New York in 1828 should his name be presented as a potential judge.[57] In this case, Van Buren wrote, 'I believe him fully competent to the discharge of the duties of the place with credit to himself and usefulness to the public that he is a gentleman of good standing in the profession, in politics sound and devoted to the cause.'[58] For some reason, his recommendation did not include the District Attorney position. Besides political scheming, Van Buren might not have favored the friendly relationship that James had with John Quincy Adams, a major Van Buren rival in New England politics.

Others seemed to share Van Buren's concerns about the District Attorney position, or they felt they would personally benefit if another held it. James received more than one letter asking him to consider if it was honorable for him to take the position, which was, up until that point, held by John Duer, whom the president wished removed because of negative statements he had made about Rachel Jackson.[59] Though James tended to be modest about his own abilities and recommend others for high positions, he seems to have remained confident in his ability to competently serve as District Attorney. He received his official appointment to the office on 10 April 1830.[60]

Van Buren's lack of desire to reward James for his service made him no less willing to request his presence in Washington for as long as James could be convinced to stay, asking more than once, 'What shall I do without you?'[61] That, combined with Jackson's pleas that, 'I think your presence indispensable,' kept James in Washington for months, though he thought his importance 'very much exaggerated.'[62] Besides the demands of Van Buren and Jackson, James bemoaned the weather. 'We are totally buried in snow here, and I fear that the roads will, for some days, be impassable.'[63]

Despite Van Buren's ingratitude, James was convinced to stay through May of 1829, but his disillusionment is clear in some of the letters he wrote during this time. In April, he wrote, 'It makes me tremble, when I reflect how unconscious we all are of our needs; and how indifferent some of our public men are to reading, and making themselves masters of principles, and familiar with striking facts in the history of our country.'[64] To another 'discreet friend' he wrote, 'I am very tired of being here, among other reasons because I am cruelly disappointed at the manner in which, and to the extent removals and appointments are made.'[65] James clearly disagreed with giving out positions based on political deals, which is possibly one of his reasons for standing firm regarding his own appointment to District Attorney, and he wished more able men filled Washington's offices. Years later, he would write in detail about presidential power to remove from and appoint to office. In May 1829, his patience was wearing thin. 'Van Buren is still harping upon keeping me here.'[66]

At other times, James enjoyed the dependency upon him and regretted his need to leave Van Buren on his own in Washington. He wrote a friend, 'I declare to you, his friendship for, and apparent dependence upon me, for his comfort (if nothing more), is so great as to make me almost sad when I think of leaving him, and particularly believing, as I do, how useful I am to him.'[67] He later admitted to 'real regret at leaving him; more, indeed, than I could have supposed.'[68]

James mentioned that Van Buren was determined to have the president name James an undersecretary of state to keep him in Washington,[69] and John Quincy Adams made a similar observation in his diary. On 11 April 1829, Adams wrote, 'Since Mr Van Buren has taken charge of the Department of State, James A Hamilton continues to attend there and do business as he did before Van Buren came,' and he believed the plan was 'at the next Session of Congress to obtain a Law, for an Under Secretary of State for the Home Department, for which Hamilton is reserved.'[70] However, James did not record why this plan was not carried out.

On 8 June, James was finally able to leave Washington to attend his own 'arduous duties' as District Attorney, but Jackson left him with parting words, 'Go to the duties of your office, and make as much money as you can; but remember, you are to be always at my command … I want you to be near me.'[71] One wonders if James considered the similarity between his relationship with Jackson and his father's with Washington as they parted ways.

Jackson would need his friends. He was about to become embroiled in an odd and long-lasting Washington scandal.

Chapter 5

The Eaton Scandal

The ticklish case of General Eaton.[1]

James A. Hamilton recorded his first correspondence regarding the Eaton Affair on 18 March 1829, scarcely a fortnight after Jackson's inauguration, which had caused a stir with its rambunctious atmosphere and lack of elegance. The letter came from the editor of the New York *Evening Post*, who asked for insight into the drama within Jackson's cabinet and encouraged James to remain in Washington to be a good influence.[2] Another acquaintance 'told me the President appeared so utterly incompetent in his new situation that fears were entertained that the Government would run down unless Van Buren could sustain it.'[3]

The scandal to which they referred would last much longer than necessary and regarded Jackson's Secretary of War, John Eaton, who had recently married a Washington widow, Margaret O'Neal (sometimes spelled O'Neil or O'Neale) Timberlake. Rumors swirled around the federal city that the two had been carrying on an affair before the death of her previous husband. Some went as far to claim that this relationship had driven him to suicide. Others accused Margaret of having affairs with countless Washington men.

Wives of Jackson's other cabinet members were determined not to socialize with a low woman like Margaret, but the president saw in Margaret his own Rachel and the public abuse that he believed had killed her. Jackson staunchly defended his friend's wife and refused to hear anything against her, creating a deep divide in Washington society.

The most significant falling out caused by Jackson's selection of Eaton for his cabinet was between him and his vice-president, John C. Calhoun. Calhoun was one of the most influential and well-known politicians of the day with presidential hopes of his own, and it was his wife, Floride, who began the boycott of Margaret Eaton before returning to her home in South

Carolina, making her shun complete. Jackson punished Calhoun for his wife's actions, leaving him out of government matters and later replacing him as his running mate in his re-election campaign.

More difficult for Jackson to understand and cope with was the stance of his own family. Emily Donelson, Jackson's niece, accompanied him to Washington to serve as his hostess and unofficial First Lady after the sudden death of his wife. Emily and her husband joined the forces lining up against the Eatons until Jackson asked them to return to Tennessee rather than continue to embarrass him, though he did eventually welcome them to return.

Determined to follow in Jackson's footsteps as the next president, Van Buren, as Jackson's Secretary of State, did take Eaton's side in this social drama. It was easier for him to do so as a widower with no wife to be smeared by acquaintance with the new Mrs Eaton. Still, Van Buren was not free of frustration in the matter. He wrote in his autobiography that 'the Eaton imbroglio' was 'a private and personal matter which only acquired political consequence by its adaptation to the gratification of resentments, springing out of the formation of the Cabinet, and, as was supposed, to the elevation or depression of individuals in high positions.'[4] When he mentions it again, Van Buren laments that the excitement over Eaton's unconventional wife was

> kept alive by feelings of the bitterest character and soon directed to the accomplishment of political as well as personal objects it maintained for two years a foothold at the seat of the Federal Government, a plague to social intercourse, destructive in many instances of private friendship, deranging public business and for a season, at least, disparaging the character of the Government.[5]

James seemed to have had greater concerns than the virtue, or lack thereof, of Margaret Eaton. He was concerned about the 'great distrust of the fitness of the two Secretaries to manage the affairs of this great Country; – a distrust which, with all my regard for the President, I cannot help indulging.'[6] He likely believed the uproar about the Secretary of War's wife would soon fade and did not consider it important enough to worry about.

In his book on the Eaton scandal, historian John F. Marszalek quotes James as writing to Van Buren, 'For God knows we did not make him president to work the miracle of making Mrs E an honest woman.'[7] However, an examination of this letter dated 16 July 1829 reveals it to have been written by James Hamilton Jr of South Carolina, not James Alexander Hamilton of New York.[8]

On 23 April, James wrote to a friend, not regarding the Eaton Affair, but on a much more important topic. 'I am very tired of being here, among other reasons because I am cruelly disappointed at the manner in which, and the extent removals and appointments are made.'[9] Jackson, who had accused Henry Clay of a 'corrupt coalition' when he became Secretary of State for John Quincy Adams in 1824, was unashamed of his own habit of making appointments to office based on his own connections.[10] James would later write a pamphlet on the legal limits on the president – any president – when it came to removing people from office in order to appoint one's own selections. In 1829, he had not yet grown so bold but attempted to advise Jackson and the members of his cabinet in a positive way.

In a letter on 8 September, Van Buren attempted to convince James that 'the utmost harmony and the kindest feelings exist' between the President and his Cabinet.[11] Despite this reassurance, he writes again just a fortnight later with a full report on the ongoing scandal, beginning with the claim that he 'would rather pull a tooth than say a word.'[12] Regardless of this apparent reluctance, Van Buren goes on to describe a story that had been related to the President before his cabinet appointments were made. 'General Jackson had been informed by his friend Dr Ely, that he had been told by a Presbyterian clergyman of standing, that Mrs Eaton had had an abortion produced of a child, of which Eaton was the father.'[13]

Far from feeling warned against association with a woman of loose morals, Jackson roared against any who repeated what he felt were vile rumors. Rather than just ignore the story, Jackson was passionate about disproving it, spending time and resources on collecting testimony and records to prove that Margaret's husband had not died at his own hand and that any pregnancies she had experienced could be tied back to his times at home. Van Buren wrote to James that Jackson had 'unlimited confidence in his [Eaton's] honor and integrity' and insisted 'that Mrs Eaton was a virtuous and persecuted woman.'[14] Senator Henry Clay was more cynical, remarking that 'Age cannot wither nor time stale her infinite virginity.'[15]

From New York, James may have believed that the scandal would dwindle, as they often do, so he was surprised when he returned to Washington in June 1830 and found 'this matter is in greater extreme now than heretofore.'[16] In a letter to a friend, he admits to spending the evening with Jackson, 'the greater part of which we passed in conversation about Ingham, Eaton, Branch, McLane' – the President's cabinet.[17]

In another letter to Louis McLane, at that time serving as Minister Plenipotentiary to Great Britain, James admits that he advised replacing Treasury Secretary Samuel Ingham. It is certain that James thought more of Ingham's lack of credentials for the job than any wrong done to John Eaton or his controversial wife. He was preparing to advise a new Treasury Secretary and requested that McLane, who would eventually serve as one of Jackson's treasury secretaries, send him copies of 'the act establishing the Bank of England, Drummard's Treatise on Currency, and any other good works on Banking.'[18]

Jackson, writing to James from the Hermitage on 12 July 1830, demonstrates that he saw only what he wished to see by stating, 'I am always happy to hear of Major Eaton's increasing popularity and prosperity. I have long known him, and a more virtuous, honest man does not exist.'[19]

In April 1831, his cabinet was disintegrating as members began resigning. When James heard that Martin Van Buren had left his post, he was offended to not have been told directly by his friend, perhaps wondering if Van Buren wished to ensure that James did not take the Secretary of State position back up as his own. However much of a scandal the resignations may have been, James reflected that changes could only strengthen the administration and that they had been 'the most unintellectual and uneducated Cabinet we ever had.'[20]

Jackson had created an unenviable position for himself as his re-election campaign began, giving rivals like Henry Clay reason to believe he could be defeated. However, with Martin Van Buren at his side, Jackson secured a second term, seemingly untouched by scandal or his own bad policies that had caused deep political divisions. James maintained that the entire scandal had been a plot by 'Mr Calhoun and his friends' perpetrated out of 'fear of Mr Van Buren's power and influence.'[21] Blaming any negative consequences on the cabinet members who were now gone, James maintained his loyalty to the president.

Calhoun did indeed make a firm stand against Jackson, and his home state of South Carolina cast its electoral votes for their senator rather than the incumbent president in 1832.[22] Calhoun became more devoted to his state and continuation of the slave economy, distancing himself from some fellow legislators with whom he had previously been able to compromise and find solutions.

Despite the undying support of the president, Margaret Eaton met an unhappy ending. After her husband's death in 1856, she foolishly married a 19-year-old dancing teacher named Antonio Buchignani, who ruined her financially and eventually ran away with one of her grandchildren.[23] She died in 1879.

Chapter 6

District Attorney

To have the life or death of a human being in one's hands was a most painful condition.[1]

James A. Hamilton was never the outspoken public figure that his father was. However, when serving as the District Attorney for Southern New York, he did demonstrate that he inherited Alexander Hamilton's erudite legal mind. He also had several opportunities to defend the Constitution, taken in its literal form, as he would have been sure that his father would have done based upon his *Federalist Papers*.

In his *Reminiscences*, James mentions only a few cases from his time as District Attorney. They are interspersed between his trips to Washington and correspondence with leading men on a variety of issues of the day. It comes, perhaps, as no surprise that James did not fill the position for long, as he was pulled in so many directions.

Upon taking up the employment, James recorded the challenge 'that they involved an accurate knowledge of the laws of the United States; of the course of commercial affairs; of the laws particularly applicable thereto; and also of the criminal law.'[2] Though he modestly questioned his ability to fulfill the role, his knowledge of each of the areas he lists is clear in his papers. He was also confident enough in his abilities to take on his youngest brother, Philip, as an assistant and pass down the family tradition of practicing law.[3]

The first case James documented in his *Reminiscences* is that of Edward Livingston, who he claimed as a friend. He was 'indebted to the United States to a large amount, for which there was a judgment on record against him.'[4] When Livingston came to James in August 1829 with a letter from a treasury agent discharging the debt, James 'could not enter satisfaction of that judgment' based on his understanding of the law, regardless of his friendship. Ever one for sticking to the letter of the law, James pointed out that 'no officer of the Government had a right (unless authorized by an act of Congress to do so) to receive anything but money in payment of a debt.'[5] Therefore, he would not put his name to an agreement to discharge Livingston's debt based on the assignment of property in New Orleans.

James recognized that government affairs were often conducted 'ignorantly or loosely' in regard for the rules, but that would not be his way.[6] It could not have been easy to stick to his ideals when Livingston 'earnestly urged me to obey the order of the agent, insisting that it was not my duty to look into the kind of settlement which was made.'[7]

Edward Livingston was forced to travel to Washington and obtain a letter from the Solicitor of the Treasury before James was convinced to settle the debt. He would not have anyone accuse him of using his position to benefit his friends.

Not everyone shared Hamilton's passion for integrity. James and Martin Van Buren had advised President Jackson against the appointment of Samuel Swartwout as Collector of the Port of New York, but Jackson was ever loyal to those he considered friends and refused to see their faults. It was not long before his role as District Attorney brought James into contact with Swartwout, who he stated was 'so entirely ignorant of the laws which regulated his duty, and of the course of the business of his office, that he required the District Attorney's services in resolving questions and difficulties for day to day – so much so, that I was requested to come every morning to the Custom House to aid him in the administration of his duties.'[8]

James was able to observe the casual embezzlement that Swartwout would not be officially accused of until years later. After watching Swartwout hand a $5,000 check to a known speculator without receiving a receipt, James 'was convinced that this was an appropriation of the public money to his private use.'[9]

He did not confront the collector directly but considered the issue before deciding that 'it was a great wrong – and asked myself what my duty as a public officer and a personal friend of the President required me to do.'[10] James decided to write to Jackson.

Jackson seems to have at least forwarded the concerns to the Treasury Department, because James received a letter 'asking me to give him the scheme which I believed would prevent the misappropriation ... I did so, and nothing further was done.'[11] Samuel Swartwout eventually embezzled over a million dollars but managed to evade prosecution in one of the largest early American cases of government fraud. Jackson did not take corruption as seriously as he took challenges to his authority, so even significant deceptions such as Swartwout's did not get much attention from the president.

One of the most interesting cases in which James became involved as District Attorney was that of the jewels of Her Royal Highness, the Princess of Orange. On 15 June 1831, a ship arrived in the Port of New York carrying Constant Polari and Susanna Blanche, who was posing as his wife. The couple was discovered to be smuggling jewels within a hollow walking stick and umbrella case. They were found out by the infamous Swartwout, who called upon James as District Attorney.[12]

Polari was arrested, but Swartwout's true interest was in the disposition of the smuggled goods. Standard procedure would have seen half of the value rewarded to the Collector, but James perceived that the jewelry of exceptional value was that which had been reported stolen from the palace of the Prince of Orange in September 1829, and should, therefore, be returned to their owner without penalty. It was not only the legally correct solution but was necessary for good foreign relations and 'the honor of the country.'[13]

James was ordered by the Secretary of the Treasury, Louis McLane, to 'appear for the Prince of Orange as owner and claimant … You will use the same zeal and diligence in sustaining before the Court this claim, as if it were a claim of the United States.'[14] Swartwout was apparently not discouraged by the Jackson administration's clear desire to see the case decided in favor of the Netherlands' royal family and continued to stake his own claim. McLane left room for Swartwout's right to file his claim, but left the result to James's skill in court, writing on 6 October 1831, 'But, as the rights of all must be respected, it is not intended that the interposition now directed on behalf of the Prince or Princess of Orange shall preclude any measures which the officers of the Customs or others interested may think proper to take for sustaining before the Courts any claims which they may assert in the property.'[15] Undeterred, Swartwout wrote that he had 'the honor of informing' James on 15 October, that he had retained John Duer as his counsel. This was the lawyer James had replaced as District Attorney.[16]

A letter to James from his friend, Edward Livingston, who had by that time replaced Van Buren as Secretary of State, indicates that the case was occupying the time of many top government officials. Livingston's involvement apparently also increased the stance that the jewels would be returned to their owners without penalty. On 12 November 1831, McLane wrote with increased certainty regarding the rights of the Prince and Princess of Orange and that 'notice will of course be given to the Collector, and all the other requisites of the Act be complied with.'[17] Roger B. Taney, who Jackson would later name as Chief Justice of the Supreme Court, also wrote his opinion on the 'case of the U States v a box of diamonds' and concurred with James's opinion.[18]

The jewels were finally delivered to the representative of their owner in January 1832, and James was thanked for his services on their behalf. The thick file of correspondence between himself and multiple cabinet members evinced the time and diplomacy required to reach this end. Therefore, James was understandably disappointed to receive only $69.32 in compensation for his months of labor in this complex and sensitive case.[19]

Later that same year, James was forced to perform 'one of the most painful events of my life' when 'three persons were arrested and brought into New York charged with, and who were unquestionably guilty of, most atrocious piracy and murder.'[20] The three being the survivors of a stranded vessel upon which the crew and captain were killed, James was responsible for choosing one to give the evidence that would convict the other two.

He describes the three only as a man named Gibbs, 'a black man, and a boy of about sixteen years.'[21] With no clear letter of the law to guide his decision, James was forced to decide 'which of these three persons should be saved from death. To have the life or death of a human being in one's hands, was a most painful condition. I deliberated much and most anxiously.'[22] Determining the case could not be tried without the testimony of one of the three, James selected the 16-year-old boy as the least guilty. He did not remark upon the fact that the black man's testimony might not have been considered sufficient to convict the others, so we cannot know if this impacted his choice.

Gibbs and the unnamed black man were tried and executed, but the teenager was freed and allowed to return home. James believed him to be 'very penitent and very grateful to me for saving his life.' It may have been a balm to his conscious after having to make such a difficult decision.

On 13 December 1833, James resigned from the District Attorney post, citing his health.[23] The years of long hours and traveling between New York and Washington had apparently caught up with him, though he gives no details of his ailment and lived several more active decades of life.

Also in New York in 1833, William Lloyd Garrison and Arthur Tappan founded the American Antislavery Society. Though there is no evidence that James was involved in this abolitionist group, he must have been acquainted with Tappan, since he had married Fanny Antil with whom James had been raised. James's recorded comments on slavery at this time were limited to constitutional issues – the problem of the three-fifths compromise and the lack of federal power to intervene. He did not record his opinion on the abolitionist movement that was becoming more vocal and active in his area of New York. Later, the Democratic party's devotion to slavery would drive James and others to form and support other parties, such as the Whigs and Republicans. It may also have played a part in ending his friendship with Martin Van Buren.

Chapter 7

Defending Hamilton's Bank

In the hope that I might be useful.[1]

James was not at his District Attorney duties for long before he received a message calling him back to Washington. His assistance was needed regarding the president's annual address and, in particular, what he should say about the Bank of the United States.

The issue at hand was not the Bank of the United States that Alexander Hamilton had formed and fought for at the nation's founding. The First Bank of the United States did not operate like the modern Federal Reserve, but it did stabilize the US economy through its management of bank notes. Its charter had been allowed to expire in 1811, despite the recommendation of Albert Gallatin that it be renewed, because the party of Jefferson and Madison believed it was an example of too much centralized power held by the federal government. By that time, Alexander Hamilton was dead, and his bank expired after a vote in the Senate with Vice-President George Clinton casting the tie-breaking vote.

The War of 1812 convinced James Madison that he had been wrong about the bank. Increased federal debt and a limping economy led to the establishment of the Second Bank of the United States in 1816. It held the deposits of the federal government and held banknotes of other institutions as well as issuing its own. Strategically managing these notes helped lower inflation and expand the economy while stabilizing the currency in the same way as its predecessor. However, Jackson had never changed his mind that a central bank was unconstitutional. He campaigned that the bank benefited the rich at the expense of common men and vowed to see it brought to an end.

James hoped to convince the president that the bank was a vital part of the US economy that could not simply be eliminated, but it was an uphill battle that he would eventually lose. When James arrived in Washington on 28 November 1829,[2] Jackson provided him with a guest room in the White House in order to take the greatest advantage of his time. James was provided with a draft of the address and immediately got to work and remained so 'until about four o'clock in the morning.'[3] James found that 'the Bank of the United States was attacked at great length in a loose, newspaper, slashing style.'[4]

The next morning, after sleeping only three hours, James met with Jackson, who wanted to know what he had written about the bank. In place of the original tabloid-style attack, James had written a few basic facts about the bank and that its charter would expire in 1836. Jackson was surprised that was all James thought should be said, but James replied, 'I think you ought to say nothing at present about the bank.'[5]

Henry Clay, who had run for president against Jackson in 1824 before becoming John Quincy Adams's Secretary of State, may have seemed a strange ally for South Carolina's John C. Calhoun, but Jackson's war against the Bank of the United States and abuse of executive authority caused them to set aside their differences to form a loosely connected political party that became known as the Whigs. Clay determined that a bill to recharter the Bank of the United States should be voted on before it was due for renewal, forcing Jackson to act upon it. By making a stance, he would be losing votes on one side or the other. Clay reasoned that if Jackson vetoed it, as he was likely to do, he might fail in his 1832 re-election campaign.

'The President will most certainly veto it,' James wrote, though he had reason, as the son of Alexander Hamilton, to wish to see the president support it.[6] He wrote to Jackson on 28 February 1833 to warn him of the inevitable consequences of failing to recharter the bank and 'the immense injury to the whole nation resulting from that event' and the resulting 'stronger public feeling in favor of a recharter of the Bank as the only means of restoring a sound currency.'[7] James agreed that corruption must be dealt with, but he understood better than the president that financial troubles would arise with the removal of the national bank's influence.

James would defend until the end of his days that his father had created a perfect financial system when he formed the First Bank of the United States, though it was the Second Bank that Jackson was attacking. Jackson was not convinced as other anti-Federalists like James Madison had been that the country required the stability that the First Bank had provided.[8] Unfortunately, those who had been placed in charge of the Second Bank were not as altruistic and made corporate decisions for their own financial gain rather than with public interest in mind. 'Whereas the First Bank of the United States had served as a check on the expansive monetary policies of commercial banks, the Second Bank and its branches instead added fuel to the fire with their own loose banknote and loan policies.'[9] For now, Jackson gave in to James, saying, 'Oh! My friend, I am pledged against the bank, but if you think that is enough, so let it be.'[10]

James was still in Washington on 3 December, when he wrote that the president had approached him, saying, 'Colonel Hamilton, I named to you that I wished to have a confidential conversation with you; what I am now going to say, I never breathed to any human being. You must know that the public mind is turned to Van Buren as the President of the United States.' Jackson believed that, to that end, Van Buren would soon leave his post, and he was 'determined you shall, if you will, take his place.'[11] James replied, 'I can only say that there is no situation in which you can place me that I am not willing to serve you.'[12] However, when Van Buren did resign in March 1831, Jackson did not name James to the post, and it was his friend, Edward Livingston, who filled it.

By 19 December 1829, James had returned to New York, where he received continued correspondence from Jackson regarding the bank issue. In one letter, the president writes, 'You are surely aware of my exalted opinion of your virtue and honesty, and this must convince you that I think you incapable of any thing dishonorable, dishonest or unfair.'[13] Given the lengths Jackson was going through to defend his Secretary of War, John Eaton, in the midst of scandal, James must have been pleased to have such strong support from the president.

The same could not be said for Nicholas Biddle, who was attempting to reform and recharter the Second Bank of the United States. He 'centralized control of the Bank, no longer allowing its branches the freedom of issuing loans and banknotes that had helped to fuel speculation.' Like the First Bank had done, Biddle 'used the branch system to help regulate the nation's money, expanding and contracting supply in different parts of the country as needed to stabilize demand for specie.'[14] But it was too late in Jackson's mind. He had declared war on the bank and would not back down. Or, as historian Daniel Walker Howe put it, 'That the modern twenty-dollar Federal Reserve Note should bear Andrew Jackson's portrait is richly ironic. Not only did the Old Hero disapprove of paper money, he deliberately destroyed the national banking system of his day.'[15]

Jackson was not alone in his distrust of banks. 'Some Americans worried about the corrupting potential of concentrating such vast economic power in the hands of one monopolistic institution.'[16] The bank may have been adding stability to the nation's economy and financial system, but it had too many political enemies. Jackson was determined to take away the bank's power by removing government deposits, which made up much of its reserves.

James advised Jackson regarding the bank in a letter on 4 January 1830. His 'few hints on the subject of Banks' are, in truth, lengthy pages of advice on the establishment of a uniform currency and the general operations of the treasury, though he closes with, 'I do not mean to extend this letter to a dissertation upon Banking.'[17] One can discern when reading it that James was truly his father's son. Learning the lesson of the Second Bank of the United States' corruption, James proposes government management of the considered bank or offices of deposit rather than entrust any individual with the duty and even provides details on the length of terms for which commissioners should be appointed – one year for not more than three successive years.[18] Finance expert Albert Gallatin, who had succeeded Alexander Hamilton as Secretary of the Treasury, agreed that the Bank of the United States had a positive impact on the economy.[19] However, no banking expert had the power to convince Jackson.

Demonstrating some concern for what Jackson would decide to do, James wrote again on 16 March 1830. He shared feedback from London, hoping the opinions of unbiased outsiders might sway the president. James wrote that 'these gentlemen deservedly rank first among their countrymen as to wealth and intelligence' and that they believed if the 'establishment should be dissolved, we suppose Government will have to make some arrangement to carry on its concerns.'[20] Simply disbanding the Second Bank was not a real solution, according to James, but he knew Jackson was not convinced.

By the end of the month, he was in Washington again, where he discussed appointments and the bank situation with Jackson. The president invited

James to lodge with him at the White House, but for reasons he did not record, he decided to stay with Van Buren instead.[21] They had apparently patched up their differences over the District Attorney appointment.

James was forced to balance duties as District Attorney with constant demands from Washington. In November 1830, he was called upon again to assist with the writing of Jackson's annual message. His frustrations are demonstrated in his notes. 'The suggestions as to the Bank I do not approve; his plan is impracticable; I made efforts to amend and omit – neither would do … I am a prisoner in the house, condemned to unceasing labor.'[22]

However, James and some of his correspondents also had concerns about the Bank as things stood. It did not operate with the same concern for the public good as had the first bank created under Alexander Hamilton, but it was still 'indispensable to preserve a sound currency.'[23] This brought James to his next question. Could the state banks perform this function if Jackson got his way, as he usually did, and the Bank of the United States was not rechartered? James directed this question to Isaac Bronson, who had served during the American Revolution and since become a co-founder of the New York Life Insurance and Trust Company and one of the era's leading financiers. Bronson's reply was not encouraging. 'I should say not,'[24] adding, 'The history of our currency during the late war will tell the rest.'[25] It had been the financial disaster of the War of 1812 that convinced President James Madison to change his mind about the need for a Bank of the United States.

When James asked about the probability of charter renewal despite the veto of the President, Bronson and Clay were of one mind. Bronson stated that nothing 'would be so gratifying to the Bank' than an act from the President resulting in public outcry. 'The community would be the victim' of such an action and demand for recharter would increase.[26] Clay voiced a similar choice between 'the will of one man and that of twelve million people.'[27] But they had underestimated the will – and the popularity – of President Andrew Jackson.

James and Secretary of State McLane were disappointed when Van Buren announced that he was determined to support the president in the removal of the federal funds from the Bank of the United States, as he had supported him in the Eaton Affair. Sticking with Jackson had served Van Buren well, and he made his decisions politically rather than for the greater good. Instead of recording his own thoughts, James shared McLane's who found 'this recreancy on the part of Mr Van Buren was most painful' and 'very unworthy.'[28]

Thankfully, Jackson was open to advice from James, and asked him for copies of what his father had written 'on the subject of changing the deposits to prevent runs upon the Bank' and 'such information as is in your power, showing the pressure of the United States Bank on the State Banks.'[29] While he was determined in his course of action, the president at least made an attempt to research the likely consequences.

James responded with the information he had been gathering from various sources, making a somewhat Washington Irving-type observation, 'The business of the country generally has been very prosperous, and, as is almost always the case, it has produced a sort of an infatuation among the money-makers of all descriptions (and who is there in our Country who is not of that class?).'[30] James also took the opportunity to quote Jackson's own words back to him. 'It is surely the duty of the Executive to administer the government for the benefit and protection of all, and not for the few.'[31] But would they agree on what path forward provided those benefits and protection? Unfortunately, James was also aware that the national bank was willing to use its power to make the financial situation difficult for the state banks and President Jackson. Therefore, he was left defending the idea of a national bank while warning against plotting by the leaders of this one in particular.[32]

Jackson had asked if the state banks could carry on fiscal operations in place of the Bank of the United States. James states the possibility but also his 'fears whether they will not, unrestrained, run into excesses which will inflate the currency, and consequently make it unsound.'[33] This, of course, is precisely what happened when Jackson set aside all expert advice, including James's when he suggested, 'whatever speculations of theories there may be indulged on this subject, experience is a better guide.'[34]

Jackson did not accept the guidance James provided regarding the banking system. Such a plan would not be put into place until the Civil War under Treasury Secretary Salmon P. Chase. Instead, Jackson issued what one historian considers 'the most important presidential veto in American history' when he refused to recharter the Second Bank of the United States on 10 July 1832.[35]

Jackson, unlike the men who had served before him, appealed to the timeless prejudices against the wealthy, rather than facts and reason, in his veto message. He claimed that 'the rich and powerful too often bend the acts of government to their selfish purposes' and that the bank was an example of this.[36] In general, the people did not understand the economy well enough to demand to know how the president planned to replace the important work that the bank performed. As time would tell, however, Jackson had not eliminated corruption from the banking system with his veto, only removed the oversight that the Bank of the United States had provided. Without it, smaller banks created more unreliable notes that were difficult to value outside of their local area.

That did not happen immediately, because the Bank of the United States had applied for its recharter early. Therefore, even though Jackson had vetoed its continuance, it was chartered through 1836. That was not soon enough for Jackson, so he decided in March 1833 to remove federal deposits from the Bank of the United States and distribute them among regional banks operated by loyal party members.

When asked by Jackson for his opinion on removal of federal deposits from the Bank of the United States, James insisted that he needed more time to deliberate since 'the subject was one of such vast importance.'[37] However, 'My first impression is that the measure proposed was a very questionable one, and must lead to great disturbance in commercial affairs.'[38] James did not take the duty lightly. He conferred with New York's 'most distinguished bankers,' former Treasury Secretary Albert Gallatin, Secretary of State Louis McLane, and others in an exhaustive quest to keep Jackson from making a disastrous decision.[39] Gallatin 'insisted that a Bank of the United States was an indispensable fiscal agent of the Treasury' and 'expressed the most decided opinion against the removal.'[40]

James sent a lengthy questionnaire to Isaac Bronson, one of the most trusted experts on banking of that era. Bronson's response, in part, reads, 'There is perhaps no operation in banking more universally understood than that, a Bank in a single city reducing its loans, others in the same city must reduce likewise. And that so soon as this affects the price of commodities, more distant Banks are compelled to contract their credits and circulation.'[41] This was the basic banking truth that James needed the president to understand.

The dual duties of advising the president and serving as District Attorney were too much for James, and he resigned his position at the end of 1833. As a friend had written, 'The Bank question absorbs all others,' and this was certainly true for James.[42]

The president had come up against another problem related to his plan to destroy the national bank. Only the Secretary of the Treasury could move the federal deposits, and only after reporting to Congress that there was a legitimate reason for doing so. Treasury Secretary Louis McLane refused.[43] To counter this difficulty, Jackson reassigned McLane to be Secretary of State to replace Edward Livingston, who was made an envoy to France. This allowed Jackson to name William Duane to the opening in the Treasury Department in May 1833. He must have been unpleasantly surprised when Duane also refused to remove the deposits. Duane felt that the move was unconstitutional and would cause a financial panic. Besides these objections, Duane insisted that Jackson required the consent of Congress.

A man who refused to back down until he got his way, Jackson removed his new Treasury Secretary after only four months and replaced Duane with Roger Taney, who was already Jackson's Attorney General. Although the appointment was never confirmed by Congress, Taney took action and transferred the government's funds from the Bank of the United States to commercial banks hand-picked by Jackson. Twenty-four years before Taney, in his role as Chief Justice, would write the horrific Dred Scott decision that stated black Americans could not be citizens, he helped Andrew Jackson send the US economy into financial panic by removing federal deposits from the Second Bank of the United States.[44] The loyalty this action demonstrated was one of the reasons Jackson later named Taney Chief Justice.

The action caused Louis McLane and Lewis Cass to resign from Jackson's cabinet, and the Senate passed a motion to censure President Jackson on 28 March 1834.[45] It is the only time in US history that the Senate has done so, and the censure was purged from Senate record on 16 January 1837. Unfortunately, it was an empty gesture. The Bank's fate had been decided. Ironically, with his dismantling of the national bank, Jackson, avowed enemy of all banks, only caused an explosion in the number of smaller banks in the country.[46]

Despite the fears expressed by James, Jackson's treasury secretaries, and others, the president maintained, 'I am determined to test it, and have no doubt but it will work well in the end.'[47] In response to the president's rejection of any and all plans, James presented to alleviate the concerns regarding the Bank of the United States without causing a fiscal disaster, he records his frustrations in his *Reminiscences*. 'These efforts to enlighten the President, made at his request, were wholly unavailing. He had determined, before he came to Washington, to destroy the Bank of the United States … The result was a most disastrous inflation of the currency, reckless speculation, and the extended ruin of 1837.'[48]

Jackson caused serious decline in the US economy with two pivotal decisions in his second term, once the Second Bank of the United States had been dissolved. The Deposit Act of 1836 returned federal surpluses to the states, expanding the money supply to an inflationary extent. Jackson's Specie Circular, an executive order which required people to pay for land purchases with silver or gold, caused people to doubt the value of bank notes and left the American fiscal system floundering.[49] His fiscal policies led to the Panic of 1837.

Chapter 8

Nullification Crisis

First, the preservation of the Union.[1]

In addition to the fight over the national bank, Jackson's Washington became embattled over the issue of nullification. Martin Van Buren wrote, 'It is difficult to imagine a more critical condition than that in which I found the country involved at the moment of my arrival at Washington on the 26th of February 1833.'[2] Modern Americans tend to think of secession as solely a Civil War issue, but the action had been threatened more than once before the Southern states started leaving the Union in 1860.

Nullification was one of the issues that brought America to the brink of civil war almost three decades earlier. Jackson referred to this problem in a letter to James on 12 November 1831.

> There is a party in that State under a certain influence that would dissolve the Union rather than not effect their ambitious views I have no doubt; but that influence can obtain a majority in South Carolina to effect this wicked purpose I cannot permit myself for one moment to believe, though should the crisis arrive you will find my energies equal thereto, and that the Union will be preserved.[3]

James was in Washington, as he often was at the end of the year, to assist with Jackson's annual message. John C. Calhoun was leading the nullifiers as a strong proponent of state rights. To him, this meant that the states had the power to nullify any federal law that they did not believe benefited their state. In this case, tariffs hurt the South and aided the North, so Calhoun did not believe South Carolinians should have to pay them.

The Ordinance of Nullification, passed by the South Carolina legislature, declared the federal Tariffs of 1828 and 1832 'null, void, and no law, nor binding upon this State.' It went on to state that we, the people of South Carolina, to the end that it may be fully understood by the government of the United States, and the people of the co-States, that we are determined to maintain this our ordinance and declaration, at every hazard, do further declare that we will not submit to the application of force on the part of the federal government, to reduce this State to obedience.

Any forceful action taken by the federal government would absolve South Carolina from 'further obligation to maintain or preserve their political connection with the people of the other States' and cause them to 'proceed to organize a separate government.'[4]

James wrote from Washington of his fears for the country in a letter on 14 March 1832. 'The unpatriotic spirit manifested here, renders me impatient and unhappy. The opposition are so bent upon pulling down this administration, that to do so they are anxious to frustrate every measure, however deeply it may wound our beautiful system.'[5]

From Calhoun's point of view, he was protecting the Union and the rights of states. If South Carolina had the right to nullify federal laws with which it disagreed, secession would not be necessary. It would also ensure that the federal government could not enact laws in opposition to slavery for as long as states kept it legal. However, South Carolina was prepared to protect its rights with force and called up 25,000 militiamen to prove it.[6]

Jackson, not one to take any type of disagreement lightly, was furious in his response. Though he was a slaveholder and considered himself a supporter of the South, Jackson believed strongly in his constitutional duty as president to preserve the Union. He wrote to James on 2 November 1832 about South Carolina, admitting to 'weep[ing] for its fate, and over the delusion into which the people are led by the wickedness, ambition, and folly of their leaders.'[7] He reassured James, once again, that the Union would be preserved as 'there has been too much blood and treasure shed to obtain it.'[8]

South Carolina had not only voted to overrule federal law, but had claimed its ability to defend the right to do so. Jackson could not be silent when 'the raising of troops under them to resist the laws of the United States is absolute treason.'[9] He did not, however, wish to go to war, but to 'cause the good citizens of South Carolina to retrace their steps, and adhere to that Constitution of perpetual union they have sworn to support.'[10]

On 10 December 1832, Jackson responded formally to South Carolina with his Proclamation regarding Nullification, handling this problem with greater skill than he had managed the problems in banking. In it, he states, 'The ordinance is founded, not on the indefeasible right of resisting acts which are plainly unconstitutional, and too oppressive to be endured, but on the strange position that any one State may not only declare an act of Congress void, but prohibit its execution.'[11] It allowed for no appeal since South Carolina also denied the authority of the Supreme Court. Jackson pointed out that 'If this doctrine had been established at an earlier day, the Union would have been dissolved in its infancy,'[12] before offering examples of other laws that had not enjoyed unanimous support by the states. He called the act 'impracticable absurdity' and the ideas it proposes 'incompatible with the existence of the Union, contradicted expressly by the letter of the Constitution, unauthorized by its spirit inconsistent with every principle on which it was founded, and destructive of the great object for which it was formed.'[13] President Jackson was not one to hold back. With this proclamation he made a strong stand for the Union and denied any state's right to claim authority greater than that of the federal government.

Jackson had firmly put South Carolina in its place, and it gave his re-election campaign a boost. Then, on 1 March 1833, Congress passed one of Henry Clay's famous compromises, assuaging South Carolina's concerns and maintaining the Union for a bit longer.[14] Tariffs were reduced and the Ordinance of Nullification repealed, but many of the underlying issues remained.

Although Jackson is remembered as 'the people's president,' part of his Proclamation demonstrates his pandering and elitist attitude toward the people over whom he ruled when he said,

> Let me not only admonish you as the first magistrate of our common country, not to incur the penalty of its laws, but to use the influence that a father would over his children whom he saw rushing to a certain ruin. In that paternal language, with that paternal feeling, let me tell you,

my countrymen that you are deluded by men who are either deceived themselves or wish to deceive you.[15]

He may have been the first to proudly claim the title of Democrat, but Andrew Jackson believed he knew what was best for those beneath him as much as many other men who have held power over others.

Vice-President Calhoun took the opportunity to strike back at Jackson in his role as of president of the Senate. After Martin Van Buren's resignation from his position as Secretary of State at the conclusion of the Eaton scandal, Jackson was determined to see him named minister to Great Britain, but the appointment was rejected by Calhoun's tie-breaking vote.[16] Calhoun thought he had landed a great strike, but Martin Van Buren went on to take Calhoun's spot as vice-president before becoming president himself, a position Calhoun never achieved.

Writing to President Jackson regarding his proclamation on nullification, James praised his message, 'expressing my entire approval, and, I may add, the pride I feel in all you have done on the subject to which it refers.'[17] He also went on to encourage others in New York to publicly express their support for the president and therefore discourage any further talk of nullification or secession.[18] Little did he realize that it was far from the last time he would address the topic of secession.

Chapter 9

Family Life

My dear child.[1]

Employed as District Attorney and at the beck and call of the President, James A. Hamilton also had a family that was transitioning into new stages as his children reached adulthood. Although James did not leave many records of a personal nature, the diary of John Quincy Adams gives us a peek at a Hamilton party in December in 1830. He wrote:

> I went about nine, and was the first person there— The company soon began to come— It was a Ball, and I found myself out of my Element— Most of the company were of the second generation after me—but Mr Hamilton's mother was there— His daughter, about seventeen was one of the belles—with a bell hoop— He introduced his Son to me, a boy of 12 or 13— Mr and Mrs Davis, Mr James King; Mr Dominic Lynch, and Edward Coles were of my acquaintance— As the company thickened I retired about ten O'Clock to my Lodgings.[2]

John Quincy might have left early, but he recorded a few days later that another acquaintance had stayed 'till 3 the next morning.'[3]

It is likely that the party John Quincy records was not an unusual occurrence for the Hamilton family, especially as James's children neared adulthood. The year 1832 was one of many changes. As James celebrated his 44th birthday, his daughters were courting, and his son began his studies at West Point.

On 14 March, Eliza, who was now 20 years old, received a lengthy letter from George Lee Schuyler. Eliza was visiting Washington at the time, and George bemoaned that New York was 'dull and stupid' in comparison. Or, perhaps, he simply missed Eliza herself, since he gushed, 'I shall be truly rejoiced when you get home – there are a thousand things I want to talk to you about which I cannot cram into a sheet of letter paper.'[4]

James did not share Eliza's enjoyment of Washington. While she was writing to George of the good times she was having, James wrote to a friend that 'The unpatriotic spirit manifested here renders me impatient and unhappy.'[5]

George and Eliza were not the only ones with their minds on romance that year. The second Hamilton daughter, Fanny, turned 19 and married George Richard James Bowdoin in October. George had been born a Sullivan but changed his last name to Bowdoin in order to inherit through his maternal line.[6] They went on to have three children through whom James A. Hamilton has descendants to this day.

Alexander was 16 years old and a cadet at West Point. Letters between Alexander and James demonstrate their close relationship. His son felt comfortable enough to ask his father's advice regarding intimate issues encountered at the academy. Alexander wrote on 10 July 1832, 'I thank you for your advice as to petting but have adopted a way of preventing it different from yours, which I find succeeds tolerably well, whenever a man walks up to me & becomes too familiar without saying a word I march off and he generally takes the hint.' Alexander goes on to say, 'I have already discovered there is nothing like making a standard for yourself & acting up to it if you wish to gain the respect of your associates.'[7] He wrote to his sister, Eliza, the next day with descriptions of his day and inquiries about mutual acquaintances without the personal details he shared only with his father.[8]

A year later, Alexander was no less attached to his father, writing, 'I had determined to defer the pleasure of writing to you until tomorrow but as I find I have still a half hour left before ten, I cannot help availing myself of it.' In this letter, he grows philosophical. 'How time flies the brilliant points alone are retained by the mind like milestones on the great journey of life.'[9]

James must have felt this phenomenon even more strongly than his teenaged son. With Alexander at West Point, one daughter married, and another being courted by her future husband, the Hamilton home likely felt somewhat empty to James and Mary. Their remaining daughters, Mary and Angelica, also spent frequent time in Washington, either with their father, family friends, or their grandmother.

Elizabeth Schuyler Hamilton (not to be confused with her granddaughter, who would soon become Elizabeth Hamilton Schuyler) was 75 in 1832, and she remained active in philanthropic work and defending her late husband's name whenever necessary. She had assisted Dolley Madison with establishing an orphanage in Washington after the War of 1812, just as she had previously founded such an institution in New York. In a letter to James, President Jackson remarks upon seeing Eliza walking to the Capitol for her daily exercise and that 'she retains all her faculties, and has clear recollections of our past history in which her deceased husband acted so conspicuous a part.'[10]

Eliza had no intention of slowing down any time soon. In 1837, she took a steamboat ride to the Wisconsin Territory to visit her son, William Stephen, who had established a lead mining settlement called Hamilton's Diggings.[11] He had settled in the area years earlier and been part of the Black Hawk War in 1832. His Hamilton's Diggings is current day Wiota in Wisconsin's Lafayette County.[12] When Eliza wrote home during her travels, she wrote of the Ohio River's beautiful shores and 'no beauty but good buildings' in Pittsburgh.[13] She inquired, 'particularly respecting Angelica,' her oldest daughter who struggled with mental illness, and made multiple mentions of 'your beloved Father' as if Alexander had not been dead for more than thirty years.[14]

Eliza was also present at the laying of the cornerstone of the Washington Monument on 4 July 1848, when she was 90. She sat alongside Dolley Madison. The elderly ladies were, by that time, symbols of another age.

We can only imagine the conversations between Eliza and her grandchildren as they were coming of age and deciding who to marry. Eliza was passionately devoted to the memory of her husband and never considered remarriage. Perhaps she instilled the same ideals in her granddaughters. In 1833, William Lloyd Garrison established the American Anti-Slavery Society, and perhaps the community-minded Hamilton women discussed this as well.

George Lee Schuyler and Eliza Hamilton were married on 18 February 1835 at the home at 64 Varick Street by the Episcopalian Reverend Henry Anthon.[15] They went on to enjoy a happy marriage and close friendship with Eliza's father. James wrote to them both for the rest of their lives with terms of endearment and demonstrations of trust.

Later the same year, James received a touchingly personal letter from President Jackson. He seems to envy James his happy family situation when he writes, 'Your present situation, surrounded as you are with your amiable and promising family, enjoying all the amusements and sweets of rural life, must afford you more real enjoyment and happiness than ever has flown or can flow from official life.'[16]

After Alexander completed his time at West Point, he went on to serve as secretary of legation to Spain under Washington Irving alongside J. Carson Brevoort, son of another of Irving's friends.[17] He wrote long, detailed letters to his father during his time away. Later, Irving would write about his time with Alexander and their shared longing for 'the glorious sunsets of the Hudson and the purple outlines of its Western hills.'[18] The young Hamilton may have flirted with some European ladies while in Irving's company, but he returned home to marry Angelica Livingston on 10 December 1845.

The remaining Hamilton daughters, Mary and Angelica, would not get married until their middle age in the 1860s when they each married widowers. Angelica became the third wife of the much older Richard Milford Blatchford in 1860. Mary did not become a wife until 1869 when she married George Lee Schuyler, six years after her sister Eliza's death.

Chapter 10

Nevis

His was always a bright, a happy home.[1]

In 1834, after resigning his position as District Attorney, James purchased property north of Manhattan from Stephen B. Tompkins for the building of a family home. His mother had sold Hamilton Grange the year before, and perhaps James wished to establish his own estate for his children. The land had previously been owned by Jonathan and then William Odell. The historic Odell Tavern in Irvington retains their name. James purchased his portion of the Odell property on 6 April 1835, receiving 203.25 acres, known as the Cox farm, for $20,728.[2] On 12 June 1835, James increased his holdings by purchasing another 86.92 acres parcel to the north of the land acquired two months earlier.[3]

One of the several Alexander Hamiltons in the family, this one a son of John Church and nephew to James, recalled the naming of the property that was in an area at that time considered part of Dobbs Ferry. It was farmland and meadows with a single chestnut tree that the young Alexander remembered for 'beautiful views of the noble Hudson up and down the river.'[4] There was also a pond, then called Hamilton's Pond, where the family harvested ice in the winter and piped water from in the summer. His nephew recorded an anecdote of James asking his friend and neighbor, Washington Irving, to suggest a name for the estate, to which Irving replied, 'his face wreathed in smiles, "call it Single Tree Hall."'[5] The nephew Alexander remembered both home and uncle fondly. It was

> a fine house, and where, with liberal heart and hand, he entertained troops of friends, among them the great men of the day, both of our own and foreign lands ... His was always a bright, a happy home; my Aunt, his wife and his lovely daughters, by their rare personal and mental

attractions and accomplishments, making every one at ease, and with their father's generous, genial nature, made all visits too short.[6]

James had other ideas besides Irving's for the naming of his estate and called it Nevis after the tiny southern Caribbean island where his father had been born in 1755. The passing of time has resulted in the Hamilton home usually referred to as Nevis with a short vowel sound, as in 'ten' or 'egg,' while the island is pronounced Nevis with a long vowel sound, as in 'feet' or 'meat.' James was not the only one to honor Alexander Hamilton when naming a family home. Almost a century after James built his house, his daughter Fanny's Bowdoin descendants purchased a home in Oyster Bay, Long Island that was also called Nevis.[7]

James's Nevis was built in the Greek style with Doric columns across the front of the two-story square structure. Wings were added in 1851 by James and 1884 by his son, Alexander.[8] James lived at Nevis until his death in 1878, when it was inherited by Alexander, who was only weeks apart in age from his cousin and close companion of the same name. The estate is currently part of Columbia University's Nevis Laboratories, and the house is used for conferences and temporary housing.

In contrast to the traditional Federalist style of Nevis, Washington Irving's Sunnyside, built the same year, is a creative combination of European styles. Both homes enjoyed views of the Hudson River. Irving wrote of his riverside home a whimsical description of the Hudson Valley that James likely shared. 'There is a charm about that little spot of earth; that beautiful city and its environs, that has a perfect spell over my imagination. The bay; the rivers & their wild & woody shores; the haunts of my boyhood, both on land and water, absolutely have a witchery over my mind. I thank God for my having been born in so beautiful a place.'[9]

Today, Sunnyside is separated from the riverside by busy train tracks, and the view from Nevis is forested. It would be interesting to know what conversations the neighbors had regarding the changing landscape as tracks were laid and the Croton Aqueduct was built.

Nevis was described in 1886 as 'roomy and comfortable' and containing 'various articles historically interesting, such as a picture of General Washington, said to have been painted by Gilbert Stuart ... Washington himself presented the picture to his friend, General Hamilton.'[10] Nephew Alexander, who described James as 'my God Father, not only in name but in deed,' also recalled Nevis as 'a fitting Depository for the Treasures of our Grandsire.' Besides the Stuart portrait, he listed another gift from Washington, 'a silver tankard,' General Alexander Hamilton's library, a collection of family portraits, and mementos from President Andrew Jackson, who had 'especially distinguished' his uncle James.[11]

In a letter dated 17 September 1835, Andrew Jackson wrote the 'description you have given me of your farm, your stock, and your improvements, surrounded as you are with your amiable family, brings fresh to my memory the happiness with which I was surrounded at the Hermitage, when I had first the pleasure of being introduced to you.'[12] Jackson invited James to visit, but understood that being at home with family 'must afford you real enjoyment' as he himself waited for the end of his term and the opportunity to 'joyfully return' to Tennessee.[13] It is no wonder that Jackson longed for home, considering the dramas that characterized his presidency and an assassination attempt in February 1835.

Some changes besides improvements to the house took place at Nevis during James Hamilton's lifetime. In 1847, he conveyed two acres on the Hudson River to his daughter, Eliza, and her husband, George Lee Schuyler. A nine-acre plot was given to their daughter, Angelica, when she married Richard Blatchford in 1860. When the aqueduct and railroads went through, they also changed the landscape of the Hamilton property. The Hudson River Railroad Company compensated James with $2,450 for the parcel taken to accommodate the modern mode of transportation.[14]

In 1855, James conveyed 21.25 acres to John Steward, possibly in payment of a debt owed. Another 12 acres were conveyed to Elias Underhill in 1857, along with water rights to Hamilton Pond. Another parcel was sold to George Taylor in 1859, again including water rights. Other small conveyances were made, some to grandchildren, leaving Alexander with a smaller estate upon his father's death than what James had one time owned. The estate was further broken up following the death of James in 1878 in order to provide inheritances to the grandchildren named in his last will and testament.[15]

In James's obituary on 26 September 1878, Nevis is described as a strikingly simple Greek structure, such as was considered exactly the thing in those days, having five weather-beaten Doric columns on either front, the one colonnade overlooking the Hudson, the other facing a shaded country road embowered in forest trees ... At the rear a noisy little brook purls through a deep, wooded ravine, winding through the grass like a strain of music.[16]

During his long life at Nevis, James and his brother Alexander were also vestrymen together at Zion Episcopal Church, which had been organized just a year before James purchased the land for his home.[17] While many streets, counties, and the like now bear the name Hamilton, the area where James A. Hamilton's Nevis still stands is known as Irvington.

Not far from Nevis and Sunnyside, Washington Irving is buried at the Sleepy Hollow Cemetery his story made famous. A short walk from the Irving family plot is the one shared by James, his wife, three of his daughters, his son, and several grandchildren. The fourth daughter, Fanny, is in the Bowdoin plot not far away. George Lee Schuyler is buried between the two Hamilton sisters he married.

Chapter 11

The Great Fire of 1835

As I got the powder, I must have the first shot.[1]

James A. Hamilton was staying at the City Hotel with his family when he was roused in the middle of the night on 16 December 1835 and 'told a great fire was raging in the lower part of the city; that the Merchants' Exchange was in danger, where was the statue of my father by Ball Hughes; and that I might, by going there, be useful in saving that work.'[2]

The marble statue of Alexander Hamilton had only been recently installed in the Merchants' Exchange. Robert Ball Hughes had portrayed Alexander in a toga, as was popular at the time when memorializing America's founders. It had been unveiled on 18 April, just eight months earlier.[3] Some men from the nearby Navy Yard attempted to move the statue, but they were forced to flee as the building collapsed around them. The domed ceiling crashed down and crushed everything below it.[4]

Charles King was also on the scene to evaluate the status of the offices of the *New York American*, the newspaper he had started with James years earlier. Some of the equipment was retrieved before flames took hold, but the structure was lost along with the offices of six other city newspapers.[5]

James quickly realized that there was much more at stake than a statue of his beloved father or his friend's offices. 'I was told that nothing could be done to arrest the fire for want of water; the engines, their leaders and the hydrants being all frozen.'[6] 'The cold was so excessive that the engines and the ladders were frozen; the firemen were exhausted and demoralized.'[7] Part of the reason for their exhaustion was the practice of New York firefighters of pulling their engines by manpower rather than with horses or steam engine.[8]

James was determined to do whatever he could, even if that did not include that task that was closest to his heart. 'I immediately said, powder must be used, and went to the fire.'[9] Convincing city aldermen that a firebreak was necessary and obtaining the necessary powder, James identified the first structure to be sacrificed in order to save the city. In the cellar of a four-story store on Garden Street, a cask of powder was placed with calico set as a trail. Then James volunteered to light it. 'As I got the powder, I must have the first shot.'[10] And so those with him agreed, and he lit it. The blast was followed by one set up in the adjacent building, and the volunteers made their way down the street.

Throughout the night, they battled frigid cold weather in contrast to the heat of the flames. James recorded the ongoing work on a firebreak in the absence of flowing water. As he was arranging the fuse for another explosion, he was faced with a volunteer from the Navy Yard.

> The sailor, with a lighted candle in his left hand was, with a hammer, endeavoring to knock in the head of the barrel of powder. Seeing that this would be inevitable destruction, I took him by the arm in which he held the light, drew him over before he struck a second blow, and drove him out of the cellar. Putting the candle far out of reach of the powder and the dust which flew up when the head was driven in.[11]

His less than helpful assistant gone, James set the barrel for firing.

James recorded that 'The night was clear, excessively cold, a very high wind, a bright moonlight,'[12] and some residents watched the efforts of those fighting the fire. When James lit the fuse for the barrel he had set up and began walking away. Some spectators, not realizing the length of the fuse, shouted at him, 'Run! Run! Why don't you run.' Even in the midst of chaos and tragedy, James saw the humor in this. 'This was a little affectation of fearlessness on my part; well knowing that it could not burn down to the train of powder before I could get well away.'[13]

Once the firebreak proved effective, James returned to his rooms as the sun rose in the morning. 'My work was done. My cloak was stiff with frozen water. I was so worn down by the excitement that when I got to my parlor I fainted.'[14]

Although 'the scene of desolation and demoralization was most distressing' to James and other New Yorkers,[15] the Great Fire of 1835 cleared the way for the modernization of Lower Manhattan. While damage was widespread, only two people were killed, the area consisting mostly of the financial district, warehouses, and few residential buildings.[16] The struggles of the firefighters also caused New Yorkers to finally raise water access to the position of a top priority. Increasing population had long created a shortage of available water in New York City but having none when it was needed to save residents' homes and businesses brought the issue to the forefront.[17] Work on the Croton Aqueduct began on 16 May 1837 after the city accepted an engineering plan and purchased the required land to transport water from the Croton River into the city.[18]

James was, perhaps, not happy that the aqueduct ran through his Westchester County property where he built his Nevis estate, but it improved quality of life for those living in the city by providing access to water like the residents had never enjoyed before. Not only would it help protect against fire, but against illnesses such as the cholera epidemics that regularly broke out within the unhygienic conditions in the city.

Charles King compiled and printed a record of the construction of the Croton Aqueduct, which he published in 1843. He begins with a history of aqueducts back to Biblical times in support of the one built in New York. Therefore, his passion for the topic is clear. The aqueduct was a brick tunnel based on ancient Roman design that began at the Croton River in Westchester County and steadily declined 15 inches per mile for 41 miles to deliver water to the Murray's Hill reservoir at 42nd Street and Fifth Avenue, where the Stephen A. Schwarzman Building of the New York Public Library stands today.[19] A northern segment of the aqueduct is in service to this day, though most of it was long ago replaced by larger, modernized systems.

John Church Hamilton's son, John Cornelius, was an assistant engineer on the Croton Aqueduct project before he moved with his wife, Angeline Romer, to Illinois, where he was close to another Hamilton brother, William Stephen.[20]

Even before James A. Hamilton's involvement in New York's Great Fire of 1835, he had been impacted by frequent destruction by fire in the city. James was a member of the New York Association, along with men like Henry Astor, in collaboration as owners of the Bowery Theatre.[21] When it burned down in 1828, the investors immediately agreed to rebuild with no inkling of the larger tragedy they would soon face. Incidentally, the Bowery Theatre would burn down several more times, but not in the Great Fire of 1835.

Chapter 12

Hamilton in Europe

My father's name alone was my best passport to society.[1]

James A. Hamilton traveled to Europe for the first time, leaving on 10 October 1836 on a ship called the *Quebec* with his wife, Mary, and youngest daughter, Angelica, who was 17.[2] Also on board was Lewis Cass, who had served as territorial governor of Michigan and as Jackson's Secretary of War, along with his family. Cass had been named minister to France and traveled for that purpose. Jackson had provided James with 'a general passport to the good offices of all our official representatives in Europe.' However, James remarked that 'I did not use it, because I did not need their services. My father's name alone was my best passport to society.'[3]

Perhaps James had some desire to distance himself from the president he had once been eager to advise. The bank was not the only issue on which they disagreed. Indian Removal remains a dark stain on the Jackson presidency, and increasing animosity surrounding Southern slavery was causing deep divides in the country the Hamiltons sailed away from. Shortly before their departure, James's brother, Alexander, had represented Eliza Jumel in her divorce from Aaron Burr, an irony that James likely appreciated.

James carried with him a letter from his mother, Eliza, for Charles-Maurice de Talleyrand, who had counted Alexander Hamilton as a friend.[4] He also received a letter from Eliza upon his arrival, demonstrating that a mother never stops worrying about her children regardless of their age. Eliza wrote to her 48-year-old son, 'How devotedly have I in my mind's eye followed the movements of the ship that contained the favorite son of my beloved departed husband.'[5]

The letters that James wrote to his daughter, Eliza, and her husband, George Lee Schuyler, shortly after his arrival in Europe demonstrate his affection for them both and the trust he placed in his son-in-law. Eliza is addressed as his 'very, very dear child' while George is 'my dear George' and asked to take care of some business for James while he is away.[6] By 5 January, when he again wrote to Eliza, James was in Florence. He wrote, 'I have taken care to make notes of every thing I see,' and said that he considered putting his travel experiences together as a book. However, James admitted that the fact that 'I write so badly as to be scarcely legible,' was an obstacle.[7]

While in Florence, James met with the Duke de Denon, who presented him to King Jerome, the youngest brother of Napoleon Bonaparte.[8] Jerome Bonaparte had set aside his young American wife and firstborn son in order to do the bidding of his older brother and marry Princess Catherine of Württemberg, for which he was rewarded with royal titles. James recorded the meeting as full of pomp and circumstance, 'although Jerome was living upon the generosity of others' by this time.[9]

It is possible that James met Jerome in 1804 at the Grange when he was 16. A letter from Alexander to Eliza Hamilton indicates that 'Bonaparte & wife' were expected for Sunday dinner, and 'we shall be 16 in number.' In the same letter, Alexander asks Eliza to have James act as messenger and 'bring me an answer in the morning. He is promised the little horse to return,' indicating that James was home and not away at college at the time.[10] James does not mention this incident in his *Reminiscences*.

The Duke also spoke to James of Talleyrand, who looked forward to receiving the son of General Hamilton. They had missed each other as James passed through Paris, but both hoped another opportunity would arise. It eventually would. In the meantime, James took hold of the invitations and opportunities as they presented themselves to meet other notable men and ladies of Europe, taking copious notes and commenting on how the kingdoms compared to his home country along the way.

On 11 February 1837, James visited the Vatican Library and became acquainted with the librarian, Mezzofanti, who was an Italian priest. James called him 'the greatest polyglot in the world,' who claimed to speak almost three dozen languages.[11] Alongside ancient copies of Cicero and the Bible, James was shown Henry VIII's 'Defence of Catholicism,' written before the king was ready to set aside his faith in order to do the same with his wife. Mezzofanti then showed James two letters written by Henry to Anne Boleyn, which James wrote were 'quite absurd love-letters in French.' Mezzofanti agreed, saying, 'When Henry got into the hands of a woman, he was lost.'[12]

While in Rome, James took the time to write to Andrew Jackson, who had retired to the Hermitage, having handed over the reins of the country to his preferred successor, Martin Van Buren. James wrote, 'In all my wanderings, I have met with nothing that has equalled my appreciation of my own country, its Government, and People.'[13]

James wrote from Rome about his observations in scrawling, and now fading, script to his daughter, Eliza.[14] He wrote of crossing the Alps and shared highlights of the places he had visited so far. He found beauty in the hilly countryside and vineyards, but nothing that could surpass, for him, the appeal of his own Nevis. In a second letter to Eliza, he delved deeper into the society in Rome, the politics, and his own opinions. 'Gambling is practiced by the people in the open streets continually,' he observed, including a weekly lottery that accumulated considerable government revenue, 'the corruption in all departments' of which 'was so open and shameless.'[15]

By 7 April 1837, he had arrived in Naples and was writing to Eliza from there of the corruption, customs, poverty, and his opinion that Italy would benefit 'in the hands of an English government.'[16] He wrote that 'The villages are like all others in France & Italy I have seen, dirty and the abode of poverty and wretchedness.'[17] Another letter, written to Eliza just two days later, includes a small sketch of the Gulf of Naples, which he labels as 'bay,' and the Castel dell'Ovo, which he had the opportunity to sail around with the Grand Duke. He also writes about 'rather dull' entertainment he paid 40 cents to attend and an 'exhausted volcano' that he visited during a trek into the mountains.[18] A postscript to one of his letters to Eliza asks her to tend to his garden while he is gone, and 'make a large bed of strawberries & raspberries & currants, I want a very large quantity.'[19] He signs his letters to her with a familiar 'JAH' or 'papa.'

A letter to son-in-law George Lee Schuyler, marked 'Private,' addresses the financial panic that had begun and was increasing as a result of former president Jackson's destruction of the national bank.[20] James had a rare gift for understanding how international politics and economics could impact the United States, and he shared his observations with George along with instructions on selling or holding particular investments in their portfolios to weather the ongoing storm. He feared many would 'suffer immensely' and worked to protect his own family finances, possibly wondering if there was more he could have done to convince Jackson that his fiscal policy would cause this disaster.[21]

His *Reminiscences* add political observations to the remarks he wrote to family, noting that the king collects millions of dollars from his impoverished subjects by controlling monopolies, even over water and snow. 'No person is permitted to take water from the sea, lest by evaporation salt should be made.'[22] He left Naples on 25 April 1837 to travel through Venice and Milan on route to London.[23]

While traveling, James wrote frequent letters to Eliza and George. On 21 June 1837, a letter to George considers the building financial panic. 'The Question then is what can and what will Congress do. The Administration will have some quackery to play off.'[24] This comment indicates loosened ties between James and the man he previously considered a close friend, Martin Van Buren, who was the newly elected president. In the same letter, James wrote about the problems facing city banks in the absence of the Bank of the United States and news of failures that had reached him. In a letter sent to George a few weeks later, James admitted that he believed the Democrats, 'the Party in Power,' would be defeated in the next election, and, in fact, that 'such would be my cause if I were at Home.'[25] His ties to Jackson and Van Buren were no longer sufficient to cause him to support their party.

He entrusted his business and financial dealings to George while he was gone, even sending a power of attorney giving George authority to sign documents in his father-in-law's place.[26]

Arriving in London for the first time in his life, James had the unique experience of observing an election before he even reached his lodgings. 'The scene was animating' at the Guildhall, and James 'was taken into the hustings.'[27] Before 'several inspectors and registers,' each voter 'announces the names of the candidates for whom he votes, the agents thank him, he passes on and out.'[28] The scene must have felt comfortingly familiar to James after months of royal courts and undemocratic tyrants. In general, his recorded observations of London are much more detailed and positive than those made regarding other European destinations.

James spent several evenings at Holland House, the estate of Henry Vassall-Fox, Baron Holland. His home was a gathering place for Whigs, including many whom James met – Viscount Melbourne William Lamb, Viscount Palmerston Henry John Temple, and Queen Victoria's attorney general John Campbell.[29] They discussed and compared the recent elections in England and the United States, and Lord Holland brought out documents to show James. 'He took me into his office, and showed me the manuscript letters of George III to Lord North, insisting upon the continuance of our war. He said, "I show you these letters to remove from North the opinion generally entertained in your country, that the war of the Revolution was continued by his obstinacy."'[30]

On his way to Scotland, James stopped in Holkham, Norfolk, where he stayed with 'a substantial farmer and extensive breeder of short-horn or Durham cattle' named Mr Whitaker and purchased a bull and a cow to be sent to Nevis.[31]

Mr Whitaker also educated James on the taxes he would be charged upon those cattle and how England's manufacturers benefited from it. The 'poor laws' enabled a laborer to apply to the justice of the peace if his wages were less than 10 shillings per week, and the amount would be made up if his plea was successful. James guessed how this law was exploited. 'Thus the manufacturers were induced to reduce the wages of their operatives to the lowest possible sum, well knowing that the taxes upon the land-owners and others would pay, in part, for his work … It tends to degrade the laboring classes, by impairing their independence and self-reliance.'[32]

The pinnacle of the trip came when James reached Scotland. 'My most interesting visit was to Grange, in Ayrshire, the residence of Alexander Hamilton, who was a cousin of my father. My grandfather, James Hamilton, had lived on this place – not in the house the Laird now occupied, but in a large stone house of which the ruins still remained, covered with ivy.'[33] This was the James Hamilton for whom James was named, though he had never met his father's father. 'I am the only descendant of my grandfather who ever visited the home of his ancestors, which he left probably more than one hundred years before to seek his fortune in the West Indies.'[34]

While at the original Grange, James made a discovery that many since his time have shared when visiting Scotland. 'The whiskey was far better than any I had ever tasted,' so he inquired how he might purchase some to send home.[35] The elderly Alexander Hamilton responded, 'Cousin, that is a question never asked nor answered in this part of Scotland.' James felt that 'I had made a blunder,' but the Laird of the Grange continued, 'Cousin James, tomorrow morning before breakfast, if you go down to the entry you will probably find on the marble table a few black bottles well corked, and if you go round the house you may encounter a naked-legged Highland man.'[36] James 'was up early' and followed his cousin's instructions to find the transaction handled in this mysterious way to 'escape the vigilance of the excise man.'[37]

James returned to London to begin his homeward-bound journey. While there, he made what became the first of many visits to Samuel Rogers. He was a well-known poet whose works included *The Voyage of Columbus* and *The Pleasures of Memory*. Rogers was also a banker, so he and James had plenty in common to spur on conversation. The obliging host told James that he remembered, upon hearing of the Declaration of Independence, his father, including 'a prayer for the success of the Colonies, which he repeated every day until peace' in the family's prayers. James wrote that Rogers 'believed the feelings which prompted this prayer were more common in England than is generally supposed.'[38] Rogers also requested that James provide the names of his five children so that a copy of the poet's works could be inscribed and sent to each of them.[39]

Not all his London hosts were quite so accommodating. James records in his *Reminiscences* a dinner that hit on a particularly sensitive topic. Another guest asked if James was an American, to which he replied, 'Yes, sir, I have the honor to be an American.'[40] When the man stated, 'Well, sir, there is an account up there [pointing with his forefinger] which your country will find it very difficult to settle,' James knew exactly to what the man referred – slavery.[41] James responded with some standard talking points of the era, which he would have reason to regret years later.

> If that account is properly entered, your country must settle it. You brought slavery upon us, and when, as Colonies, we asked to be permitted to abolish it, our parental government refused to allow us to do so. And let me add, too, in India the English Judges have decided that the

Hindoo law which sanctioned slavery was the law of the land, the law of a British territory. If I recollect aright, we are informed by the best authority that, in a great famine in British India, the women sold their children to obtain bread.[42]

What James said was true, but, of course, did not excuse the continuation of slavery in the United States, a truth he would come to recognize later. As this dinner conversation grew heated, the attention of others was drawn and apologies were made.

Although James wrote his *Reminiscences* after the Civil War and included his own outspokenness against slavery in the 1860s, this record of his own defense of the institution, choosing accuracy over the temptation to hide the fact that he ever believed such a thing, may help modern readers understand the change in mindset that had to occur in those years between the American Revolution and the Civil War. James was far from the only American to evolve in his attitude toward slavery and state rights before becoming an abolitionist.

Abolitionists had quite the battle for public opinion through the early 1800s. They were called wicked, not only by Southern slaveholders, for their attempts to undo the careful balance of society and traitors for speaking out against state rights that were confirmed by the Constitution. Their fight for human rights was unpopular, and severe actions were taken to stifle their message.

In 1835, postmasters refused to deliver abolitionist materials sent through the mail, effectively censoring the anti-slavery message in the hope that it would not reach those enslaved in the South.[43] They defended this action by claiming that the mailings were 'exciting the negroes to insurrection and to massacre.'[44] As historian Daniel Walker Howe wrote, 'The southern practice of ignoring inconvenient federal laws in order to preserve white supremacy was established long before the Civil War.'[45] Democrats attacked Whig voters and kept them from voting stations in order to keep pro-slavery politicians in power.[46] William Lloyd Garrison, founder of *The Liberator* newspaper and the American Anti-Slavery Society, was almost killed by a Boston mob on 21 October 1835. The abolitionists' fight became even more challenging when Jackson packed the Supreme Court with pro-slavery judges and named

Roger B. Taney as Chief Justice. Taney's infamous Dred Scott decision was still twenty years in the future, but abolitionists and free blacks struggled to even be heard in court and experienced few victories.

Martin Van Buren was also speaking out against abolitionists at this time, which may have been part of the reason his friendship with James seems to have become distant over time. He organized demonstrations in New York City opposing abolitionists and opposed the captives of the *Amistad* in 1841 when John Quincy Adams defended them in the Supreme Court. As a leader and organizer of the Democratic party, Van Buren moved toward state rights, and therefore rights of slaveholders, as James moved away from the party he had supported during his younger years.

James Fenimore Cooper, a famous New York novelist, spoke passionately against the abolitionists in his state. He wrote *The American Democrat* in 1838, asserting that slavery was 'no more sinful, by the christian code, than it is sinful to wear a whole coat, while another is in tatters.'[47] He, like other supporters of slavery, insisted that the enslaved were better off than the working poor and incapable of caring for themselves if suddenly freed. Northerners like Cooper encouraged Southerners that their way of life was secure despite the extremist activity of abolitionists.

Still in England, James also had a conversation with Lord Brougham, who served in the House of Lords, and Lord Denman, Chief Justice of the Queen's Bench, during his time in London. Denman asked to 'talk with you frankly upon an interesting subject to your country if you will give me leave.' James, again, knew what was coming. 'Certainly, my Lord, slavery, I suppose,' he responded.[48] This time, James gave a more thoughtful, reasoned response. 'Let me say, I consider it a great social and political evil and a crime; here we all agree, and now the only point worth discussing is, how to get rid of it, and I now put the whole power of the Government into your hands, and call upon you to say how we can get rid of it.'[49]

When asked why the Government did not abolish it, James pointed out that only State Governments could do so, and 'men who controlled the States were slaveholders to a man, and that it could not be expected they would pass a law which would break up their whole social system, and consequently impoverish them and their children; surely, that is more than can be expected from poor human nature.'[50] He had not yet, as was the case with most Americans, considered the fact that the federal government might do something. When Lord Brougham asked about this, James responded, 'That Government has no power under the Constitution to do so.'[51]

In this instance, James defended the stance that the federal government had no power to abolish slavery in the states and no power to alter the Constitution to make it possible. He would come to change his mind when the Southern states rebelled and seceded.

Before boarding the ship *Westminster* for the return to America, James purchased two terriers for £5 and made one more attempt to connect with Charles-Maurice de Talleyrand in Paris.[52] After so many failed attempts, James was tempted to believe 'that perhaps he did not care to see me,'[53] but, having been assured that was not the case, he and his son, Alexander, arranged to join him in Valençay.[54]

His concerns were immediately assuaged when Talleyrand greeted him with 'evident feeling' saying, '"Thank God, I see the son of my dearest friend!"' James offered his hand and Talleyrand 'took it in both of his.'[55] When James later recorded the event, he wrote, 'This was conclusive. I had done him injustice. Nothing could be more kind and affectionate than he was during the three or four days I remained with him.'[56]

Talleyrand had spent time in the United States and become friends with Alexander Hamilton in the 1790s when James was just a child, now Talleyrand was white-haired and aged. He died less than a year after the visit, so James must have been gratified that he had persevered in his efforts to make the meeting happen. Talleyrand had written his memoirs, which 'were not to be published until thirty years after his death.' In them, 'he speaks of all the distinguished men he met with in your country, and particularly of your father,' James was told by another guest who had been privileged to see them.[57]

Talleyrand shared a story with James that was also included in his, at that time, unpublished memoir. He had been in Dover, traveling to the United States, when he met with an American gentleman. 'Being anxious to learn something more than I knew of the country to which I was going,' Talleyrand pursued conversation and 'found the gentleman well informed of the localities and of the distinguished men of the country, all of whom he spoke frankly and sincerely.' Offering to deliver any letters or messages to friends in America, Talleyrand discovered the identity of his new friend, who replied, 'I am of all men the least likely to have a friend in America.' It had been Benedict Arnold.[58]

One can only imagine what James must have thought of this story, as he surely knew that his father had been with General Washington when Benedict Arnold's treason had been discovered. Alexander Hamilton had also made an attempt to see Arnold traded back to the Americans for punishment in exchange for British Major John André, who had been captured after conspiring with Arnold. The exchange was refused, and André was hanged. Arnold escaped punishment and lived out his days in England and was involved in other unsuccessful escapades.

James recorded another portion of their visit when Talleyrand invited him to his office. 'I offered him my arm,' and Talleyrand took it, saying, 'I cannot be better supported.' Once in the room, Talleyrand 'took from the mantel a miniature on Sevres china.' The image was that of Alexander Hamilton. 'It was younger than when I knew my father, but was very like.'[59] As if seeing the miniature of his father was not poignant enough, Talleyrand also informed James that he had been, in 1801, looking forward to hosting his older brother, Philip. 'I had his rooms all prepared at my hotel, and the vessel by which I expected he would arrive brought the news of his death.'[60]

Another story involved then Vice-President Aaron Burr, who had asked to meet with Talleyrand, at that time Minister of Foreign Affairs for France, in Paris. Not feeling that he could refuse due to his position, Talleyrand sent a note that Burr would be received 'but he thinks it is due to Col. Burr to inform him that the miniature of General Hamilton always hangs over his mantel piece.' Burr did not come, and Talleyrand was grateful. 'I hated him; he had deprived me of my dearest friend.'[61] James certainly concurred.

James soon returned to New York. A few months later, he received news of Talleyrand's death along with a lock of hair and a pair of his glasses as mementos.[62] The miniature of his father was also included.

Chapter 13

Portents of War

The extraordinary events on our frontier call upon every citizen to render such services as may be in his power.[1]

James returned to a United States with President Van Buren at the helm. Though the two had been friends since they were much younger men, James did not participate in the Van Buren administration, and he makes little mention of it in his *Reminiscences*. He does record the incident of the *Caroline* and related tensions with Great Britain regarding Canada, but he includes just a single letter written to Martin Van Buren during his tenure in the White House.

Rebellion against British rule in Canada was at the root of the dispute that led to the *Caroline* crisis. It was not uncommon for Canadian protestors to be immigrants from the United States, and some Americans still hoped for the eventual annexation of Canada to the United States. Therefore, Britain was not entirely unreasonable in their suspicions that US citizens were aiding the Canadian rebels.

A group of Americans led by Rensselaer Van Rensselaer numbered in the hundreds and set up camp on an island in the Niagara River, ready to join the rebellion.[2] The *Caroline* was a steamship bringing supplies to this island, which happened to lie within Canadian waters. On 29 December 1837, Canadian militia attacked the *Caroline*, setting it afire before sinking it while it was on the US side of the river.[3] It was up to Van Buren to deal with this international incident.

James offered his services in the case that tensions escalated into war. 'I beg leave to say that if I can be of use to the State, either in a civil or military capacity, I hope you will command me,' he wrote to Governor Marcy on 7 January 1838. He added that, 'Our course is a plain one: to repress aggression on the part of our own citizens, to fulfil our duty as neutrals by enforcing

James Alexander Hamilton by Aimée Thibault, miniature in Mrs Helen Bowdoin Spaulding Collection.

James Alexander Hamilton, undated portrait in the private family collection of Helen Hamilton Spaulding.

Mary Morris Hamilton, undated portrait in the private family collection of Helen Hamilton Spaulding.

Mary Morris Hamilton by Aimée Thibault, miniature in Mrs Helen Bowdoin Spaulding Collection.

Alexander Hamilton II by Daniel Huntington, 1890, Astor Library (NYPL).

Mary Morris Hamilton (Schuyler) by Richard Morrell Staigg, 1860, miniature in New York Historical Society collection.

Elizabeth Schuyler Hamilton by Henry Inman, 1825, photo of miniature, Frick Art Reference Library.

Frances Hamilton Bowdoin, undated portrait in *The Bowdoin Family: Including Some Account of the Belgrave, Grinnell, Hamilton, Howland, Irving, Kingsford, Ligon, Means, Morris, and Sullivan Families* by Russell E. Train.

William Stephen Hamilton… or is it Philip? This undated portrait is included in Allan McLane Hamilton's *The Intimate Life of Alexander Hamilton* and described as 'Philip Hamilton (The First) Age 20.' It is often used online, and even at Hamilton Grange, as Philip's image. However, author A. K. Fielding researched the image and believes that it is actually William Stephen Hamilton, and her case for this identification is included in *Rough Diamond: The Life of Colonel William Stephen Hamilton, Alexander Hamilton's Forgotten Son*. Either way, we might wonder if James looked at all like this brother in his younger years.

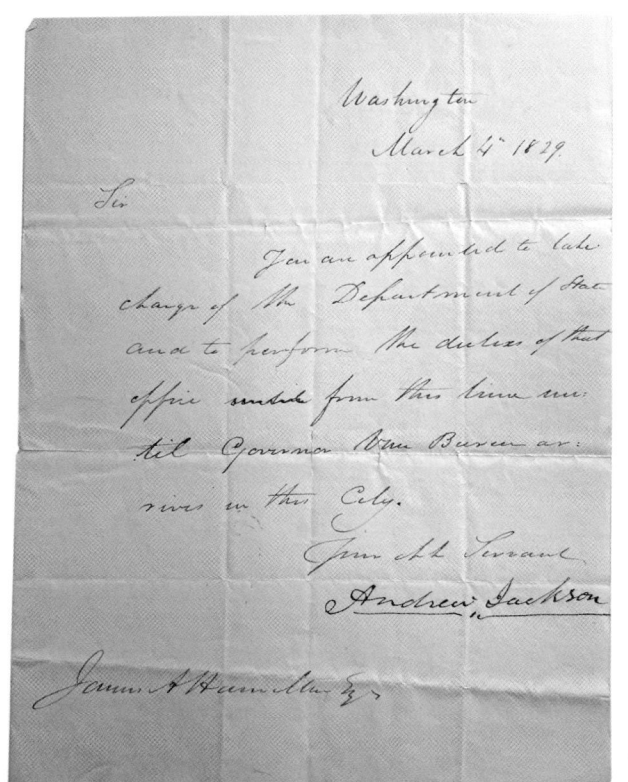

President Andrew Jackson to James A. Hamilton, 4 March 1829, written by secretary and signed by Jackson, 'You are appointed to take charge of the Department of State and to perform the duties of that office from this time until Governor Van Buren arrives in this City.' James A Hamilton Collection at NYPL. (*Author's photo*)

OBITUARY.

JAMES A. HAMILTON.

James A. Hamilton, son of Alexander Hamilton, Secretary of the Treasury under Washington, died on Tuesday last at "Nevis," the old Hamilton mansion on the Hudson, near Irvington, at the advanced age of 91 years. James A. Hamilton was born in the year 1788, while his father was engaged in the Constitutional Convention, and was 16 years of age at the date of the famous rencounter with Aaron Burr. Two years previous his elder brother, a young man of 20, had lost his life in a duel. The second son, John C. Hamilton, wrote the life of his father in two volumes. The name of the deceased, James A., is familiar in the literary world, also, as the author of a work, published in 1870, entitled *Hamilton's Conduct as Secretary of the Treasury Vindicated*, in which considerable documentary evidence of importance is adduced in defense of his father's financial policy. He married a grand-daughter of Robert Morris, of Revolutionary fame, and retired from active life after the Administration of Andrew Jackson, of whom he had preserved many striking reminiscences. Nearly 50 years ago he built the mansion on the Hudson, a mile from the busy village of Irvington. It is a strikingly simple Greek structure, such as was considered exactly the thing in those days, having five weather-beaten Doric columns on either front, the one colonnade overlooking the Hudson, the other facing a shaded country road embowered in forest trees. The house was originally brown, but, not having been painted for years, has something grim and stern about it. At the rear a noisy little brook purls through a deep, wooded ravine, winding through the grass like a strain of music. The Hamilton mansion was famous in New-York society 40 years ago, and has been the scene of many a distinguished gathering. It is now occupied by a son of the deceased, a gentleman having the strong, thick-set physique of the Morrises, rather than the tall, slender form of the Hamiltons, with the Greek nose, dashed with Gallic nervousness and decision, and the sensitive mouth of that historic family. Mr. Hamilton retained the use of his intellectual faculties until within the last four or five years. His death was consequently not an unexpected stroke; but those who knew him will miss an old man's picturesque and rambling reminiscences of society and politics in old times. He remembered Jackson, and all about the great Mrs. Eaton scandal, and the ins and outs and windings of Martin Van Buren's political career. He had seen President Washington, and knew all the mythology of the heroes of the Revolution by heart. He was familiar with the inner events of New-York society as it was 60 years ago. During the last half a century he had lived the life of a retired gentleman, with scarcely an event of importance to disturb the recollections of his youth.

The funeral is announced to take place to-morrow, and carriages will be in waiting at the depot to receive friends and relatives and take them to Nevis, so named after the island where his father was born.

Site of the First Lincoln-Douglas Debate, Ottawa, Illinois, statue by Rebecca Childers Caleel dedicated 14 September 2002. (*Author's photo*)

Crew of the *America* welcomes Queen Victoria and Prince Albert, Image 28 of *The Lawson History of the America's Cup, a Record of Fifty Years*, Library of Congress (James A Hamilton is man to far left) https://lccn.loc.gov/02020245

The *America*, Schooner Yacht, New York Yacht Club, 1851. (*Public domain*)

Maquette for Statue of Alexander Hamilton, 1831, plaster form of Robert Ball Hughes work destroyed at the Merchant's Exchange in the 1835 fire, New York Historical Society.

Print issued by John Bachmann. *Birds Eye View of the New York Crystal Palace and Environs*. John Bachmann, 1853. Museum of the City of New York. 29.100.2387.

View of Hudson River from near Sing-Sing, New York by Robert Havell, Jr, 1850, Collection of the New York Historical Society at Historic Hudson Valley.

The Great Fire of the City of New York, 16 December 1835 (showing Merchants Exchange), Library of Congress, www.loc.gov/pictures/item/2004669612

Watercolor of the White House's South Grounds, artist unknown, 1827, near the time James served as Secretary of State for President Andrew Jackson, Anthony St John Baker, Memoires d'un voyageur qui se repose, Huntington Library, San Marino, California.

Washington Irving's Sunnyside, Irvington, NY. (*Author's photo*)

Nevis, east façade, 1850, before addition of wings with the Hudson River visible to the west, Nevis Laboratories at Columbia University.

Nevis, east façade, 2014, Nevis Laboratories at Columbia University.

Nevis, west façade facing Hudson River, Nevis Laboratories at Columbia University. (*Author's photo*)

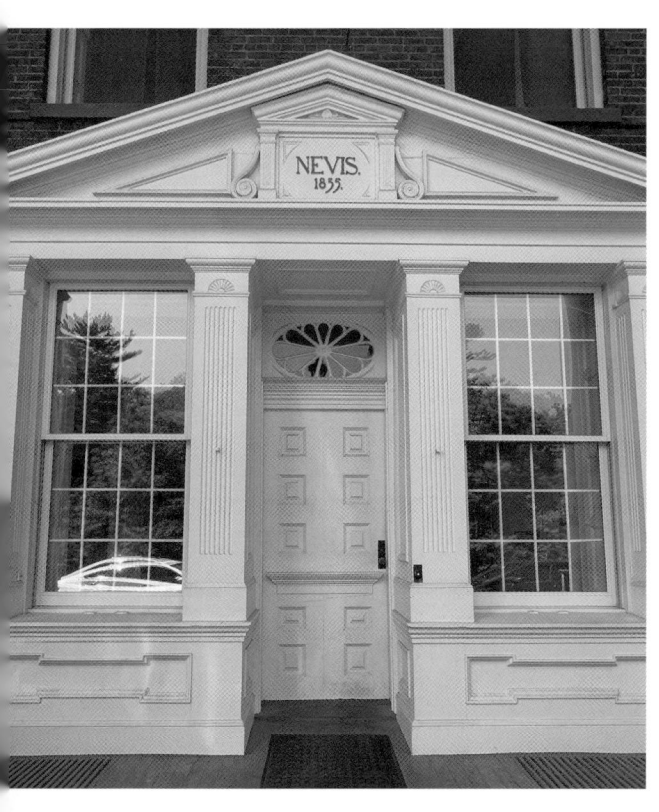

Nevis, main door on east façade, Nevis Laboratories at Columbia University. (*Author's photo*)

Hamilton Grange in New York City. (*Author's photo*)

Andrew Jackson's Hermitage in Nashville, Tennessee. (*Author's photo*)

Grave of James Alexander Hamilton at Sleepy Hollow Cemetery, weather worn but reads 'James A Hamilton, the son of Alexander Hamilton, Born April 14, 1788, Died September 24, 1878'. (*Author's photo*)

Grave of Mary Morris Hamilton (back side of stone engraved for James) at Sleepy Hollow Cemetery, reads 'Mary Morris, daughter of Robert Morris, wife of James A Hamilton, Born Dec 25 1790, Died May 24, 1869.' (*Author's photo*)

Plaque at Zion Episcopal Church, Dobbs Ferry, New York, 'To the glory of God and in memory of James A. Hamilton, vestryman 1838–1853, and Alexander Hamilton Jr, vestryman 1847–1859, sons of Alexander Hamilton, 1757–1804, First Secretary of the Treasury of the United States'

James A. Hamilton Family plot at Sleepy Hollow that includes graves of James A. and Mary Hamilton (large stone on far left), Alexander and Angelica Hamilton (flat stone in forefront), Louisa Lee and Georgiana Schuyler (matching stones in front on right), Angelica Blatchford, Mary Hamilton Schuyler, George Lee Schuyler, Elizabeth Hamilton Schuyler, and Philip and Harriet Lowndes Schuyler (back row)

the laws against previous offenders, but, above all, to be prepared to punish the recent outrage, if it is not satisfactorily atoned for, without delay.'[4] The governor's reply is not recorded.

James also must have corresponded with Jackson, who had recently retired to the Hermitage, regarding the incident, for he recorded his reply. Jackson wrote, 'I have no fear of a collision with England growing out of the Canada insurrection; our Government will continue to maintain a strict neutrality, and Great Britain will punish those who have infringed upon our nation honor and independence by the outrageous capture of the *Caroline* within our Territory.'[5]

Part of the problem was an uncertain border between the US and Canada in the northeast. James recorded that 'Van Buren sent his Maine message to Congress. It wants decision and recommends Maine to negotiate with New Brunswick, which is wholly wrong.'[6] General Winfield Scott was sent to cope with the situation, and he convinced Van Rensselaer and his followers to leave the island and return to US ground, but that did not bring an end to the dispute.[7]

James wrote to Van Buren on 25 September 1839, apparently concerned that the president might not understand the current strength of the British navy. He included

> a printed statement of the steam naval force of Great Britain which has been accumulated within the last very few years. In doing so, I have taken the liberty to presume it possible, owing to the multiplicity of your engagements, that these facts may have escaped your attention, and to express the opinion that they call for your serious attention.[8]

James emphasized that 'in the event of war' Britain's use of steamships and 'change in the mode of attack' would need to be considered in US coastal defense.[9] He did not record Van Buren's response.

Perhaps Van Buren had not responded at all, for James later wrote to Daniel Webster, at that time Secretary of State and negotiating with Britain over the border issue, with some of the same concerns that 'Great Britain is preparing to increase her Lake armaments' and 'the necessity for arming the Nation, of defending her against hostile attack.'[10] The border dispute calmed and was settled without the escalation of fighting that James feared by the Webster–Ashburton Treaty of 1842. However, the US was still seeking reparations for the destruction of the *Caroline* in 1841 under President Tyler, who took office after the death of President Harrison shortly after his election.

James wrote to President Harrison, during his brief time in the White House, warning him of Van Buren's political machinations and Swartwout's financial fraud. As was his habit, he also offered his services while denying that he sought any office or advancement.

As the risk of war decreased in the northeast, disputes heated up out west. Texas gained its independence with the help of many Americans living there, but the republic's future was not settled and many saw it as a future US state.

The federal government was also, once again, debating the future of banking with many supporting the creation of a Third Bank of the United States. As those who had come before them, they realized the error of replacing the Second Bank with regional and state banks without federal oversight. James supported this idea and wrote to Senator Henry Clay with his approbation.[11] He must have been thankful that the financial gap left by Jackson, when he insisted on elimination rather than reform of the bank, would finally be filled. When President Tyler vetoed the proposed bank legislation, his entire cabinet resigned in September 1841, with the exception of Secretary of State Daniel Webster.[12] The US went without a central bank until the creation of the Federal Reserve System in 1913, though, as we will see, James was much involved with the evolution of the financial system under Salmon P. Chase during the Civil War of the 1860s.

However, in 1841, as protestors gathered outside the White House in response to Tyler's veto of the Third Bank of the United States, James embarked upon another trip to Europe with his son-in-law, George Lee Schuyler.

Chapter 14

Hamilton in Russia

I heard 'Amerikanskey' repeated again and again.[1]

When James made his second trip to Europe he ventured even further, accompanying his son-in-law George Lee Schuyler to Russia. George was in business with his brother, Robert, and they had been commissioned to build a steamship, named *Kamschatka*, for the Russian government. When it came time to settle the account, there were questions regarding payment of the final sum, $55,089.42.[2] Therefore, it was determined that George would deliver the ship in person, not turning it over until the funds were in hand.

He asked that his father-in-law accompany him in the case that 'I must throw myself for protection upon the American Minister.'[3] James was not only respected in his own and his father's right but had a fine legal mind, as his son-in-law well knew. George wrote on 26 September 1841, 'you can easily imagine how agreeable and important to me would be your presence at St Petersburgh, to say nothing of my prospects in other countries, which would be so materially enhanced by your assistance.'[4]

James 'was persuaded by the members of my family to take the voyage' and 'sailed from New York on Wednesday the 28th September, 1841.'[5] During their ocean crossing, James and his son-in-law were caught in a fierce storm. 'The peril was so imminent, that I was requested by Mr Schuyler to ascertain how many inches of steam we were using, how many revolutions we were making, and our course; to write it down and put the statement in a bottle corked up, to be thrown overboard,' James later wrote.[6] Thankfully, the storm abated, and they arrived safely in England.

Before sailing, James had obtained a letter of introduction from Daniel Webster, who was at that time Secretary of State. (The rest of President Tyler's cabinet had recently resigned over his bank related vetoes.) James and Webster had already been in correspondence regarding difficulties between the United States and Great Britain over a revolt in Canada, which some Americans were accused of aiding. Webster, along with the requested letter, advised James on how to respond on the government's behalf to any discussion of these events, particularly the attack of the American steamboat, *Caroline*, which had been set afire and sent over the Niagara Falls in December 1837. President Tyler, who was winning the debate over whether he was president in his own right or simply an acting office holder after the death of President Harrison, was still seeking reparations for the attack in 1841. Once arrived in London, the Prime Minister, who had requested that James meet him at the Foreign Office, asked him, 'Mr Hamilton, do you believe your government wishes to get into a war with us?' James replied, 'Certainly not.' Apparently convinced, the Prime Minister said, 'I rejoice to hear you say so; for, where there is a will, there is a way,' and invited him to a party the following evening.[7]

James had written to General Winfield Scott regarding military service should fighting erupt between the United States and Great Britain once again. Scott replied

> Are you in earnest about a fighting commission in the event of war? You have certainly the highest hereditary right to military employment, and in the contingency alluded to, you have nothing to do but repeat your wishes, & if Mrs Hamilton will allow me, I shall be ready to launch you against the enemy.[8]

Thankfully, this did not become necessary, as the Webster–Ashburton Treaty of 1842 settled the northeastern territory dispute.

From England, James and his son-in-law sailed to Copenhagen, where they landed on 3 November 1841.[9] Arriving late at night, they 'hurried to the Straus Hambourgh, the best hotel in the city,' where they encountered 'domestics not speaking any language we could command, we had some difficulty but much amusement in making our wants understood.'[10] His presence made known to the Princess of Hesse, James soon had invitations to society events to occupy himself and George Lee Schuyler, where, thankfully, 'these people understood English.'[11]

On 11 November, they were in Kronstadt, Russia, and challenged by a snowstorm that kept the emperor from coming to see the ship and put it in additional danger because of ice.[12] The emperor sent men to take command of the ship, but George and James insisted that this was a violation of the agreement, and that Schuyler must retain possession of the vessel until the amount due was paid.[13] The question was settled when the ship was too broad to bring into the naval dockyard.

James recorded the incident in his *Reminiscences*. 'Their captain stood on the wheel house, and was scolding nearly all the time. When he found the vessel could not go through the opening, he threw his hat down, stamped upon it, and swore most awfully.' James calmly observed that 'it would have been much easier and wiser to have asked what her breadth of beam was, and what the measure of the opening was.'[14]

In Russia, as during his other travels, James keenly studied the people and culture that were so different from what he was accustomed to in New York. He recorded how they fought the cold with gloves, boots, and long coats, and that the Kronstadt hotel had wood stoves that were carefully and continuously tended. The condition of Russia's serfs was 'a subject of the deepest interest' to James.[15] He observed that 'almost the whole peasantry are slaves to different masters.'[16] They required written passes to travel and could be required to serve as soldiers to fulfill their owners' obligation to the government. James reflected that 'It is agreed on all hands that they do not work industriously; the nature of the system of servitude necessarily induces this, here and in my own honored land.'[17]

Russian subjects were required to 'pay a high tax for a passport.'[18] James believed the reason for this was to 'deter him from leaving the Empire. This policy is founded upon the fear of introducing liberal opinions.'[19] 'The Government fears liberal opinions more than a pestilence.'[20] His party, however, was 'treated with marked civility' and given passes to visit St Petersburg.[21] 'In my pass I was described as "formerly Secretary of State of the United States,"' and James was amused that they 'cracked me off as a most distinguished person who … probably would be President of the United States.'[22]

Travel to St Petersburg was accomplished by carriage since Russia did not yet have any railroads in 1841. Once arrived, James 'had the first opportunity to see the Imperial family' at the Theatre Michel, which he described as 'vaudeville.'[23] According to James, 'there was no manifestation by the people when he [the Emperor] entered, we were not apprized of his presence until, turning toward the private box, I saw a face which was familiar to me.'[24] After consulting Schuyler and another man in their party, it was agreed that it was indeed Nicholas, 'an uncommonly handsome man,' the Empress, and other members of their family.[25]

James and his son-in-law then returned to the back-and-forth negotiations over payment for the ship they had delivered, which went on for weeks as winter settled around them. At one point, given reason to believe the balance would be paid, James was surprised to be informed that 'where any money is paid out by any department, it is customary to pay to the chief of that department and his subordinates a small portion of the amount so received, in the nature of a compensation for their trouble.' Clarifying that the men expected to be bribed, James replied:

> I am gratified by your frankness, and now I intend to be equally frank. I know of no such practice in the United States, and am quite sure there is none such there. I understand you to say it is an accustomed practice here. Now I wish you to understand me. We intend to receive the amount due to Mr Schuyler under his agreement and we do not intend to give Prince Menschikoff, yourself, or any other subordinate in his department, a single ruble; and further, if the money cannot be obtained without making the payments suggested, that Mr Schuyler would, as owner of the ship, take her to London, and sell her for whomever it might concern.[26]

George had clearly made an astute decision in inviting his father-in-law on this trip.

While James and George believed they had gone through great trouble to simply receive what they were owed, one Russian baron congratulated them on their success. 'I knew what you came for on your arrival; and well knew that, according to the accustomed course of business here, you would be detained at least six months: and here you have got your money at the most favorable rate, in less than thirty days.'[27] The more time they spent in Russia, the more they understood the truth of this.

The jurisprudence of this country is as corrupt as possible. I have most reluctantly permitted myself to believe this, being aware, as a traveller, how readily we are imposed upon, and how imperfect, and oftentimes how unfair, are our sources of information; but I hear this from all quarters, and one resident (a man very much disposed to mitigate what was said, and to put the best appearance on all that he told me) said it was unquestionably true that the judges constantly expect and receive bribes.[28]

Only 'cases of much importance' were put before the Emperor 'who always judges and decides uprightly.'[29]

James recorded his observations of the despotic government and the police, who he 'considered the greatest rascals on earth,' despite a visit from the head of the secret police. This unnamed man wished to 'ask a favor of' Hamilton.[30] As he often did, James responded, 'I am gratified to learn that I can serve you in any way; please to let me know how.' His answer was, 'You will do me a favor if you will not permit persons who come to your rooms to speak disparagingly of this government, nor to participate yourself in such conversations.'[31] James discovered that 'our valet was undoubted a spy of the secret police,' who had been reporting on his conversations.[32]

The trip was not all negotiations and bribery attempts. James was also officially presented to the Imperial family and attended a ball at the palace. The Empress told him that if he could learn the Russian language, 'you may learn any thing; however, it is not as harsh as it no doubt seems to your ear when it is spoken in the streets,' and attempted to convince him of the truth of this by reciting lines of Russian poetry.[33] She was interested in his impressions as an American visitor and invited him to a less ceremonial visit to 'see our domestic life.'[34]

James and company left St Petersburg on 28 December 1841 by carriage. His last reflection upon Russia was that Emperor Alexander 'has performed successfully the great and glorious work his father wished to do; but could not – the emancipation of 23 millions of people.'[35]

When they stopped for a meal along the way, James had an unexpected new experience. Served a 'dark-colored meat' he 'cut a piece off it, began to eat, found it tasteless, dry and tough.' One of his companions, Captain Wright, came in then and instructed him to stop eating. 'That is horse meat.'[36]

They had 'purchased a Tallago with four wheels, four seats with a cloth covering' for their travel.[37] Arriving at Tilsit, where they acquired a different carriage, 'the keeper of the house came in, and inquired what he should do with our Tallago.'[38] James instructed him to 'sell it for what you can get for it, and give the money to the poor.' When asked who to credit for the generosity, he replied, 'an American gentleman.' James recorded that 'some years afterwards I saw Captain Wright in New York ... He told me he had been asked by divers people in Tilsit for the name of the American gentleman. The secret excited much curiosity and speculation.'[39]

They arrived in Berlin on 4 January 1842. James was excited to visit the Winter Garden, 'an establishment I have long wished might be introduced into New York,' where 'all classes of people are admitted, for the smallest copper coin ... and all were gratified by the exquisite music, and thus they were refined in their tastes. Music and painting must have that effect; particularly upon the younger and less improved classes.'[40]

The last stop before returning home was London. James was invited to dinner at Lady Holland's, 'although I have inherited from my father nothing but his illustrious name.'[41] At this event, he was put 'in an awkward position' when asked to retell the story of General Jackson's victory at New Orleans. 'The idea of an American talking about the battle of New Orleans at an English dinner-table!'[42] Yet he acquiesced, remembering to give credit to the British soldiers for their bravery, and was thanked for the tribute.[43] He was much more comfortable with inquiries regarding his father, to which he unhesitatingly replied, 'I have indisputable evidence that he wrote the Farewell Address.'[44]

Shortly after James returned to New York, his son, Alexander, embarked on his own trip to Europe, where he served as Secretary of Legation to Washington Irving. Irving was a friend and neighbor of the Hamiltons and currently serving as US Minister to the Court of Madrid. During the two years he served there, Alexander exchanged candid letters with his family regarding foreign relations, personal observations, and family finances. James wrote to his son with details of income and expenses at Nevis and American politics. On 29 August 1843, he wrote with more prophetic vision than he likely realized when he confessed to his son that, 'It is now to be feared that the Country will be torn by Civil War.'[45]

Perhaps James considered the possibility of civil war partly due to a minor insurrection known as the Dorr Rebellion that occurred in Rhode Island during the summer of 1842. Thomas Dorr had begun calling for a new state constitution and universal male voting rights in 1834.[46] In 1841, Dorr fomented widespread discontent by forming a 'People's Constitution' and held an unauthorized convention for its ratification. Then the reformers held their own election to make Dorr governor, which led to the authorized governor, Samuel King, to request federal intervention.[47]

James had potent feelings about this movement and escalation to a military matter. In his journal, he wrote,

> I suggested to Mr G.L.Schuyler that we might be of service there, and proposed that we should take the afternoon steamboat for Providence; there the parties were arrayed against each other; where the fight was to be we did not know. We arrived in Providence on the morning of the 28th of June, when we learned that Dorr had made a cowardly escape during the night, leaving over one hundred men, a part of his force, who were taken prisoners.[48]

James and his son-in-law were presented to Governor King, 'who thanked us for our good intentions.' He had felt 'moved to go on this expedition, first, because I felt it was my duty to show a readiness to risk something in support of law and order,' but he was disappointed that 'four lives were lost in this foolish and wicked outbreak; the State was put to much expense, and much hot blood had been excited' because of 'Dorr's treasonable acts and purposes.'[49]

Alexander returned from Spain two years later and married Angelica Livingston on 10 December 1845. This same year, *Narrative of the Life of Frederick Douglass, An American Slave, Written by Himself* was published, publicly revealing the experience of America's enslaved people.

Chapter 15

Texas and Mexico

I desire most ardently to serve the country in a military capacity; and if opportunity should be afforded, to end my life on a field of glory.[1]

On 13 May 1846, the United States declared war on Mexico at the behest of President James K. Polk. Americans had been emigrating to the Mexican state of Coahuila y Tejas, or what Americans called Texas, for more than two decades since Mexico had declared its independence from Spain. Then Texas declared its own independence on 2 March 1836, causing many to view it as a made-to-order US state. The philosophy that America had a Manifest Destiny to possess western territory and expand the nation from sea to sea was gaining popularity, and many believed Texas and parts of Mexico from Arizona to Oregon should be annexed to the United States. Polk's declaration of war was a technicality. Fighting had already broken out. Mexico viewed the annexation of Texas on 27 December 1845 as an act of war, and the US had not stopped there.

Americans were deeply divided on the Mexican–American War. Democratic administrations had been sending diplomats offering to purchase Texas since the 1820s, without success. American citizens living in Texas had fought and died during the republic's fight for independence, the most famous example at the Alamo on 6 March 1836, where Jim Bowie, Davy Crockett, and over a hundred others were overwhelmed by the forces of Santa Anna.

Texan independence lasted ten years, with heavy immigration from the United States. While Mexico had abolished slavery, Texas legalized it for the American Southerners moving there. Many Texans favored annexation by the US as a slave state in order to gain military protection against Mexico and to relieve the young republic's debt. Besides believing in America's Manifest Destiny, Southerners were eager to add Texas to the Union to tip the power balance in favor of slave states. They also stirred the public's Anglophobia with claims that if the US did not annex Texas, Britain might step in and take it instead. On 12 April 1844, John C. Calhoun, at that time Secretary of State to President Tyler, signed a treaty annexing Texas as a territory with the intent that it would soon become one or more slave states.

Discussion of slavery had been growing more contentious for years, as best demonstrated by the 'gag rule' in the House of Representatives. In May 1836, they had passed a resolution against hearing petitions related to slavery. Former president John Quincy Adams, who by that time served as a representative for Massachusetts, immediately and vocally opposed this rule. Adams argued quite correctly that the Constitution guaranteed citizens' right of petition. When Adams attempted to read the anti-slavery petitions on the floor of the House, he was silenced. On 25 May 1836, he exclaimed, 'Am I gagged or am I not?'[2] giving the unconstitutional ruling the name it has been remembered by. The gag rule was rescinded in 1844 due to constant challenges led by John Quincy Adams, but the topic of slavery remained one that was almost impossible over which to have civil discourse. Upon winning the hard-fought battle for freedom of speech, Adams wrote in his diary, 'Blessed, forever blessed, be the name of God!'[3]

Opposition to Calhoun's Texas treaty was raised as soon as the news reached Washington DC, and the Senate failed to approve the treaty.[4] Calhoun's goal of increasing slaveholder power was obvious, and it was left to the next administration to see it done.

James Knox Polk was elected in 1844 in a close race with Great Compromiser Henry Clay, who James had supported and hoped would be elected. Nicknamed 'Young Hickory,' Polk shared Andrew Jackson's authoritarian attitude and imperialistic ideas about the future of the United States.[5] If it were not for the third-party candidacy of abolitionist James G. Birney, Clay would have been declared president, Texas might have remained an independent republic, at least for the time being, and the US might never have gone to war with Mexico.[6] Would it have put the US on a path that could have avoided the bloody Civil War of the 1860s? We will never know.

Polk's victory and Democratic gains in Congress enabled Tyler to see the annexation completed in the twilight hours of his presidency, and it was signed into law on 1 March 1845, three days before Polk's term began. He had aggressive goals to settle Oregon, California, and Texas as America's western empire.[7] He was immediately challenged by Mexico, who saw the annexation of Texas as 'an act of aggression.'[8]

Polk did not hesitate. He sent General Zachary Taylor into the region between the Nueces River and Rio Grande. This area was generally agreed to belong to Mexico with the Nueces the boundary between them and Texas. However, Polk was keen to claim the Rio Grande as the border instead. Through this duplicitous move, he put US forces on Mexican soil while claiming they remained on Texas ground. In the meantime, Polk looked toward California and how to bring it within his grasp.

When General Taylor marched his army into Mexican territory, Lieutenant Colonel Ethan Hitchcock wrote, 'It looks as if the government sent a small force on purpose to bring on a war, so as to have a pretext for taking California and as much of this country as it chooses.'[9] And so it had. When Mexico demanded that the US withdraw, Taylor blockaded the mouth of the Rio Grande.[10] Though the US had instigated with acts of war, Polk asked Congress to declare war based on Mexico's default on debt.[11] He argued that a state of war already existed – and that Mexico was the aggressor rather than the US – and asked Congress to approve $10 million in funding.[12]

John Quincy Adams, once again, boldly led the opposition, but the number willing to follow him dwindled as congressmen worried about being the next to lose their seat if they were seen as failing to support troops that had already been sent forth. These were politicians who had watched the painful death of the Federalist Party after it failed to support the War of 1812. While John Quincy Adams was a force on his own and unconcerned about re-election campaigns, the Whigs who agreed with him in theory were determined not to repeat the Federalists' mistakes and lose power entirely. Polk had his war, which he boldly claimed was not entered into for the purpose of conquest.[13] Despite this assertion, Polk would lead the country to a greater acquisition of territory than any other president.[14]

James A. Hamilton seemed to agree with the philosophy of supporting the US in the war now that it had started. He had not desired a Polk presidency but still expressed his desire to serve his country in a letter to William Marcy, the Secretary of War, on 20 July 1847. Having heard 'that a brigadier-general is to be appointed ... allow me to beg the favor of you to present my name to the President for that place.'[15] He was 59 years old, but it would not be the last time he would offer his services to a US president.

His services not requested on the battlefield, James returned to the tasks typically required of him. He prepared a resolution at the request of Daniel Webster to be submitted to Congress. In it, he parroted Polk's lie that 'the war is not prosecuted by the United States for conquest' and that the President should be authorized to appoint commissioners to seek terms of peace.[16] Perhaps, with the war already begun, James did not see the value in writing in opposition to the president, but rather to write the resolution as it could be accepted in support of the troops. The treaty secured on 2 February 1848 ceded to the United States more than could have been anticipated, establishing a border that transferred half of Mexico's territory that would eventually make up California, Nevada, Utah, New Mexico, and portions of Arizona, Colorado, Oklahoma, Kansas, and Wyoming.

During this time, the nation was also considering its next presidential election. A major issue was whether slavery would be established in the new western lands. James 'sought advice from the best minds in the country' regarding the June 1847 Democratic Convention in Chicago.[17] Daniel Webster wrote to him on 17 June 1847, 'I am a little afraid of the results of this Convention, in a party point of view. The Whigs have now the advantage of being that party which sustains Internal Improvements.'[18] This was due to Henry Clay's 'American System' that included investment by the federal government in international infrastructure that had previously not been considered in a country where roads, bridges, and canals were state responsibilities. John Quincy Adams had promoted federally funded internal improvements during his presidency, but he had been too far ahead of his time. Since then, Henry Clay had been attempting to change the public's attitude toward federal funding for long enough that it was a pillar of the Whig party, and Webster felt Whigs had a good chance of winning the presidency. 'All that has been done for the country on these subjects has been done by the Whigs, this is now getting popular.'[19]

James attended the convention and 'played the subordinate part of taking care that the course of proceedings should be systematic.'[20] General Lewis Cass did not attend the convention but was nominated as the Democratic candidate.

Martin Van Buren ran again, this time as the candidate of the Free Soil party, but he received zero electoral votes. The Free Soil party had been formed with the help of Charles Francis Adams, son of John Quincy, in the hopes that a compromise could be found between abolitionists and slaveholders. They believed that slavery should not be expanded in the West, but that it would not be interfered with where it already existed. James also supported this option for a time and saw it as a constitutional way to keep slavery in check without interfering with the rights of Southerners. The party did not gain much ground, however, though it did take away enough votes from Democratic candidate Lewis Cass to ensure victory for Whig candidate and Mexican–American War hero, Zachary Taylor. He would be the last man to serve as president who was born before the ratification of the Constitution. The country he led was quadruple the size it was when George Washington took his oath of office, and the population had exploded from just under 4 million in the 1790 census to over 23 million people spread over thirty states in 1850.[21] It was a whole new world.

As for James A. Hamilton, he was preparing for another journey to Europe.

Chapter 16

Hamilton in Europe II

Revolutions never go backward.[1]

James planned to take a steamer to England, 'and thence directly through France to Italy, to pass the winter there' and offered to deliver any messages on President Polk's behalf.[2] He was willing to act as an intermediary, given the unrest rising in Europe at that time. Polk did not take James up on his offer. 'I received no answer, and perhaps did not deserve one.'[3] He left in November 1847, as the American debate over slavery was escalating heatedly due to the question of whether it should spread throughout the new western territory.

The ocean crossing was apparently uneventful, but James recorded an incident on the steamer that took him from Genoa to Leghorn in December. 'A drunken dandy, full of affectation and conceit' who turned out to be an East Indian Prince 'got into my berth. When I called this intrusion to the captain's notice, he begged me not to insist upon taking him out, as, being drunk, he would make a great noise; and promised that he would give me another berth as good.'[4]

In Florence, James met with his friends made during his previous trip, as well as others drawn to the Hamilton name. James recorded mixed observations of the people of Italy. In Florence, he wrote, 'The practices of the people are very dirty – no delicacy toward females ... both men and women are under size.' Yet he also observes, 'They sing, talk loud and vehemently, are very courteous to each other and to strangers.'[5] He also believed that 'the people of Tuscany are the most intelligent and independent of all the people of Italy.'[6] On Christmas Day, James was in Rome, where 'the religious ceremony made a gorgeous display,' but he was surprised that 'the people showed no interest whatever.'[7]

The reform movement was growing in Rome. On 27 December 1847, James saw a procession of people led by Angelo Brunetti. They presented the Pope with a list of twenty-eight demands. They returned days later for his answer but were turned away. When James saw the Pope later, 'he drove on a trot through the crowded streets, blessing the people – he was evidently designed, to avoid any address. He probably hopes, by time and certain influences, to divert a serious issue.'[8]

James had arrived in Europe on the eve of widespread revolution – or attempt at it anyway. Perhaps inspired by what they saw, or what they believed was true, in the United States, people in Europe demanded change. The movement began in Sicily and spread north, almost as James traveled that route. Opposition to monarchy was more popular than ever before, and the demand for republican forms of government was made by various groups throughout the continent. It was just the sort of historic event that James was eager to witness.

On New Year's Day 1848, James met with the Earl of Minto, Great Britain's Lord Privy Seal, to discuss the 'popular movements in the Papal States, tending to a revolution.'[9] James believed that Pope Pius IX 'had very good intentions' but 'was not a man of vigorous intellect.'[10] Wishing to form a full picture of current events, James also

> became acquainted with men in the popular movement, and from then learned much of their affairs and of what they complained, and the movements which were in progress ... I thus learned much more than I could otherwise have done of the working of this Government, and its various departments.[11]

As often seemed to become his duty, James prepared 'a paper containing such measures of reform as they desired ... that personal liberty, the right to be free from arrest without a written warrant ... was the only sure foundation of public liberty.'[12]

The threat to personal liberty that James referred to was the tribunal of the Vicar-General. 'The ostensible object is to investigate and punish immorality, and deviation from, or neglect of religious discipline.'[13] However, 'the whole proceeding is secret. There are no witnesses to confront the accused ... all the means of attempting to prove innocence are frustrated.'[14] James writes that the court 'by usurpation and abuse of power, is now made the instrument of revenge, and used for private gain.'[15] Being his father's son, he was glad to provide what assistance he could to those speaking out against this injustice. He believed that the Italian states had the resources to support the population but 'these advantages are, however, counteracted by bad government, a government in which the head is elected by an exclusive and privileged class, ignorant of political economy, educated despots, accustomed to implicit obedience.'[16]

On 8 January 1848, James prepared a report intended for the Pope 'at the request of a gentleman of rank in the government of the Sovereign Pontiff.'[17] In it, he addressed the twenty-eight demands, 'some deserving of consideration, and others not' with the insistence that 'it is their right and duty to express in decorous language, their grievances and wants,' and the Pope's duty to 'give due heed.'[18]

James arrived in Naples on 18 January 1848 and stayed at the Great Britain Hotel, where he dined with Ibraham Pasha, the Viceroy of Egypt.[19] They were able to communicate satisfactorily through interpreters, and the viceroy was interested in American affairs. When he informed James that he had heard 'that the union of the States would not continue long,' James defended the nation of which he was so proud, telling Pasha that 'there was no foundation for such a statement' and going as far to say that 'the wish was father to the thought' regarding the Englishman who had said it.[20] The two spent many hours together, becoming friends through their mutual interest in world politics. James and his daughter, Angelica, attended the viceroy's ball, and Pasha also escorted Angelica to the opera. He asked James to promise he would visit when he succeeded his father as King of Egypt.[21]

Those protesting against the government also reached out to James in Naples, having heard of his efforts in Rome. He was invited to meet with them, but James was reluctant to become too involved, partly out of concern for Angelica, who accompanied him. In a cloak-and-dagger style moment, he was instructed to present half of a paper heart when meeting with the group's representative to indicate whether he would join them.[22] Choosing to remain unassociated with the movement, James watched from a balcony when a government procession was swarmed by protestors. Though no shots had been fired, the owner of the house suggested he move inside to avoid injury should violence ensue.[23] The king indicated that he would grant some of the protestors' requests, including a new constitution. When it was time for James to leave the city, events were not settled. 'We must await the result,' he wrote.[24]

It is unknown what news of home James received as he traveled through Europe. On 23 February 1848, John Quincy Adams died after collapsing on the floor of the House of Representatives, where he still represented his home state of Massachusetts. Besides losing one of the young nation's greatest statesmen, the discovery of gold in California at about the same time was about to fuel great change in the United States. Even one of the Hamilton brothers was caught up in America's gold fever. William Stephen left his settlement in modern-day Wisconsin to make his fortune in California, not on mining but on opening a common goods store.[25] Unfortunately, William never returned to Wisconsin. He died in Sacramento on 7 October 1850.[26]

When James wrote to a friend on 27 February 1848, he said,

> When I turn my thoughts back from this Old World in her state of decrepitude and decay, to our happy land, so new in its institutions, but so much farther advanced towards true civilization, where the mental and physical properties of man are so much more vigorously developed than in any part of Europe, England with all her pride not excepted, the undoubted result of our free institutions, I thank God I am an American.[27]

He went on to say,

> The spirit of '76 is the pillar of light by day and of fire by night to all mankind, and without blasphemy, I hope I may be permitted to express the conviction, long entertained, that the spirit of our Declaration of Independence, practically carried out in our system of government, is the greatest boon received by mankind next to the sacred revelations of the Almighty himself.[28]

He hoped that the reformers in Italy and throughout Europe might obtain for themselves what Americans had created.

Of course, American society was far from perfect, and the debate over slavery was rising toward a boiling point. In fact, shortly before James arrived there, Frederick Douglass had given an anti-slavery speech in England, his audience more receptive and his safety more assured away from American soil. On 15 April 1848, the attempted escape of seventy-six enslaved people from Washington DC aboard the steamship *Pearl* was thwarted. The plot had been financed by abolitionists, and the ship's white crew were imprisoned while the black freedom seekers were returned to owners or sold to traders. Democrats stridently fought the abolition of slavery in the federal district amid fears that it would set a precedent for national abolition.

James was in Vienna in March 1848 when armed revolution broke out. Some people were panicking as shops closed and the military took control of the city, but James went about the city to observe as much as he could, only withdrawing some cash 'to meet all contingencies' with seemingly little fear for his physical safety.[29] He watched as the scales were torn down from the statue of Justice and soldiers attacked the crowd with guns and bayonets.[30] Rather than quell the rebellion, the violence enraged the people. When James went out again that night, he 'found the people engaged with much greater animation in endeavoring to break into the police head-quarters' and 'the gate of the city where duties were collected was torn down.'[31] Before he returned to his rooms for the night, he heard the announcement pass through the streets, 'Prince Metternich has abdicated!'[32] James left Vienna as the riots continued. 'I seemed swept along by a revolutionary tornado.'[33]

When he arrived in Dresden, the situation seemed much the same. 'The people had demanded a change of the Governor' and sent 'demands to the Emperor.'[34] Revolutionary violence had spread across Europe, with some leaders making concessions and others refusing to yield while their military slaughtered citizens. Soaring prices exacerbated the suffering of the people.

In Paris, James witnessed a barricade built in the street outside his rooms and violence between citizens and soldiers.[35] 'Royal carriages were taken, put in a line, and burned ... the names of the streets were changed.'[36] The Provisional Government pursued recognition by the United States, and James attended some of their meetings. 'The speeches were amusing; many of them quite absurd.'[37] George Washington Lafayette, son of the General Lafayette who had fought in the American Revolution, requested that James assist with the writing of a new French constitution.[38] Although James resisted and claimed he lacked the required skill, 'they urged me most earnestly to make the attempt, to which I reluctantly consented.' Obtaining a copy of the US Constitution and the *Federalist Papers*, James went to work. 'Earnestly desiring to render any service in my power to the son of the illustrious General Lafayette, and also to promote the welfare of the people of France, I endeavored to form a Constitution for France, by such alterations of the Constitution of the United States as I believed would be judicious.'[39] One notable request was that slavery not be protected in the new constitution. The resolutions James sent to Lafayette for debate in the Provisional Government, asking for it to be destroyed if they did not find it useful.

James may have thought his work in France was complete, but he was soon asked to attend the Assembly to advise them on fiscal policies. He provided them with a written list of 'hints of a plan which may relieve the political, social, and fiscal difficulties of France' that included detailed instructions, including what denominations of treasury notes should be issued.[40]

When James arrived in London, the first stage in his journey home, he found that Queen Victoria had been evacuated to the Isle of Wight for her safety from unrest, and the Duke of Wellington had obtained permission from homeowners to have soldiers placed in the upper-story windows of houses in areas where rioting was thought possible.[41]

The revolutions of 1848 ended in a variety of results. In France, the Orleans monarchy was ended and the French Second Republic created. It did not last, however, and Napoleon III was proclaimed emperor in 1852. In Germany, the Frankfurt parliament was dissolved, and the rebellions were put down by military force. Other countries did not see their monarchies brought down, but the people were able to gain some reforms that they had requested. The shift to democracy was a gradual climb, not an instant result.

The United States was not immune from the global outcry for civil rights. On 19–20 July 1848, the Seneca Falls Women's Rights Convention was held in James's home state of New York. Their Declaration of Sentiments was purposely crafted to bring to mind the Declaration of Independence, opening with 'We hold these truths to be self-evident; that all men and women are created equal' before going on to enumerate the 'abuses and usurpations' against women in the United States.[42] American women would wait even longer for the right to vote than did black men.

When he returned home, James found that demand for change was everywhere. Perhaps he found some comfort in the fact that, amid the turmoil, on 4 July 1848, the cornerstone of the Washington Monument had finally been placed. Almost fifty years after the first president's death, the honor of George Washington was one thing that most Americans could agree on. At the ceremony, Eliza Hamilton sat by Dolley Madison, symbols of the nation's birth and brief history. Few remained who remembered General George Washington from anything besides stories. These aging matriarchs raised money to see the monument begun, but they would never see it completed. The final stone was not put in place until after the Civil War, on 6 December 1884.

Chapter 17

America's Cup

Going out before the wind, the *America* took the lead.[1]

Finally back in New York, James returned to his habit of offering advice and wrote to President Taylor on foreign affairs. These observations were not limited to matters James had witnessed first-hand in Europe. Instead, he commented upon Panama and the treaty that 'for the first time departed from that sound maxim of public policy which counsels us to steer clear of entangling alliances with any portion of the foreign world.'[2]

Unfortunately, Zachary Taylor died after just over a year in office and had little time to consider anyone's advice. A hero of the Mexican–American War that had gained so much new territory for the United States, Taylor succumbed to an unknown stomach ailment on 9 July 1850. Taylor had been a compromise candidate for the Whigs, who had capitalized upon his status as a war hero in putting his nomination before that of aging statesman, Henry Clay, who had already tried and failed to win the presidency three times.

Taylor's vice-president was Millard Fillmore. He signed the Compromise of 1850 that allowed California to enter the Union as a free state but strictly enforced the Fugitive Slave Act. Putting his anti-slavery beliefs on the back burner to keeping the Union intact, Fillmore angered many but kept America out of civil war for a few more years.

It was not long before James was on his fourth voyage to Europe, this time to participate in the yacht race that would become known as the America's Cup. George Lee Schuyler was one of the owners of the schooner *America*, and when circumstances kept him from accompanying the crew to England, he asked his father-in-law to go in his place.[3] The likely reason for Schuyler's desire to remain in the country was the poor health of his mother. He wrote to his wife, Eliza, on 2 July 1851, 'The disease in incurable, but the progress uncertain.'[4] She died less than a year later.

The invitation had come to the New York Yacht Club from the Royal Yacht Squadron 'to test the relative merits' of the ships.[5] The New York Yacht Club was the only yacht club in the United States in 1851, and it had only existed for seven years, so the British challengers surely believed no great contender was likely to come from that quarter.[6] They were not counting on the ambition of the Americans to prove themselves.

It was the year of England's Great Exhibition. 'As befitted a people whose supremacy on the seas had been long undisputed, an important part of the season's program of sport was contests of speed between pleasure vessels, open to all comers.'[7] The Crystal Palace was another impressive aspect of the Exhibition that New Yorkers would soon work to replicate.

The contract for the ship that would be named *America* specified that it 'should be faster than any craft of her size afloat.'[8] Should it fail to meet that requirement, delivery could be declined and payment withheld.[9] George Steers, who, at age 30, was 'preeminent among designers of small vessels in the United States,' was the head designer of *America*.[10] Upon completion, the *America* was tested against the sloop *Maria*, which outsailed her. However, the test was considered inconclusive since the *Maria* could only reach that speed in smooth water, conditions that couldn't be guaranteed in the upcoming race. George Lee Schuyler wrote, 'As far as the trials went, the *Maria* proved herself faster than *America* – but so nearly are they matched that the builders of the *America* feel confident that with new spars of proper dimensions, and by some alterations of sails, etc., that a different result may be anticipated.'[11] He could not have known then just how correct he was. The owners agreed to a reduced sales price of $20,000 and prepared to cross the Atlantic.[12] James admitted that some were 'most urgent against our going ... as we were sure to be defeated,' but he felt 'we are in for it, and must go.'[13]

While the schooner was transported, James took a steamer to France. The *America* was refitted in Havre 'to avoid giving Englishmen too much opportunity to study the vessel before she began her racing.'[14] The first hint that *America* might be a greater competitor than anticipated was the journey from Havre to Cowes, which it completed in impressive time, unexpectedly beating the *Laverock* to their destination.[15] Despite this, the *America* 'at first gave her opponents no concern' but the US team was underestimated, and the 'simple silver cup, originally valued at $500, has come to represent the supremacy of the seas' and bear the name of the New York schooner.[16]

Before the main competition, teams challenged each other to informal matches. The *Titania* accepted the *America*'s challenge.[17] Another ship, the *Gondola*, had proposed to join the regatta, but did not appear on race day.[18] The *America* beat the *Titania* by about 7 miles in the race that required them to sail approximately 40 miles.[19]

Twenty-second of August 1851 was the day the competitors had been waiting for. 'The morning was bright, the wind very light,' James recalled.[20] Sixteen ships set off, 'breaking away like a field of race-horses'[21] at ten in the morning, and 'the Yankee vessel seeming to be excited by the responsibility of her position, rushed to the lead in beautiful style.'[22] 'In a quarter of an hour she had left them all behind, except the *Constance*, *Beatrice*, and *Gipsy Queen*, which were well together, and went along smartly with the light breeze.'[23] They raced around the Isle of Wight, a course that was said to give great advantage to those who knew the local currents and tides, but 'local knowledge could not offset the speed of the *America*, and the seamanship of her rough-and-ready crew.'[24] 'The *America* speedily advanced to the front and got clear away from the rest … from the moment the *America* had rounded St Catherine's point, with a moderate breeze at SSW, the chances of coming up with her again were over.'[25] 'The *America* arrived at Cowes at half past 8PM, and was received with the most gratifying cheers. Yankee Doodle was played by the band.'[26]

After the regatta, a story spread that Queen Victoria, in attendance on her royal yacht, asked her signal master if any yachts were yet in sight. When he replied in the affirmative, she asked, 'Which is first?' When informed it was the *America*, she asked, 'Which is second?' And her signal master stated, 'Ah, Your Majesty, there is no second.'[27] Queen Victoria decided to personally congratulate the winners.

George Lee Schuyler had chosen well to send his father-in-law for this moment. Americans were not generally held in high respect in the country they had rebelled against, but James was an ideal representative. His well-known name combined with his own intellect and diplomacy made him just the sort of man to greet the queen on behalf of his country.

Queen Victoria boarded the *America* with Prince Albert and a small party. 'To our surprise, and that of all present, the reserve and those forms generally observed in the presence of majesty were entirely done away,' James wrote. 'The Commodore took her Majesty's hand to help her to the cockpit, and then took her through the vessel, as I did the Prince. Her Majesty was particularly struck with the arrangement of the ballast, which was peculiar, and asked to see the accommodations for the crew.'[28] The friendly visit was said by some to improve relations between the two countries.

Once the *America* was docked, rumors spread that she 'had a propeller which was artfully concealed.'[29] Visitors came by the thousands to view the winning ship, some saying, 'I will give a hundred to see her bottom.' A few of the crewmembers could not resist a bit of fun and claimed that 'there is a grating which the Commodore does not allow any person to open.'[30] When the *America* was in Portsmouth for repairs, many saw the truth, but that could not stop a good story from having its day.

Before returning to New York, James took the opportunity to make some visits. A letter of introduction from Washington Irving resulted in an invitation to the estate of Sir Arthur Aston near Liverpool.[31] The gentlemen shared interests in farming and literature. James offered Sir Aston advice on using a 'horse-rake' for bringing in hay more efficiently and offered to send him one from the United States. However, Sir Aston refused 'as it would, by turning so many men out of work, create much excitement.'[32]

James also visited his friend Samuel Rogers, with whom he arranged an exchange of works. He promised to provide a copy of his father's writing, and Rogers reciprocated with a set of his own works for each of James's children.[33]

When the winners arrived back in New York, a dinner was held to celebrate the success of Commodore Stevens and his associates, including James. 'It was attended by the leading business and professional men of New York, while Commodore Matthew C Perry of the United States Navy was among the guests.'[34] They proudly displayed the trophy that they referred to as the 'Royal Yacht Squadron Cup' at that point.[35] Charles King, president of Columbia College and friend of James Hamilton, spoke, as he was often asked to do due to his skill at oratory. 'Our modern Argonauts – they have brought home not the golden fleece, but that which gold cannot buy, national renown.'[36]

While James had been away, violence had broken out over the fate of fugitive slaves in Christiana, Pennsylvania, on 11 September 1851. A shootout occurred between a Maryland slaveholder and those who were hiding the runaways. Edward Gorsuch, the slaveholder, who had shouted, 'I will have my property, or go to hell,' died in the fighting.[37] President Fillmore insisted that those involved be charged for treason, a move that only made the abolitionist movement gain sympathy. The defense attorney stated what many in the North were thinking: 'Did you hear it? That three harmless non-resisting Quakers and eight-and-thirty wretched, miserable, penniless negroes, armed with corn cutters, clubs, and a few muskets, and headed by a miller, in a felt hat, without arms and mounted on a sorrel nag, levied war against the United States.'[38] After a jury acquitted the first defendant, the remainder of the charges were dropped, infuriating Southerners.

When war broke out a decade later, the *America* was mounted with guns and used as a blockade runner during the Civil War until it was sunk in the St John's River.[39] Salvaged, she was used for training at the Naval Academy where James once gave the commencement address. Long retired, the *America* was destroyed on 28 March 1942 when the building in which she was stored in Annapolis collapsed under heavy snow.[40]

Chapter 18

The 1853 Crystal Palace Exhibition

[T]hat vast array of the triumphs of genius and industry.[1]

Americans were inspired by London's Great Exhibition year, and, being competitive in nature and inspired by the *America*'s win, a committee was formed to plan New York's own Crystal Palace. James served alongside his son, Alexander (possibly his brother, Alexander, rather than his son), and son-in-law, George Lee Schuyler, on the board of directors.[2] Called the 'Exhibition of Industry of All Nations,' it became thought of as the first world's fair in the United States. The New York Crystal Palace stood between 40th and 42nd streets, where Bryant Park is today.[3] It was next to the Croton Reservoir, which stood where today stands the Stephen A. Schwarzman Building of the New York Public Library, which houses a collection of James A. Hamilton papers.

Built with steel, cast iron, and glass, the structure was designed to be fireproof. This proved to be wishful thinking when the structure was destroyed by fire on 5 October 1858.[4] Fortunately, there were no fatalities.

It makes sense that James would be interested in being involved in New York's Crystal Palace after his experience with the crew of the *America*. At the British Great Exhibition, American industrialists had left their mark with demonstrations of Cyrus McCormick's reaper, Charles Goodyear's vulcanized rubber, and Samuel Morse's telegraph.[5] How many more would gather when not required to cross an ocean to participate? By 1852, news spread across the country about the planned world's fair, though some suggested a longer waiting period between England's 1851 exhibition and New York's.

Organizers originally planned to hold the event in Madison Square, but petitioners, concerned about the crowds and less desirable entertainments that might accompany the exhibition, caused the city council's permission to be revoked.[6] The new location was north of town next to the Croton

Reservoir, a location desolate enough that there were few to complain about its selection. The fortress-like walls of the Reservoir were a challenge to those charged with designing the new Crystal Palace, but the area around it was hastily developed to take advantage of the anticipated visitors.

Across 42nd Street from the Crystal Palace, Waring Latting built a tower called the Latting Observatory that reached 315 feet into the sky. It was the tallest building in New York City at the time, giving visitors a panoramic view of the city as had never been seen before.[7]

The New York Crystal Palace housed a wide variety of exhibitions from art, industry, agriculture, and even some that were difficult to categorize. One exhibitor displayed a woman who was supposedly a 124-year-old slave who had been owned by George Washington.[8]

James did not record his feelings about the design chosen for the New York Crystal Palace. It was much smaller than the London prototype. The plan was only a quarter of the size before the basement level was cut to save money.[9]

When visitors began arriving, New York became a tourist town for the first time, rather than solely a financial center. Hotels, diners, and ice cream shops popped up in the recently empty blocks around the exhibition, but it was still struggling to cover expenses at the 50c per person entry fee.

The Crystal Palace continued to strive for financial stability after the world's fair was complete. The venue was rented for events, but the building fell into disrepair for lack of funds. As the city lease on the land approached the expiration date, which some thought caused the building to revert to city ownership, debate about the future ensued.

The issue was settled when the Crystal Palace burned to the ground with astonishing speed on 5 October 1858, causing arson rumors that have never been proven. James's lack of mention of the project in his *Reminiscences* might cause one to wonder if he considered the entire episode a failure.

Chapter 19

Family Life II

The best of wives, mothers, and women.[1]

The *Reminiscences* of James A. Hamilton focus on his public life and correspondence with prominent men and those in public service, so it is more difficult to gain a peek into the daily life of the close-knit Hamilton family. Some letters between them have survived, as has other evidence that the members of the family had strong relationships throughout their lives.

Several letters from Eliza Hamilton Schuyler to her father have been preserved. In one, written on 12 December 1853, she writes, 'I have been sitting two hours this evening in Charles Adams' library, most interested in the Journal of John Quincy and in the manuscript letters.' When she refers to the abolitionist Charles Sumner, she says, 'I wish he would get through with his politics, that he was made of too fine material for a politician.'[2] Far from leaving politics, Sumner spoke boldly against slavery and was caned on the Senate floor for his anti-slavery statements in 1856. Years later, he was still someone James wrote to for his political views and advice.

In a document titled 'Nevis Portfolio,' one of Eliza Hamilton Schuyler's daughters gives a glimpse into the spirit of the Hamilton family. 'It was an atmosphere of love and kindness into which we came of justice and good sense; of wise understanding of us children and true consideration for us, without any spoiling.'[3] Of her mother and grandfather, she wrote, 'The tie between Eliza and her father [James] is close and intimate. She shares her confidences, his interests and his ambitions,' and his 'pride and affection for his clever, precocious daughter' are noted.[4] 'Nowhere did we have more genuine fun, more hearty laughter than under our own paternal roof.'[5]

Letters between the family members express open affection. For example, Alexander addresses letters to 'My dear papa' well into adulthood, and he writes to his brother-in-law as a close confidant as well. Alexander and James also had in common a relationship with Washington Irving. The families were neighbors along the Hudson River, and Irving built his Sunnyside the same year James built Nevis. After completing his education at West Point, Alexander served as secretary of legation for Irving, who was the United States Minister to Spain.

Several of Alexander's letters from this time survive and give a glimpse of his work and his relationships with Irving and the family members to whom he writes. He wrote long, detailed letters to keep his father informed of foreign affairs, but also wrote to his mother and sisters, sometimes in cross-hatched script to save paper. He writes to his brother-in-law, George Lee Schuyler, referring to 'our dear girls' – Alexander's sisters, one of whom was George's wife.[6] A letter written after the new year, a homesick-sounding Alexander writes, 'I do not expect to hear from you again for two or three weeks but I fill up the interval very agreeably by allowing my imagination & memory full scope, when I picture myself a happy family in a quiet comfortable home.'[7]

In some of his letters, Alexander refers to Washington Irving as 'Uncle Geoffrey,' a reference to *The Sketch Book of Geoffrey Crayon*, which Irving published in 1819–20 and includes his well-known short stories, *Rip Van Winkle* and *The Legend of Sleepy Hollow*.[8] He shares personal bits of poor Irving's life as well, such as when he writes to his father that

> Mr Irving's health begins to be affected very considerably by this herpetic disorder which has extended itself over the greater part of his body. He insisted first upon treating it himself, and went thought a course of Sulphur Baths; a violent remedy under which he did not appear to improve.[9]

It is possible that the James A. Hamilton family was not as close to the other branches of the Hamilton family. James served at Zion Episcopal Church with his brother, Alexander, and their sons, two more Alexanders, were close, but not all his siblings seem as much so. James and John Church Hamilton wrote pamphlets during the Civil War in favor of Union and in opposition to slavery, exhibiting some of their father's passion and skill. Of the other Hamilton siblings, less of their connection to James is known.

William Stephen Hamilton, almost a decade younger than James, does not seem to have retained a close relationship with his brothers. He moved to Wisconsin and established a mining settlement called Hamilton's Diggings, which was later renamed Wiota. He was involved in politics in the area which was largely untamed at the time. During the California Gold Rush, William joined the Forty-niners swarming west, though he did not look for gold. He opened a store with the intention of raising some money and returning to Wisconsin. When he died in Sacramento on 7 October 1850, it is possible that the family decided not to inform his mother about his death due to Eliza's failing health.[10]

Eliza Hamilton had visited her son in Wisconsin in an adventure happily taken on in her golden years. Whether or not she knew of William's passing is not mentioned by James in his *Reminiscences*, but he does detail Eliza's final hours. In November 1854, Eliza was living in Washington DC with her widowed daughter, Eliza Holly, who informed James that their mother 'was quite sick.'[11] The matriarch of the family was 97 years old and had lived a full life by any measure. James 'went immediately' and arrived at Eliza's bedside the next day, 9 November 1854.[12]

> I found my mother so sick as to induce a belief that she would not recover, and such, I learned from her attending physician, was his opinion ... I passed the day in her room, and in the evening my dear good sister, who was so unremitting in her attentions, said to me, 'James, I sat up with mother last night, I wish you to do so to-night; I will sleep on the sofa in the next room; there is no medicine to be given to her; should there be any change, call me.'[13]

James stayed with Eliza throughout the night. 'I took my seat at the bedside with my face to my mother's, holding the pulse of her right wrist with my right hand, and so continued about two hours, the pulse growing more feeble all the time.'[14] Checking that she was comfortable, James returned to his post.

> I bowed my head down to see if there was any change in her countenance. She put her arm around my neck, pressed me to her, kissed me most affectionately; and said, 'God bless you, you have been a good son;'

the arm was relaxed, there was a slight hiccough, a slight discharge of dark-colored liquid from the sides of her mouth, and she was dead – her pulse and breath were gone. I wiped off her mouth, kissed her, and called my sister.[15]

James was pleased to 'have almost the entire care and management of her affairs' since his older brother, 'Alexander, was away from home attending to his commercial affairs.'[16] He remembered his mother fondly both for her care of her own children and her tireless philanthropic work. 'She was a devout Christian, the best of wives, mothers, and women.'[17]

Two of James's daughters, Eliza and Mary (the two who would in turn both marry George Lee Schuyler), followed their grandmother's footsteps in philanthropic work and expanding opportunities for others, especially other women. They were involved in a wide variety of organizations, and Eliza's daughter, Louisa Lee Schuyler, also eventually joined them.

In 1852, Mary co-founded the New York School of Design for Women,[18] which provided educational and occupational opportunities to women not previously available. Mary continued her involvement with the school until it became part of the Cooper Union in 1859. That school exists to this day, and is known for hosting Abraham Lincoln's speech on 27 February 1860 that was considered vital to his presidential candidacy. Speaking out against the spread of slavery to the western states and territories, he said, 'Let us have faith that right makes might, and in that faith, let us, to the end, dare to do our duty as we understand it.'[19]

Mary, Eliza, and Louisa were all involved with the Children's Aid Society, and, when civil war broke out, the United States Sanitary Commission. The Commission was the largest volunteer organization formed in the United States at that point, a fact their grandmother Hamilton would likely have appreciated.[20] By coordinating local aid associations and working tirelessly to fill needs where the government was falling short, the women involved in the Sanitary Commission went far toward advocating for the rights of women and blacks.

Louisa, who never married, later became a principal of the Women's Central Association of Relief, an organization formed with the leadership of Elizabeth Blackwell, the first American woman to earn a medical degree.[21]

Besides the historically typical tasks of women while men were at war, such as sewing clothing and bandages, the WCAR trained nurses and strived to save men dying of disease in filthy conditions.

Louisa was 23 at the beginning of 1861 when she started a journal that combines typical entries about visits and parties alongside notations of the secession of Southern states. As if she knew that one day her diary would be part of a collection of Hamilton papers, Louisa wrote on 15 January 1861, 'With even a journal, supposed to be one's most intimate friend one has to be as careful about some things as if it was in reality an intimate friend. There are many things – thoughts rather that I don't dare to put down in black & white, any more than I should think for a moment of whispering them to anyone. Am I right?'[22] Louisa also recorded Lincoln's arrival in New York City on 19 February. She wrote that she had arrived 'too late' to catch a glimpse of him 'but saw the carriages pass & the crowd & white handkerchiefs – great enthusiasm.'[23] This was followed three days later by watching the procession for Washington's birthday from a friend's balcony.

His children grown and making their own impact, James was often asked to be involved in endeavors related to national politics and history. According to his nephew, Alexander, James was 'a very effective speaker, sought for on all public occasions.'[24] On 4 July 1853, he was asked to lay the cornerstone for a Tarrytown monument raised to honor those who had captured British Major John André. André had been hanged for his part in the treasonous plot of American General Benedict Arnold. Alexander Hamilton had attempted to save the life of André by suggesting a prisoner exchange, since he was more eager to see Arnold punished than André, but that effort failed. One wonders if James considered his father's part in André's fate as he participated in the Independence Day festivities.

Chapter 20

North and South

The exasperation of the two great sections of the country may lead to fatal results.[1]

The early nineteenth-century United States was cobbled together with compromises and agreements to set disagreements aside to be settled at a later time. Beginning with the Founding Fathers, who left slavery to be dealt with by their heirs, American leaders thought it best to focus on keeping the states united, sometimes at the expense of the liberty and freedom for which they had fought. However, that delicate balance could not last forever, though it did, perhaps, last longer than some might have anticipated. Even Alexander Hamilton expressed doubts about the longevity of the republic, or at least with the purely republican form of government, when he reportedly said to Thomas Jefferson, 'The success indeed so far is greater than I had expected, and therefore at present success seems more possible than it had done heretofore, and there are still other and other stages of improvement which, if the present does not succeed, may be tried and ought to be tried before we give up the republican form altogether.'[2]

While several issues, including tariffs, national infrastructure, property and maritime law, and others challenged legislators who were attempting to determine how to balance federal and state power, nothing threatened the unity of the states like the enslavement of black people. The founders knew that they were leaving the touchy issue for later generations to cope with. At the Constitutional Convention, slavery was discussed and purposely set aside because the framers understood ratification would not be possible with any mention of abolition involved.

When George Washington included the manumission of his slaves in his will in 1799, did he believe that others would follow suit? He may have envisioned the end of slavery with the death of his generation. If so, he would have been disappointed, because Southern slaveholders dug in their heels on the issue as those in other parts of the country – and the world at large – more vigorously questioned the peculiar institution.

James struggled with this issue and his thinking evolved just as it did for much of the country. Although he had stated more than once that he did not believe that the federal government had the constitutional authority to make laws regarding slavery, he came to firmly and loudly proclaim otherwise. He attached as much sanctity to the purity of the Constitution as anyone of the age, but even he began to question how the problem of slavery could be dealt with while holding the Union together. By the election of 1856, legislators were struggling to keep the United States together and many questioned whether they should even try.

In February, James published a 'call for a public meeting … to arrest disunion.'[3] He believed the nation could avoid civil war. He invited all, 'regardless of party or personal differences, prejudices or partialities, to meet in council,' in the interest of preserving 'our glorious Constitution' and perpetuating the Union.[4] The gathering was not intended

> to express opinions in favor of or against the various measures which are proposed in relation to the Territories, the District of Columbia, or in respect to the rights and duties of the North, or the South, the East or the West, but in commanding terms to express your solemn conviction that the Union under our Constitution is necessary to the preservation of our liberties; and our firm determination, that at all hazards, it shall be preserved.[5]

James called it 'holy work' to 'arrest this fell spirit of disunion.'[6] Unfortunately, he did not record the results of this call to action or the conversations that took place at the gathering.

In May 1856, the slavery issue became violent in the halls of Congress. Senator Charles Sumner, speaking on the debate over whether Kansas should be admitted to the Union as a free or slave state, had harsh words against slaveholders and especially for South Carolina senator Andrew Butler. 'My soul is wrung by this outrage, & I shall pour it forth,' Sumner had written to anti-slavery ally Salmon P. Chase just days earlier.[7] Mocking the senator's

Southern chivalry, Sumner stated Butler 'has chosen a mistress to whom he has made his vows, and who, though ugly to others, is always lovely to him; though polluted in the sight of the world, is chaste in his sight; I mean the harlot Slavery.'[8]

Stephen Douglas was overheard remarking, 'That damn fool will get himself killed by some other damn fool.'[9] In retribution for Sumner's passionate speech, Representative Preston Brooks, also from South Carolina, viciously attacked Sumner with a cane three days later within Senate chambers. Each man was seen as a hero for their respective cause. Charles Sumner took months to recover from his wounds, and Henry Adams, John Quincy's grandson, then a student at Harvard, offered to stay with Sumner and serve him during his recuperation on the condition that he not 'speak a word of politics' for two years.[10]

When James wrote to a friend days after the almost fatal attack, he was

> much pained by recent events. The exasperation of the two great sections of the country may lead to fatal results. The assault upon Sumner, is, as respects the man, of the least importance. The attack upon the Senate, and the freedom of debate, cannot be submitted to; particularly when we learn from the resolutions and meetings of the Southerners that they not only applaud the act but say it was committed in the right place, and that they will not submit to the expressions of opinion such as he had uttered in regard to slavery.[11]

William Cullen Bryant of the *New York Evening Post* agreed with James. He wrote, 'Are we to be chastised as they chastise their slaves? Are we too, slaves, slaves for life, a target for their brutal blows, when we do not comport ourselves to please them?'[12] Not everyone who considered themselves opposed to slavery agreed with Sumner's instigative rhetoric, but they were horrified by the lack of respect for free speech, especially in the halls of federal government. On the other hand, Butler received little admonition from fellow Southerners. His 'noble actions' against 'vulgar abolitionists' were celebrated by slaveholders.[13]

In the autumn of 1856, James participated in correspondence with Hamilton Fish that was published under the title *Fremont, the Conservative*

Candidate. In these letters, James and Fish discuss national values and which candidate fulfills them in the weeks leading up to the election of 1856. The conversation was based on the problem as expressed by Fish that 'our old, honored Whig party is temporarily disorganized, and presents no distinctive candidates for our support.'[14] These men considered voting a 'high duty' from which they could not abstain 'without a violation of duty to his principles and his country.'[15] Therefore, Fish and Hamilton were determined to discern which candidate deserved their votes during this tumultuous time.

James A. Hamilton is often described as a Jacksonian due to his service to that president. However, in a letter to Hamilton Fish on 7 March 1856, James identifies himself 'as a National Whig and as a citizen feeling a lively interest in the welfare of the country.'[16] He also often referred to himself as a conservative rather than a Democrat and would go on to demonstrate support for the new Republican party.

On the other hand, he wrote to Senator Lewis Cass on 8 August 1856, urging him to run as the Democratic candidate and 'sacrifice yourself with that party, to save it from defeat, and the Union from disruption.'[17] Whichever party was in power, James found those he could connect with in the national interest and strived to do his part to serve his country.

Cass did not agree that his candidacy was the answer to the nation's problems, but he appreciated the 'evidence of personal esteem.'[18] In his response, Cass demonstrates his respect for James. 'Certainly there is great force in your argument, while a spirit of patriotism pervades your letters, which is refreshing in this day of our troubles. You bear a glorious name, and may boast of a proud descent, which gives you a right to speak to your countrymen.'[19] James believed the Missouri Compromise required reinstating for the sake of the Union. Cass disagreed and 'long held that the Missouri line was unconstitutional.'[20]

Hamilton Fish, however, was of one mind with James, and together they were determined to select a candidate who could defeat the Democratic candidate, James Buchanan, whose candidacy Fish believed demonstrated that 'what once was the National Democratic party' has been converted 'into a mere sectional Southern party.'[21] James agreed that the Democratic party had become the chosen party of slaveholders and that the success of Mr Buchanan would be more to be deplored than that of either of the other candidates. I cannot express in terms too strong, my contempt for the spirit of unmanly compliance, which has induced him to lay down his identity, to become the inanimate representative of a party platform. Commencing in such a spirit of submission to party dictation, no man can tell where he will end.[22]

These were strong words from James, who typically strived to be more controlled in his writings than his father had been and tended to have friends of broad political persuasions. James and Fish were disappointed that Millard Fillmore had abandoned the Whigs to run for the American party, also commonly referred to as the Know Nothings, with vice-presidential candidate Major Andrew Jackson Donelson, nephew of the former president.

They considered the possibility that the election would be decided by the House of Representatives, something that did not seem as outlandish in 1856 as it does today, since that was how John Quincy Adams had been elected in 1824. Fish believed it was 'an event at all times to be deprecated' regardless of the outcome.[23] He, perhaps, had a point. John Quincy Adams never quite recovered from the 'corrupt bargain' that made him president and had failed to be re-elected to a second term, despite being possibly the most eminently qualified statesman of the day. James did not believe it was 'barely possible that the election may go to the House of Representatives – an event deeply to be deplored at all times, but particularly when the parties there are so deeply excited against each other.'[24]

John Charles Fremont, the candidate determined to be most qualified by Fish and Hamilton, had the timeless disadvantage of being too moderate, called anti-slavery by Southerners but pro-slavery by abolitionists in the North.[25] Had Fremont won, the Southern states may have begun seceding from the Union four years earlier. A suggestion that Fish called 'unpatriotic and disloyal.'[26] James was more confident that 'the good and true men of any section of our country' would not allow a step as terrible as secession, but was sure that 'the will of the majority must govern' and 'such fearful consequences' could be avoided.[27]

Fremont was a Free Soil candidate, meaning he believed in limiting the expansion of slavery in the west but would not pursue eliminating slavery in the states where it existed. To the modern reader, this seems not progressive enough, but to many in the nineteenth century, including James A. Hamilton, the federal government did not have the constitutional authority to make these state-level decisions, though it could impart limits upon territories.

Many Southerners were not content with this plan and insisted upon the expansion of slavery into the west, possible annexation of Cuba, and some even had hopes of conquering Mexico and overturning its anti-slavery laws. As historian and great-grandson of John Adams, Henry Adams, wrote, 'Whenever a question arose of extending or protecting slavery, the slaveholders became friends of centralized power and used that dangerous weapon with a kind of frenzy.'[28] Southern papers portrayed Fremont as an anti-slavery tyrant who would cause the South to become inferior to the North and West. Fremont was called a 'Black Republican' just as Abraham Lincoln would be four years later. The press also printed accusations that he was Roman Catholic, which was not true, but anti-Catholic sentiment was widespread in the United States until the election of John F. Kennedy a century later.

James was concerned about the development of what John C. Calhoun had called 'the Great Southern Empire,' which included not only the annexation of Texas 'under the imbecile Tyler' but 'the conquest of Cuba.'[29] He was confident that 'the Union will not be dissolved, or attempted to be, by the election of Mr Fremont, or at all, until the range of our Southern boundary shall be extended, so as to embrace all the States and Territories required to form an imposing confederacy.'[30] James placed somewhat too much hope in the leaders of the Southern states, understanding the disadvantage they would experience if they were to attempt to stand on their own.

'The highest duty of an American citizen is loyalty to the Union and devotion to the Constitution,' James declared.[31] Unfortunately, this was not a conviction held by all Americans, and certainly not all Southerners. Almost five years before the shots at Fort Sumter, James feared the sectionalism in the United States 'would plunge us into civil war; and every other step would bring along a dark and dreary waste of crime and misery.'[32]

Talk of disunion was not necessarily new and had been threatened several times throughout the young country's existence over multiple issues, but this time it would not be resolved through negotiation and legislation.

James Buchanan stated, 'the Black Republicans must be ... boldly assailed as disunionists'[33] and his fellow Democrats took up the cry, failing to see the irony in blaming the failure of the Union on someone besides those determined to secede.

Buchanan won the election of 1856, appeasing the slave states for another four years, but disappointing James and increasing the polarization between North and South. For all his admiration of and work in service to President Jackson, James saw Buchanan's rise as directly tied to 'when "The Northern man with Southern Principles" was appointed Secretary of State by General Jackson.'[34] He was disillusioned with the lack of 'moral and political principles' held by the parties or demanded by the public. Instead of 'great virtues and duties,' politicians demanded 'absolute, unhesitating obedience to the dogmas of the party; in the name of the Democracy ... all this is done in order that a few men may enjoy power and place, and fatten on the plunder of the public Treasury.'[35]

Civil War may have been temporarily avoided by Buchanan's election, but it did not resolve the divide that was growing deeper between those who wished to abolish slavery and those who wished to protect and expand it. In addition to this issue, a run on the banks began with the failure of the Ohio Life and Trust Company, causing the Panic of 1857. A variety of factors contributed to this financial panic, including the end of the Crimean War and the impact that had on global supply chains and prices. America was also experiencing changes relating to westward movement that required adjustments to how commodities were distributed and priced. Some blame may also be placed upon land and railroad speculation. James continued to lobby for a return to financial control under a centralized bank as his father had created. He wrote, 'It is a remarkable fact, that the treasury system established in 1790 for the United States, when the population was about three millions, and the area was not one-fourth part what it now is, should have the capacity of extension to such large proportions as the commerce and revenue now require.'[36]

James corresponded with the first Republican New York Governor, John A. King, regarding the run on the banks and discussed the part of the railroads in causing financial crisis. James wrote in December 1857, 'As to the capital or credit of a bank being loaned to build railroads, or to make or sustain stock operations, that is entirely out of the question, and any bank which should be found doing either, should be discredited.'[37] Had more of this financial advice been put into practice, some of the financial scandals involving railroads might have been avoided.

They also corresponded regarding the situation in Kansas, where those on both sides of the slavery issue were fighting for dominance. 'It has occurred to me,' James commented with more prescience than he likely realized, 'the course of the President and his Southern backers may drive the people of that territory into civil war.'[38] At this point, James still embraced the state's 'right of self-government ... whether with or without slavery' and did not believe 'the President, or any other power of Government' should force Kansas in one direction or the other.[39] He based this upon his understanding of constitutional law rather than his personal feelings regarding slavery. The majority of people in Kansas were in favor of status as a free state, but conflict continued during the period sometimes called 'Bleeding Kansas' until 1859 and escalated again in vicious violence during the Civil War.

One of the anti-slavery participants in the unrest in Kansas, John Brown, became famous for his raid at Harpers Ferry, Virginia, on 16 October 1859. He anticipated that local abolitionists and slaves would flock to support him if he took a bold stand and provided weapons and leadership. The misjudgement cost him his life and that of two of his sons.

Widespread violence and voter fraud perpetrated by the Democrats in Kansas challenged the legitimate government to the extent that it delayed statehood until 1861, when it was welcomed into the Union to counter Southern secession. With free and legal elections, Republicans held large majorities in Kansas, where people had seen the extent Democrats would go to in order to spread the power of slaveholders.[40]

In response to these events, James wrote a pamphlet on the power of the president. He abhorred the habit, started by Jackson, of removing hundreds if not thousands from government positions in order to appoint those who were being rewarded for their votes and campaign work. Feeling that the monetization of elections went against everything men like his father had worked toward, James decided to speak up.

In his *Examination of the Power of the President to Remove from Office during the Recess of the Senate*, James states that 'making the offices of government "the spoils of victory" has degraded the country by corrupting the parties and the people.'[41] He also points out that selections are 'not guided by their fitness for the places, by their integrity or intelligence' – a truth James had complained about back during the Jackson administration.[42] However, the question was not whether the practice was morally correct, James wrote regarding legality.

He argued that the President alone held 'no such express power.'[43] James believed Congress had erred in permitting presidents to remove appointees for partisan reasons and that such removals should require concurrence of the Senate. He quotes his own father in the *Federalist Papers*. 'One of the advantages to be expected from the cooperation of the Senate, in the business of appointments' is 'that it would contribute to the stability of the administration. The consent of that body would be necessary to displace as well as to appoint. A change of the chief magistrate, therefore, would not occasion so violent or so general a revolution as might be expected if he were the sole disposer of offices.'[44] According to the Constitution, the president has power to fill a vacancy during a Senate recess (without concurrence), but he cannot create a vacancy by removing someone from office.[45]

James goes on to argue that the president also 'cannot create an office by making an appointment or otherwise, because "all other offices must be established by law."'[46] James quoted statesmen such as Daniel Webster and John C. Calhoun in his pamphlet to demonstrate the bipartisan agreement on this issue.

The problem of appointments and removals from office had been going on for decades, and James chose the wrong time to address it. 'The threatened secession rendered any change for the present hopeless.'[47] James, at age 78, took up his banner in opposition to cronyism once again in 1866. The Tenure of Civil Office Bill was passed in March 1867.

Chapter 21

The Private Side of James A. Hamilton

I employed most of my time with my books.[1]

The *Reminiscences of James Alexander Hamilton* provide valuable insight into the early decades of the United States. What it does not always offer is information about the personal lives of the Hamiltons. However, James does include a few rare glimpses of his family life and love for his home on the Hudson River.

> Between the autumn of 1851 when I returned from the Yachting expedition, until July, 1858, when I made another voyage to Europe for the benefit of my health, I employed most of my time with my books; in utilizing the advantages of my country residence by bringing the water from the pond I had formed to this house, a distance of over four thousand feet, and conveying it to a reservoir which contains 132,000 gallons; and also building an addition to my house; with the accustomed attention which every man of leisure gives or ought to give to public affairs by promoting the success of the party of his choice.[2]

Some of the improvements to the estate James mentions can be viewed at Nevis to this day. A large room on the main floor facing east would have had a view of the Hudson River in the 1850s. Today, the area between the house and the railroad tracks that run along the riverside is heavily wooded, but within this room are glimpses of the life James lived in the built-in bookshelves that line the walls. They are stained a deep, rich color, and arched at the top, demonstrating a desire for beauty as well as practicality.[3] One can imagine the volumes that James would have collected on the bountiful shelves.

The house is not maintained as a historic sight, but it retains some hints of the family that once happily filled the rooms. A large gilded mirror, said to have been purchased by James's son, Alexander, still hangs on one wall, and elaborate wainscotting and trim testify to the home's grand past and the care that went into its construction.[4] An elaborately carved handrail leads to a second floor is original construction. The main entrance is topped by a plaque that reads: 'Nevis. 1835.'[5]

Although James clearly took comfort in this home he had built and the family that surrounded him there, he left it to make his fifth voyage to Europe. He seems to have made the journey a bit spontaneously, writing to a friend from Paris on 30 September 1858, 'The fact is, I decided one Sunday morning, after a very bad night, to try what the ocean would do for me, and I sailed on Wednesday.'[6] James's sister, Angelica, had died the year before at age 72, ending her lifelong battle with mental illness. Perhaps this reminder of mortality encouraged James to be impetuous about doing something he simply wished to do.

This was probably the first ocean crossing where James might have enjoyed food provided in the cost of passage. Before this time, passengers were often expected to bring food to feed themselves. The trip was made for the sake of his health but had an inauspicious start.[7] 'The bounding billow was not a match for dyspepsia, and rendered me no service. On the contrary, I was worse when I landed than I was before my departure. However, under the advice of an English physician in London, Dr Eliottson, I am much better.'[8]

As he had done during his previous travels, James enjoyed recording his observations and experiences. In contrast to other trips, his *Reminiscences* include more leisurely relaxation than meetings with diplomats and world leaders. He reflected, 'I think the Parisians love noise and talking better than any thing in the world.' They talk and 'do so most vehemently at all times, under all circumstances, and upon the most trifling occasion.' The friendliness of the people and 'charming' weather enabled James to spend many agreeable hours where 'here they talk and eat and drink.'[9]

He, perhaps, could not help delving a bit into politics during his visit. He remarked upon the 'fruitless' revolutions of 1848, which he had witnessed first-hand.[10] Napoleon III ruled at this point, and James observed that the French villages were organized on a feudal system, much as they would have been before France's several attempts at revolution. In discussion with a French diplomat, James observed the limitations on education 'before people learn their rights and duties' and 'will not patiently bear their burdens, social, civil, or ecclesiastical, and they may attempt to throw them off.'[11]

He also expressed a rare moment of disillusionment with the United States as he reflected upon events in France. 'What can be said in favor of popular government? I confess I have fearful forebodings. Of one thing I am quite sure, that universal suffrage in our cities, with our foreign and pauper population, whose votes are directed by the worst men, is a complete failure, and most of the good and sensible in New York now believe it to be so.'[12]

When James returned to New York from his trip, he was ready to begin speaking out against the failures he saw in the US government, starting with political cronyism, a practice he believed resulted in offices 'given to the relatives and dependents of those who hold offices, executive and legislative, and thus your legislatures are poisoned at the same time.'[13] He also prepared to respond to the Dred Scott decision of the Supreme Court and the extent to which it empowered the slave states to manipulate the federal government.

Chapter 22

Slavery and Secession

These facts prove incontestably that it was the deliberate purpose, not of individual members alone, but of the Convention, to exclude from the Constitution, not only the hated word 'Slave,' but the detested thing 'Slavery.'[1]

James A. Hamilton wrote that the only saying more offensive than 'to the victors belong the spoils' was 'that the black man has not any right which a white man is bound to respect.'[2] Up until this point, James had been supporting the Free Soil party. He did not believe in expanding the institution of slavery, but he did not believe the federal government had the power to eliminate it in states where it was legally protected. His thoughts began to evolve when the Dred Scott decision brought to the forefront that the South would never be content with that compromise and free black people would always live in fear of losing liberty, even if they lived in a 'free' state.

Dred and Harriet Scott sued for their freedom in St Louis Circuit Court in 1846. Since they had spent time living in the Wisconsin Territory, which was free, the Scotts argued that this residency made them free and they could not be re-enslaved upon return to Missouri.[3] Some cases had been decided this way, but Missouri judges were reluctant to set such a precedent in their state. After battling in court for over a decade, the case was decided by the Supreme Court and pro-slavery Chief Justice Roger B. Taney. He wrote, 'the right of property in a slave is distinctly and expressly affirmed in the Constitution,' in an attempt to remove all legal protections from blacks regardless of the state in which they resided. James responded that this argument was 'wholly groundless.'[4]

The majority opinion stated that 'enslaved people were not citizens of the United States and, therefore, could not expect any protection for the federal government or the courts.'[5] It went even further to state that 'Congress had no authority to ban slavery from federal territory.'[6] Suddenly, the idea that free soil might exist anywhere in the US was in doubt. Free states had been required to enforce fugitive slave laws, endure kidnappers who claimed they were retrieving runaways, and now they could not even offer citizenship to the black people living within their borders. Southerners had made clear that they wished for a weak federal government, except when it meant enforcing their will regarding slavery.

Two Supreme Court justices, Benjamin Curtis and John McLean, dissented. They pointed out that constitutional rights of free blacks had been upheld many times since the country's founding. When the Constitution was ratified in 1788, five of the thirteen states had included the legal votes of free black men.[7]

James began his own argument where one might expect, with the Constitution. 'The Chief Justice has not quoted those parts of the Constitution on which his judgment is founded,' he writes, and one can almost envision him shaking his head. Not one to make the same mistake, James intended 'to prove beyond all question' that 'it was the purpose of all' at the Constitutional Convention 'to exclude Slavery, and all idea that there could be property in man from that instrument.'[8] He also reminds readers that it was 'unanimously resolved that the words "Slave" and "Slavery" should be stricken out' at the Constitutional Convention.[9]

The specific provisions of the Constitution that James quotes include Article 4, Section 2, Clause 3. 'No person held to service or labor in one State, under the laws thereof, escaping into another, shall, in consequence of any law or regulation therein, be discharged from such service or labor.' He might seem here to be making his opponent's argument for him, but he goes on. 'The right to a person's service or labor comes very short of the right to the person himself. The right of service of an apprentice or a redemptioner does not make either a slave.'[10]

He goes beyond the Constitution to demonstrate that philosophers throughout history have denounced slavery, quoting, among others, Plato, 'Slavery is a system of the most complete injustice,' and Locke, 'Every man has a property in his own person; this nobody has a right to but himself.'[11] Of course, he includes America's favorite hometown philosopher, Benjamin Franklin, 'The wise and good men throughout all time, and the Christian

Church throughout all the world, with an important exception during a brief period in our own country, have denounced "Slavery" as "an atrocious debasement of human nature."'[12]

Even the Supreme Court could not reverse 'the established law of Nature.'[13] To the contrary, James insisted that US law 'distinctly disaffirms all idea of Slavery or property in man, by natural law, by the Constitution, or by the action of Congress.'[14] He turns the South's own argument on them. Those who had been long proclaiming that other states' laws could not impact slavery where it was legal were now told that they could not extend their pro-slavery laws into free states. Could an enslaver prove that a fugitive slave owed him labor 'under the Constitution of the United States,' he asks before answering his own question: 'Most certainly not.'[15]

Not holding back, the way he might have done when he was younger, James wrote:

> The Chief Justice of the Supreme Court of the United States has declared that their being 'purchased and held as property' within the States and under the law, is 'sanctioned and authorized by the Constitution.' Respect for the high office he holds forbids us to intimate the cause of this palpable judicial perversion. Recent discussions as to the arbitrament of that Court upon the meaning of a deceptive party platform, are pregnant with painful suggestions.[16]

He also encouraged his readers to stand firm, even when Southerners threatened the Union with destruction. Their demands were 'a lust for power' by states that already held extraordinary power due to the infamous three-fifths compromise that gave them representation on behalf of the enslaved who could not vote.[17]

James was 'confident that a large proportion of the people and statesmen of the South are as true to their interests and their patriotic impulses as were their ancestors,' who would agree with him that 'Disunion is a word of mighty import.'[18] He hoped they would 'return to the wise counsels of the illustrious dead, and unite with their brethren of the North, as they did in the better days of the Republic … and sternly rebuke the profligate extravagance and gross corruption of the present Administration.'[19]

Outcry in opposition of the Dred Scott decision was not the only example of James, and the American public, becoming more outspoken regarding the rights of black citizens – beginning with their right to be considered citizens. As the 1850s came to a close, it became more difficult for politicians or voters to remain neutral on the issue of slavery. The most commonly held opinions of the day were thoroughly expressed and disputed in the debates between Abraham Lincoln and Stephen Douglas during their fiercely competitive Senate race in 1858.

Political parties had long been trending toward regional division, rather than the traditional split between more or less federal power. The Lincoln Douglas debates demonstrate this. Like many who found themselves in the new Republican party, Lincoln considered himself a Whig and had been a great admirer of Henry Clay. Lincoln stated that the abolition of slavery had been a goal even of the Founding Fathers, who had stated that 'all men are created equal' and established limits on the institution that they had hoped would quietly fade away on its own. He admitted that Southerners were 'no more responsible for the origin of slavery' than those in the North, and 'that it is very difficult to get rid of it,' while denying 'that there can be moral right in the enslaving of one man by another.'[20]

Douglas tried to walk along a moderate line, defending the 'sacred right of self-government' that gave the Southern states tyranny over the black people they held enslaved.[21] At the same time, however, he said the law of the Dred Scott decision was worthless 'unless sustained, protected and enforced by appropriate police regulations and local legislation.'[22] Douglas realized, as many politicians would soon discover, that appeasing constituents in the North and the South was becoming nearly impossible. He continued to argue that the Union could continue as it had with each free and slave state 'perfectly free to do as it pleased,' but that delicate balance was becoming less acceptable to both those who saw slavery as a moral wrong that should be corrected or those who defended it as a moral right that should be expanded into new territory.[23]

Many thought Lincoln won the debates despite losing the senatorial race. His future held greater things than he probably imagined as those results came in. Soon newspapers were calling for change, such as the *Chicago*

Tribune's declaration, 'Let the next President be Republican, and 1860 will mark an era kindred with that of 1776.'[24]

Before this landmark US election, James experienced more personal loss. His sister, Eliza Holly, who had been with him as they cared for their mother on her deathbed, died on 17 October 1859. She was a month shy of her 60th birthday and had been a widow for more than a decade. Four of the eight Hamilton siblings remained as civil war approached: Alexander, James, John, and the younger Philip.

On the other hand, there were family moments to celebrate, such as the marriage of James's daughter, Angelica, to Richard Milford Blatchford. She was his third wife. Angelica had waited until relatively late in life, age 40, before marrying, and they had no children together.

The election of 1860 was unique in US history in the regional breakdown of the issues and voting results. The South, where slavery was once called a necessary evil, now boldly defended their peculiar institution. One South Carolinian insisted that slavery was preferable to the situation endured by laborers in the North because 'slaves are hired for life and well compensated,' but those working for wages were 'hired by the day, not cared for, and scantily compensated.'[25] When Southerners pointed to strikes and labor issues in the North as evidence that slavery was the superior system, Lincoln retorted, 'I am glad to see that a system prevails in New England under which laborers can strike when they want to. I like the system which lets a man quit when he wants to and wish it might prevail everywhere.'[26]

With the Southern states threatening secession in the event of a Republican victory, one might think that Lincoln was an outspoken abolitionist. Such was not the case in 1860, and he only slowly and reluctantly came to see the benefits of emancipation over the long years of war. In 1858, Lincoln clarified that when he said slavery would ultimately be eliminated, he envisioned a gradual process. 'I do not suppose that in the most peaceful way ultimate extinction would occur in less than a hundred years at the least; but that it will occur in the best way for both races in God's good time.'[27] Even this assertion was too radical for most Southerners and many Democrats, but the rate of change brought on by the war escalated the pace of emancipation.

Since the country was so staunchly divided along regional lines, the 1860 election became a battle between North and South. In the Northern states, voters saw a rematch of the Illinois senatorial race between Abraham Lincoln and Stephen Douglas, while Southern states did not put Republicans on the ballot. Instead, they looked to John Breckinridge, who had served as Buchanan's vice-president and would later serve as Secretary of War for the Confederacy. Southern states threatened secession if Lincoln was elected, 'the old game of scaring and bullying the North into submission to Southern demands,' said the mayor of Chicago.[28]

Lincoln won by a healthy margin in the Electoral College, though with only 40 per cent of the popular vote and without carrying a single Southern state. Charles Francis Adams, son and grandson of two of the five non-slaveholding presidents to serve the US before Lincoln, wrote, 'The great revolution has actually taken place ... The country has once and for all thrown off the domination of the Slaveholders.'[29]

South Carolina seceded from the Union on 20 December 1860, and it was promptly followed by ten other slaveholding states. The immediate question asked by most Americans had nothing to do with slavery. They wondered if the right to secession was constitutional or if the Southern states were in rebellion.

Chapter 23

Civil War

The following pages relate to the most interesting period of my life – the Rebellion.[1]

James A. Hamilton had no doubts that secession was unconstitutional and that the rebellion of the Southern states opened up a new case for abolition of slavery. He wrote, 'I was sternly opposed to slavery because I knew it to be a great crime and a great evil to the oppressor as well as the oppressed. I had learned this from the writings of the wise and good men of all times.'[2] James had not always boldly stated this, but his study of history and law, combined with the corrupt forces he witnessed at work within the government, brought him to this point.

> It was well understood, that slavery should not be interfered with directly by the Free States. I therefore did not permit myself to become an abolitionist. As soon, however, as the Slave States threw off their allegiance, freed from my constitutional obligations, I became a most determined abolitionist, and prepared by all means in my power to abolish slavery throughout the land … My whole time and all my faculties were directed to the work; stimulated by the conviction that should we abolish slavery and crush the rebellion, cost what it might, we should thus be made a wiser, better, and happier people.[3]

As firmly as James began to stand against slavery, he had also inherited his father's passion for preserving the Union. In 1785, when Rufus King, a friend of Alexander Hamilton's, had advocated the abolition of slavery, it was dismissed to accommodate Southern slaveholders. In January 1860, when there was still hope of avoiding war, James wrote to Representative John Cochrane, urging him to use his influence within the Democratic party, 'compelled by your duty to your constituents, but above all by your devotion to the honor and welfare of your government and country' to that end.[4] James recognized that to do such was 'so signal a personal sacrifice' that would be rewarded by 'the commendation of the good and the wise in all parts of this country and of the world, and, above all, of your own conscience.'[5]

Cochrane's response was not encouraging. 'I cannot write you of any definite prospect. Indeed there is none.'[6] Although he agreed that, 'The country begins to sway fearfully in the storm that is upon us, Party should be forgotten now.'[7] He was as disappointed as James, writing, 'opinion fluctuates here exceedingly, but the steady tendency is toward the inevitable approach of dissolution.'[8]

James understood better than most that the Constitution had been a compromise. 'Slavery, from its inherent feebleness from moral as well as political causes, as long been a bold aggressor upon the rights of the North, and with such complete success as to have become reckless of consequences,' he wrote in his *Reminiscences*.[9] He felt that 'declaring extra-judicially the Missouri Compromise law unconstitutional – have manifested so clearly the purpose of the slave power – we mean the oligarchy of slave-holders – to govern the Union, not by force of numbers, but by combinations hostile to Republican government.'[10] Rather than participate in what had always been a compromise, the slaveholding states, what James and his brother John called the 'slave power,' strove to increase their domination of the country through westward expansion. Repealing the Missouri Compromise, which limited the extent of the expansion of slavery into the western territories, was a step in that direction. Because of the poorly conceived three-fifths compromise, the more people enslaved, the greater the political power of those who held them.

James even attempted to correspond with Charles Cotesworth Pinckney, son of Thomas Pinckney, regarding the importance of maintaining the Union. The Pinckney family had been involved in governance since the birth of the nation, and Thomas's brother, Charles, had been a general during the American Revolution and participant in the Constitutional Convention. James wrote:

> The names of our fathers were associated, in former times of anxiety, of danger and of struggle, in the service of their country, and the labors of

those whose names we bear, seventy years ago contributed in no small measure to form the Government under which we have grown to our present stature among the nations of the world. United, we take the rank of a first-class power; respected, feared, and deferred to by the rulers of Europe, of Asia, and of America.

After a lengthy list of the country's accomplishments in that time, he continues, 'The expectation of those men in your State who are endeavoring to plunge South Carolina into secession is, that other States will be drawn by her into the same disastrous condition; and thus that a Southern Confederacy will be formed. What would be our future in that event?' James encourages Pickney to realize that

prejudices have thus been excited by politicians to promote their selfish ends ... we ask you in the name of all that is dear to us both to pause; to trust to the strong conservative feeling of the North, to our respect and affection for our southern brethren as part of our glorious country, to our common memories of the past and hopes of the future.[11]

Pinckney, apparently unconvinced by the patriotic sentiment, did not respond to James but did publish pamphlets in favor of secession. From Pinckney's perspective and that of many other Southerners, they were fighting for their freedom in the spirit of 1776 for their right of self-government. This seems irrational to our modern perspective, given their fight to keep black people enslaved, and it did so to many in the North at the time as well. William Cullen Bryant wrote that 'Their motto is not liberty, but slavery.'[12]

Seeing the likelihood of secession on the horizon, James wrote to President Buchanan, who he had previously encouraged those in Congress to impeach, with advice on 'the treatment of secession.'[13] Given his feelings about Buchanan, James must not have held much hope that the president would follow his advice, but he was tireless in his efforts, even in reaching out to Southerners and their supporters.

James reminded Buchanan that a president is 'compelled by his oath to protect and defend the Constitution, and by that Constitution to take care that the laws be faithfully executed.'[14] His first instruction was, 'As secession by South Carolina is now understood to be a determined purpose, it has become the imperative duty of the President without delay completely to garrison Fort Moultrie.'[15] He provides examples of Washington's handling of the Whiskey Rebellion and Jackson's refusal to allow South Carolina to secede during the nullification crisis. 'These examples of two of the most illustrious predecessors of President Buchanan ought to command his respect,' James wrote.[16]

James spent Christmas Eve 1860 addressing another letter to President Buchanan. 'My duty to the President, to my country, and to the truth compels me to inform you that very many intelligent and discreet men of all parties in this State, condemn the inaction of the Secretary of war in relation to the forts in Charleston harbor.'[17] His opinion was that the forts, Moultrie, Pinckney, and Sumter, should have been secured months earlier, but now that South Carolina had voted to secede, no further delay could be condoned.

James included an essay titled 'Secession – Its Treatment – A Peaceful Solution' with the letter.[18] In the essay, James wrote, 'When South Carolina shall, by her Convention, declare that her people are no longer subjected to the Constitution and laws of the United States, they will be in the condition of rebellion. The laws which affect the people of South Carolina, particularly which regulate commerce, establish the judiciary and the mail service.'[19] It was the President's duty, he felt, to close the South Carolina ports, forcing them to export through Georgia, hopefully deferring that state's secession.[20] By forcing South Carolina to see great disadvantage in independence, James thought a peaceful reunification might be possible. He sent more detailed plans and advice on the closing of Southern ports to Representative Cochrane.[21]

Bold action was required, James and others believed, to squash the idea that states could dissolve the union for any reason. The Declaration of Independence and the Constitution that followed created a perpetual union, as its language made clear. 'On the other hand, where can be found any article of these instruments, or any fact or circumstance connected with their formation, which can be tortured into an admission of the right of a State, or the people thereof, to secede?'[22] States had surrendered rights 'to make war or peace; to enter into any treaty, alliance, or confederation; to grant letters of marque or reprisal; to coin money; emit bills of credit' among countless others in favor of federal domain over these laws.[23] James was convinced that, 'After a careful examination of the Constitution of the United States, and the sovereign rights of States, we are compelled to declare, that after surrendering specifically the sovereign powers above enumerated, it is absurd to speak of the States of this union as sovereign.'[24]

James was willing to take action himself. On 28 December 1860, he wrote to General Sanford of the New York militia, offering to take men to South Carolina himself.

> The President having exposed a handful of brave men now in Fort Moultrie to slaughter, and the flag of our country to disgrace, there can be no violation of law or duty of any kind, should citizens volunteer to go to Charleston harbor in a steamer, chartered for the purpose, in order to reinforce Major Anderson.[25]

Kentuckian Major Robert Anderson, the unfortunate officer in charge at Fort Moultrie, remained loyal to the Union, despite his personal Southern sympathies.[26] Offering to pay for the steamer and provisions himself and intending, at age 72, to be one of the 400 volunteers, James was 'deeply disappointed' when General Winfield Scott insisted 'the military needs of the country require no appeal to militia or volunteers.'[27]

Not only did James feel he had been 'thus deprived of an opportunity, in a noteworthy manner of rendering an essential service to my country; and of connecting my name creditably with this the greatest chapter in the history of our country,' but the federal forts in Charleston were not reinforced. Anderson requested reinforcements, which Buchanan refused to send.[28] Without waiting for orders to do so, Anderson was forced to abandon Fort Moultrie and move what men he had to the more defensible Fort Sumter.[29] There, the first shots of the Civil War were fired by South Carolinians on 12 April 1861.

As the country hastened toward armed conflict, President Buchanan chose inaction, and the states of Mississippi, Florida, Alabama, Georgia, Louisiana, and Texas followed South Carolina into secession in January 1861. One can only imagine the combination of pride and fear that James felt as his only son, Alexander, volunteered for service and became an aide to Major General

John Ellis Wool. In the journal kept by James's granddaughter, Louisa Lee Schuyler, the first months of 1861 include notes of the secession of states alongside her schedule of parties and family dinners. On 9 January 1861, she recorded Mississippi's secession along with the message, 'there seems to be a tacit agreement that we mean to frolic during these three months.'[30] One of the last entries she records is on 12 April. 'Heard of attack on Fort Sumter by Extra at 10pm.'[31] She began working for the Women's Central Relief Association on 6 May.[32]

Louisa's mother, Eliza Hamilton Schuyler, the daughter with whom James had shared so many letters during his travels, in her own diary about this time makes the reference, 'illness first appeared & medical advice was taken.'[33] She volunteered for the Union effort as long as her health allowed but died of cancer before the end of the war.

Even as states joined the Southern Confederacy, 'As long as there was a hope of avoiding an appeal to arms, I was earnest in my endeavors by compromise to avoid that dire necessity, and at the same time to preserve the Union and the Constitution,' James wrote.[34] Recalling again the three-fifths compromise made for the same purpose, James encouraged the president-elect, Abraham Lincoln, to 'hold fast the Border States.'[35] This was a concern that Lincoln shared, and he walked a fine political line to keep the border states of Missouri, Kentucky, Maryland, and Delaware within the Union while maintaining Republican support. Along with his advice, James wrote, 'I love the Union and the Constitution, as I do the memory of my father (Alexander Hamilton), one of the chief architects of the last.'[36]

In February 1861, Congress voted on a proposed Thirteenth Amendment, designed to appease the South. It granted constitutional protection to slavery in the states that legalized it. Before the states had the chance to ratify this amendment, the country was at war, and this proposed compromise was abandoned. The eventual Thirteenth Amendment abolished slavery rather than protected it.[37]

On 27 February, James wrote to Lincoln again, days before his inauguration, to 'present to your consideration an important suggestion upon which the more I reflect, the more confirmed I am of its wisdom.'[38] His suggestion was to retain John Dix as Treasury Secretary. Dix had served since Philip Thomas resigned due to South Carolina's secession. However, Lincoln named Salmon P. Chase, an anti-slavery politician from Ohio, with whom James would correspond a great deal throughout the war.

In what appears to be his first letter to Chase on 18 March 1861, James spelled out much of what he had already sent to Representative Cochrane and others regarding controlling the Southern ports as well as some advice on appointments.[39] He closes the letter with, 'I want no office, and would not receive one. Although advanced in years, I am anxious to promote the success of this Republican administration and the public interests. What there is left of me at 73, is at your service.'[40]

James also wrote again to General Winfield Scott after receiving the news of shots fired at Fort Sumter, despite having his services denied months earlier, asking,

> Permit me to ask if a hale man, of seventy-three years of age, can be useful in any way, that you will command my services? To cut off the remnant of an inglorious life by a glorious death in the service of our country to which my ancestors of two generations devoted their best services, ought not be considered as an event to be avoided.[41]

General Scott did not put the elderly James into uniform, but he was invited to join a committee to advise the president 'as to the course to be pursued to suppress the rebellion.'[42]

Having 'left New York without delay,' James 'called upon the President ... on the evening of my arrival' and was 'introduced to him by Secretary Chase.'[43] James, perhaps with the boldness that tends to come with age, asked Lincoln 'whether he intended to give as well as receive blows, in order that my fellow-citizens of New York might understand what their duty was, and be prepared to perform it.'[44] Lincoln's reply he recorded as 'I intend to give blows. The only question at present is, whether I should first retake Fort Sumter or Harper's Ferry,' and James was 'glad to hear that he had determined to coerce the rebels into obedience.'[45]

At this meeting, James read a 'plan of military operation' he had written titled, 'No Truce, No Compromise – One or the Other: Slavery Must Conquer Freedom, or Freedom Must Conquer Slavery.'[46] He, once again, advised an immediate blockade, because, 'by destroying commerce, the pecuniary resources of the enemy are cut off.'[47] He also suggested 'driving the negroes from their work, it would cut off their crops and thus impoverish and distress the whole Southern Atlantic region.' He named three targets of attack: Charleston, Virginia (through West Virginia), and New Orleans.[48] He believed, 'These measures taken promptly; effectively and unrelentingly carried out, would crush the enemy in one year.'[49] We have no way of knowing if his confidence in his plan was well placed, because the war was not taken to the enemy promptly or effectively and would drag on for four years.

General Scott did march troops into Virginia and take possession of Arlington House after Robert E. Lee resigned his army commission and defected to the Confederacy. General Charles Sandford of New York was selected to take charge of the estate that today is Arlington National Cemetery.[50] Under his command was Major Alexander Hamilton, son of John Church Hamilton and nephew to James.[51] Shortly before they arrived, the family of Robert E. Lee had vacated the property, including the general's son and his visitor, Henry Adams, grandson of John Quincy.[52] Henry had grown up calling his grandfather 'the President,'[53] now he was a first-hand witness to a rupture in the nation so many Adamses had dedicated their lives to building.

A collection of western counties in Virginia did not wish to be a part of the Confederacy, so they voted against secession and were accepted into the Union as the state of West Virginia on 20 June 1863. As James wrote in his *Rebellion Against the United States by the People of a State is Its Political Suicide*, 'The people of Western Virginia, holding the opinion that their State Government was abolished by the treason of the people in other parts of the State, with the organs of that Government have formed another government, which has been recognized by the United States as the existing government of that State.'[54]

When Secretary Chase read James's report on slavery and the federal government's response to it, he asked if 'you intend to free the negroes as you go along?' To which James replied, 'Certainly, and to make them soldiers.'[55] On this point, Chase agreed with James more enthusiastically than their president, who would not support the raising of black troops until later in the war. When James returned to New York, tasked to help raise funds there, he had found a new friend in Salmon P. Chase.

Chase wished for federal treasury notes to be sold at par, a tough sell for James to entice New York bankers with. He advised Chase to take out loans and prepared a lengthy report on what amounts, rates, and terms Chase should accept. By offering different note denominations, rates, and redemption periods, Chase could raise the funds needed and appeal to a wide variety of investors.[56] James apparently took to the work of treasury as passionately as his father had, sending Chase pages and pages of reports and suggestions over the course of the war.

In addition to treasury notes, James recommended increasing taxes to cover the interest payments and eventual debt retirement. Duties on imported goods proposed included one on tea, 15 cents on each pound of black tea and 25 per pound of green.[57] An income tax of 1 per cent was also suggested. The United States did enact an income tax of 3 per cent on all income over $800 in 1861, which was repealed in 1872.

James similarly wrote with advice to Secretary of War Cameron, Secretary of the Navy Welles, and others, including President Lincoln, but few seemed as appreciative of his insight as Salmon P. Chase in his unenviable position as Secretary of the Treasury. Taxes had long been a touchy subject for Americans, and Chase suddenly needed to raise tens of millions more than the country's usual budget.

James was not intimidated by the office of the presidency and wrote to Lincoln more than once to point out where he had not done as James thought proper. Once, for his making wartime appointments to office without the consent of the Senate, something James had written at length about during the term of James Buchanan.[58] In August 1861, he wrote again to insist that it was Lincoln's duty to remove a man from office whose name he redacted from the transcript of the letter included in his *Reminiscences*.[59] The redacted name is likely that of David Wilmot, since James recommends Joseph Holt, a previous Secretary of War, as his replacement. James insists that his removal is 'demanded by the voice of the country' as demonstrated by 'the hesitation yesterday of the bankers and capitalists in New York … owing to a want of confidence in further expenditures by the [redacted] Department. We will not advance money to the Government to be wasted, or perverted to private gain.'[60] After promising that 'Mr Holt's appointment would touch the heart of the nation by inspiring full confidence,' James signs the letter 'your, perhaps too bold, but honest friend.'[61] James did also write when he believed Lincoln had performed admirably. On 17 December 1861, he wrote:

> Your moderation, firmness, and wisdom will, I have no doubt, by the blessing of the almighty, carry us through this wicked conflict with success by bringing all the rebellious people into subordination to laws, preserving the Union and the Constitution. I congratulate you upon having the honor to be placed in the foremost position in this the most interesting chapter, not only in the history of this country, but of the world.[62]

Lincoln also received support from some unexpected sources. Stephen Douglas, who had fiercely debated with Lincoln in the 1858 Senate race and then again in the 1860 presidential campaign, spoke out in favor of Lincoln and Union until his death on 3 June 1861. 'There can be no neutrals in this war,' he exclaimed to Northern Democrats who did not support Lincoln, 'only patriots or traitors.'[63]

In September 1861, James offered his services to Governor Morgan of New York. Demonstrating his offense at being declined, he wrote:

> I am very anxious to be employed in any situation connected with military affairs where I can be useful. I acquired some knowledge of staff duty in the war of 1812; I confess that at the age of (73) seventy-three, I have not physical power to serve in the field, as my friend, General Scott, very frankly told me, when at the commencement of this life and death struggle, I volunteered to be one of his staff; still there is much work in me.[64]

Since it was Chase who welcomed and appreciated his efforts, James seems to have focused on supporting the Treasury Secretary. He wrote to bankers in New York and other states, encouraging them to support the United States war effort and made the treasury notes a common topic of conversation. He also wrote to Chase about issues unrelated to finances, perhaps because they shared convictions or because Chase was an eager correspondent. In fact, one of Chase's letters to James states, 'I am much obliged to you for your promise of some financial suggestions with reference to my next reports. Please let me have them at as early a day as practicable.'[65]

On 20 November 1861, James wrote to Chase regarding the treatment of slaves in the case of a successful invasion of South Carolina. 'Should they be enlisted in large numbers, formed into companies and battalions, to be used at first in manual labor, drilled and prepared to receive "their freedom with their swords," they would make useful and most efficient soldiers.'[66] Chase, long known for supporting the legal cases of free blacks, agreed, adding that afterward they should receive enfranchisement.[67]

James did not record his thoughts on extending voting rights to free blacks, but he did write to his friend, Charles King, who was serving in Congress, regarding their responsibility. 'First, that Congress should exert its unquestionable power to abolish slavery in the District of Columbia' and 'that Congress should at once take measures to alter the Constitution; first by expunging the Fugitive Slave Clause; second, by changing the 2d clause of Sect. 2, Art. 1, so as to exclude three fifths of all other persons (slaves) from enumeration in ascertaining the ratio of representation and the apportionment of direct taxation.'[68] He believed 'this would destroy slavery, inasmuch as it only exists by virtue of State or territorial laws.'[69] He wrote similar letters to other members of Congress, encouraging these law changes, 'and when this shall be accomplished readmit these conquered people to be States of the United States under the Constitution of Government so altered.'[70]

An important project that James discussed with Secretary Chase was the establishment of a national paper currency. Up to this point, the United States minted gold and silver coins, but banks issued private notes, which could be difficult to accurately value outside their home region. Chase established American 'greenbacks,' which were issued without the backing of gold or silver reserves. They were legal tender, rather than a treasury notes with specific repayment terms.

Alexander Hamilton's image appeared on early US $5 bills. On 18 January 1862, Chase wrote to James, 'I wish a better engraving of your father for the United States notes than that which appears on the fives.' He then requests permission to use an engraving that James had sent to be copied for that purpose.[71] James, always eager to see his father honored, immediately agreed and took 'the Talleyrand miniature (a photograph of the same miniature which my dear mother wore on her breast, with the letter last addressed to her by her husband, until her death)' to be copied for Chase's purposes.[72] Chase had James approve the new image before it was used on several denominations of notes. Alexander Hamilton did not appear as has become familiar on $10 bills until 1929.

Pleased with Chase's accomplishments and the inclusion of honor to his father, James wrote on 19 May 1862, 'It affords me very great pleasure to congratulate you on the triumphant success of your financial system.'[73] Chase's management of the Union's wartime finances turned out to be one of the North's greatest advantages over the cash-poor Confederacy and served to correct what James had long thought were errors made by the Jackson administration. The Legal Tender Act and National Banking Act of 1863 finally put into action much of James's advice from decades earlier.

At the same time, Congress was freed from Southern opposition to legislation that expanded federal power and internal improvements first promoted by John Quincy Adams in the 1820s. Despite the fact that a war was raging, bills were passed to grant western settlers acres of land, sponsor higher education, construct railroad lines, and, eventually, to emancipate the enslaved.

Chapter 24

Emancipation

Man was created in the express image of his Maker – a responsible being, having an immortal soul. No power less than that which created him, less than omnipotent, can reduce him from his condition of a man to that of a brute, a chattel.[1]

On 6 March 1862, James A. Hamilton made a speech at the Cooper Institute, in which he spoke boldly about the abolition of slavery. It was the same venue where Abraham Lincoln had spoken during his 1860 election campaign that had thrust him into national prominence on the platform that combined Henry Clay's old American System with anti-slavery and pro-Union sentiment.

James began with a reference to his father.

> The honor of presiding at this thronged meeting of those who represent the intelligence, the wealth, the enterprise, the mechanical skill and labor of this great city excites my sensibility from the conviction, that your choice has been induced not by considerations personal to myself, but from respect to the memory of him whose name I bear.[2]

Slavery had been the vice of the nation's formation but need not continue to be so.

> Let us under the hallowed influence of patriotism – of a sense of our duty to the oppressed of this nation – treat this great subject so decisively as that the echo of your voice may come up from the loyal people in all parts of the nation, in tones which cannot be mistaken or disregarded by their representatives.[3]

'Has the Government the power to destroy slavery?' When James asked this question of the gathered crowd, he must have recalled the instances when he had answered no. On this day, he said,

> We are engaged in a war which involved the life or death of the nation. A blow on behalf of slavery has been struck at the national existence. Every Government, whatever may be its Constitution, is necessarily armed with all the powers required to preserve its life ... The people of the loyal States have, with unequalled patriotism, devoted their lives to the service of the country. The Government, through its various departments, has formed an army and navy of vast proportions and the most efficient character, with a promptitude and skill most honorable to them. Now let the people require that this accumulated power shall be used not only to crush out armed rebellion, but its malignant cause.

Here, the applause of the crowd caused him to pause before saying, 'Your military and naval forces, with rapid blows, are destroying the military power of your enemy; but unless the last blow which is struck strikes off the fetters of the slaves, the work of restoring the Constitution and the Union will be mockery.'[4]

Next, James encouraged those who might not have yet experienced his evolution in thought.

> I may here remark, that although I detested the system of slavery as a great crime and a great social and political evil, I was not an abolitionist, because I well knew that when the Constitution of the United States was formed and adopted, it was well known that slavery might and would continue in all the States which should so decide ... I therefore believed, in the true spirit of this understanding, that I was inhibited from interfering with the accursed thing. But as soon as the slaveholders threw off their obligations under the Constitution, I was freed from mine.[5]

From our twenty-first century point of view, this ongoing debate over the constitutionality of slavery can be difficult to understand. We are tempted to wonder how they did not grasp the human rights issue at hand and move more quickly to correct it. Today, it is common for the federal government to take on many responsibilities that it did not control before the Civil War, and state rights were historically more important. It took long years of discourse and, unfortunately, a bloody war for this mindset to shift.

While her father was engaged in his fight to see the Constitution altered to see the complete abolition of slavery and the slave trade within the United States, Mary Morris Hamilton was involved in her own cause. She had clearly inherited many of the characteristics of her father and grandmother. Eliza Hamilton was famous for her philanthropic work that included founding a home for women and orphans and a public school. James quietly but unceasingly concerned himself with guiding those who were forging the country's future. Mary followed these examples when she joined the fledgling Mount Vernon Ladies' Association in 1858.

Ann Pamela Cunningham headed the effort to save George Washington's family home, and she gathered women from each state to help raise funds. Washington's lack of direct descendants left Mount Vernon in the hands of his step-grandson, George Washington Parke Custis, and then other extended family, who had not been able to manage its upkeep. Cunningham despaired, 'I was painfully distressed at the ruin and desolation of the home of Washington, and the thought passed through my mind: Why was it that the women of his country did not try to keep it in repair, if the men could not do it? It does seem such a blot on our country.'[6]

Mary Hamilton agreed with Miss Cunningham and went to work in her home state of New York. She was just the sort of woman Cunningham needed on her team, well-connected and intelligent with family ties to the American Revolution. Mary went above and beyond her share of fundraising, eventually raising $40,000 toward the purchase of Mount Vernon, which was transferred from John Augustine Washington III to the MVLA in 1859 as Civil War loomed over the country Washington had sacrificed so much to establish.[7]

The rebellion of the Southern states was another hurdle for the women to overcome, as they realized that the $200,000 they had raised for the purchase price of Mount Vernon was just the beginning of what would be needed to complete extensive repairs. The war removed vital Southern support for Mount Vernon, which was perched near the boundary between the armies of North and South. The women must have wondered if the estate they were working so hard to preserve would survive the war.

The challenges caused a break between the ladies. Mary was convinced that Mount Vernon should be turned over to the federal government, which had greater resources to ensure its restoration, but this idea did not have much support among the other vice-regents.[8] Cunningham, still serving as regent of the MVLA, was indignant and quick to point out that the association's deed only allowed the estate's reversion to the state of Virginia, which had seceded from the United States. Despite these differences, Mary continued to assist the MVLA in selecting and purchasing furnishings for Mount Vernon.[9]

During the war, Mary volunteered at the Office of the Commission and tried to use her contacts to the advantage of Mount Vernon. She worked to have boat service restored to the property, which was difficult to visit by land, especially during wartime. If the fear of spies or other enemy activity kept the government from allowing their boat service, Mary wrote, 'I wish to ask a sum equivalent to that we are losing by the absence of the boat.'[10]

Mary's concerns for Mount Vernon's finances and her conviction that the estate should be transferred to the federal government did not abate. She wrote to another vice-regent, 'You know that my preference is, if practicable, to place the property in the hands of the US Government, but I shall be thankful to sustain you in any plan which is equally good or better … I suggest this as a matter of sheer necessity.'[11] This caused some tension within the association, and Mary eventually accepted that she was a lone voice on the position and resigned her position in 1866. She at least left the project knowing that it had survived the war.

James and many others understood that one question of freedom for slaves was, 'When the slaves are freed, what is to become of them?'[12] He dismissed the idea of colonization. 'This cannot be coercive; it will not be voluntary.'[13] James believed, 'Should the black race remain, which I assume will be the fact, will they trust and be willing to work for their old masters, and if they should be, by what course of legislation can their freedom be secured?' Here he hit upon the challenge of the Reconstruction era, two years before it began.

His concern was not solely for newly freed blacks but also for poor Southern whites who felt threatened by equality. Both 'are to be cared for' and 'educated, and thus be raised by profitable labor to the condition of independent and industrious citizens.'[14]

On 24 July 1862, James wrote to President Lincoln. 'I implore you as a duty to yourself, to your country, and to your God, immediately to issue such a proclamation ... that all the rights of the property of rebels of every kind, slaves included, shall be destroyed.'[15] He also wrote a Circular to the Governors of the Loyal States in which he encouraged state leaders to urge the president toward such a proclamation regarding emancipation.[16]

In September 1862, James participated in a committee to report upon the conduct of war. On the 10th, they met with President Lincoln and expressed their dissatisfaction with General McClellan's appointment to the command of the Army of the Potomac and the desire for a proclamation freeing the slaves.[17] James recorded that the conversation regarding General McClellan 'became a sharp encounter' that he attempted to calm by suggesting that 'it would be best to defer what he had to say to a future interview.'[18] Since Lincoln declined, James went on to state that Secretary of State Seward's 'policy was not to wage war against the rebels with vigor, but in such a way as to be accompanied with as little suffering as possible to them,' which Lincoln felt was 'undue criticism.'[19] James again suggested a break in the conversation to cool tempers.

> I came here for no man, nor with ill feelings against any man. I look only to the country and in this I am moved by the same interests and feelings which excite your solicitude, Mr President, to preserve the Union ... My father, sir, was one of the architects of this government, and he was one of those who gave it its first impetus. Should our system of government now fail under its present pressure, his reputation would suffer.[20]

Lincoln agreed to break until the next day, saying, 'If I am permitted to be here,' which James only realized later was a comment revealing his fear that Washington might be taken by enemy forces at any moment.[21]

When James had his opportunity to present his evidence against Seward the following day, 'the President was silent,' but James did not relent.[22] 'To talk of a short war, accompanied with the purpose of making as little suffering to the enemy as possible, is an absurdity.'[23] He also pressed his second point, 'a proclamation declaring that the laws of Congress confiscating and freeing the slaves should be enforced by the armies.'[24]

James was undoubtedly pleased when Lincoln asked if James would draw up such a proclamation. 'I certainly will.'[25] Hard feelings apparently assuaged, Lincoln left James, saying, 'Mr Hamilton, it will give me pleasure to see you whenever you come to Washington.'[26] James immediately returned to New York to draft his version of Lincoln's proclamation.

Lincoln issued a preliminary Emancipation Proclamation on 22 September 1862, the same day James sent his draft, and the official version was announced on 1 January 1863. In it, Lincoln stated 'that all persons held as slaves within any State or designated part of a State, the people whereof shall then be in rebellion against the United States, shall be then, thenceforward, and forever free.'[27] The version James wrote was more verbose, giving the legal background of slavery, justification of its abolishment, and listing various conditions of the enslaved, before declaring them to 'forever thereafter be free.'[28]

The Emancipation Proclamation may be praised today but it was by few at the time. Abolitionists were disappointed that it freed slaves only in the rebellious states. Was it an empty gesture to outlaw slavery in a territory over which Lincoln currently held no authority? He was still concerned about the border states, those slaveholding states that had remained in the Union. The Emancipation Proclamation did not impact them. Others were unwilling to fight a war to free slaves. They had been sacrificing much to preserve the Union but were not willing to sacrifice so much for the sake of emancipating the enslaved.

And, of course, the Confederacy reacted in fury. Jefferson Davis vowed to execute captured Union officers for the crime of 'inciting servile insurrection.'[29] While this threat was not carried out, many blacks captured by Southern troops were summarily executed. The Confederacy refused to treat them as prisoners of war and would not include them in prisoner exchanges.[30]

In the North, the losses of war caused a need for the raising of additional troops, but the Emancipation Proclamation made some men less willing to volunteer. Low unemployment caused by war industry also gave those who had not already joined up for patriotic reasons incentive to stay home. In

James's home state of New York, Democrats began calling the war 'illegal, being unconstitutional, and should not be sustained.'[31]

Learning that the military volunteers for his county were well below the quota requested, James wrote an open letter 'to the supervisors, assessors, magistrates, and other officers, civil and military, and all other loyal citizens of the second assembly district of the county of Westchester' reminding them that 'it becomes the duty of all good citizens not only promptly and truly' to abide by a draft given the shortage of volunteers.[32] For one who had volunteered his services so many times, often to be declined, James must have bristled at the shortage of volunteers, and he tried to inspire in others the duty he felt.

> We will rise as one man with God for our strength, and crush the barbarous hordes fighting to establish an aristocracy founded upon slavery, and will thus vindicate the Constitution and the Union, and the great principle upon which all our political systems are founded: Popular Government and the Freedom of all mankind.[33]

The Emancipation Proclamation was not the last word on abolition, however. It was limited to slavery in the rebellious states, but the slave states of Delaware, Kentucky, Maryland, and Missouri remained in the Union. The argument James had used regarding the Confederate states, that they had forfeited their constitutional rights and authority, could not be applied to these four, but that did not stop him from drafting an act to abolish slavery. In part, he wrote,

> The existence of slavery in any part of the United States is in direct and manifest violation of the sublime principle of liberty on which the Government of the United States is founded, and whereas the existence of slavery in certain States of this Union by the laws thereof has caused and continues the criminal rebellion which now threatens the national existence, it has become a matter of indispensable necessity on the part of the Congress in the exercise of its war powers, and in defence of the Constitution of the United States to abolish slavery.

Furthermore, free blacks 'shall stand before the courts and be considered and treated therein as entitled to full and complete protection in their persons and property as any white person does … and that hereafter the crime of slavery and all its consequences to those who were heretofore held as slaves, is obliterated and forever destroyed.'[34]

In addition to this, James published *The Constitution Vindicated* to establish his expanded argument on the government's right – and duty – to abolish slavery throughout the United States once and for all. He first gives a history of states' rights and the negative impact upon the nation the sovereignty of states has had, pointing out that during the period before the Constitution was ratified only one state (New York) contributed the full dollar amount requested by the federal government while Georgia, South Carolina, and North Carolina 'did not contribute one dollar to the National Treasury.'[35] The Constitutional Convention was meant to solve for the destructive force of state sovereignty, he insists. 'In denial of these historical truths, the secessionists, or the State Rights Democrats who sympathise with treason' and believe 'the States have a right to secede, is so like "the baseless fabric of a vision," as justly to be denounced a base imposture.'[36]

After enumerating the powers of Congress, James emphasizes the power 'to make all laws which shall be necessary and proper for carrying into execution the foregoing powers.'[37] In this vein, he hoped to prove 'beyond all controversy, that the Congress has power to abolish Slavery throughout the United States.'[38] He quotes both James Madison and John Quincy Adams where they had written that Congress has power 'to provide for general welfare,' and this is where the duty to abolish slavery is derived.[39] 'The highest object committed to the care of the Government is to preserve the life of the Nation and next to that is, "to provide for the general welfare."'[40]

He also quotes the Declaration of Independence and its statement that 'All men are created equal,' adding that 'it does not mean to assert that all men are equal in their physical, mental, or moral qualities; but that all are equal before the law, and equally entitled to protection for their lives, their liberty, and in the pursuit of happiness. It declared that great Christian truth, "The brotherhood of man in fellowship with Christ."' By promptly abolishing slavery, 'some atonement will be made for the past; the Union will be restored, reinvigorated; the general welfare will be promoted and secured, by the blessing of God, to future generations.'[41]

Slavery would not be fully abolished until the Thirteenth Amendment was signed by President Lincoln on 1 February 1865. The latest recorded emancipation of enslaved American people occurred in Galveston Bay, Texas on 19 June 1865 with the arrival of Union troops, a day that became known as Juneteenth and became an official federal holiday in 2021.

The Union had other issues to deal with as the war inevitably dragged on longer than anticipated and the need for soldiers became desperate. In March 1863, the Conscription Act became law, enacting a registration and draft system for all male citizens and immigrants between the ages of 20 and 45. Coming on the heels of the Emancipation Proclamation, some felt unfairly treated to be forced to fight for someone else's freedom. Exemptions were only offered to those who were the sole support for widows, aging parents, and motherless children. It was also possible to pay a $300 fee for a substitute. That was an amount that most people could not afford, but it had been selected to keep the amount paid for substitutes from soaring out of control as it had in the South.

The tension of the situation exploded in the New York City Draft Riots during the summer of 1863, shortly following the bloody Battle of Gettysburg. Mobs formed in Manhattan, burning buildings, especially government and military structures, in the hope of destroying draft records. Men took out their frustration over the war evolving into a fight for abolition by lynching black men. The Colored Orphan Asylum on Fifth Avenue was burned to the ground, though the children were all saved. Violence and destruction continued for several days, leaving over one hundred people dead.

In the meantime, Lincoln continued to insist that the primary goal of the war was not to emancipate slaves, but that it was a strategy that brought the North closer to victory. 'My paramount object in the struggle is to save the Union, and is not either to save or to destroy slavery. If I could save the Union without freeing any slaves I would do it; and if I could save it by freeing some and leaving others alone, I would also do that,' he wrote.[42] Lincoln's strategy may have been sound, but it continued to alienate both those who were passionate about abolition and those who did not care to fight for emancipation. However, he had the support of the fighting men, as the next election would demonstrate.

On 16 July 1863, James wrote to Edwin Stanton about the feelings in his area of New York, near Tarrytown. 'At present, all is quiet, with threatenings, however, at all the landing places along the River. There is a large foreign population at Yonkers, in the pistol factory and other manufactories, who will be compelled to yield to the rioters, and may be brought into the field against us.'[43] In his typical style, James went on to offer lengthy suggestions for putting down the riots, including the number of soldiers needed to establish peace, the recommendation to hold the draft at the White Plains Court House ('It is in an open space, incapable of being burned'), and instructions for the current District Attorney of the Southern District of New York to make arrests.[44]

James was a strong supporter of the draft and its purpose of expanding the number of Union troops to a level that could end the bloody war. His father had served in the American Revolution, and many of the Hamilton men had followed Alexander's example in the War of 1812 and the Mexican–American War. The next generation, including the Alexanders that were James's son and nephew, enlisted in the Union forces. While the rioters argued that the draft was just another form of slavery, James saw military service as every American's patriotic duty. He wrote, in the aftermath of the riots, 'I admit that a law authorizing a draft will never be obeyed with pleasure, and yet I believe that there may be occasions when that mode of raising troops must be resorted to, and that such is the case at this moment.'[45] He also felt that it was important to stand firmly by the law rather than 'yield to the demands of a mob, and pusillanimously to refrain from carrying into effect a law because of the threats of violence of a mob.'[46]

The South was having similar problems with enlistment and conscription, with two more weary years of war to come. The Confederacy had the advantage of a people fighting for their homeland, but they struggled against the Union's advantages in population, industry, and economy.

In the midst of all this, James received a letter from his daughter, Eliza, on 9 October 1863, in which she writes of her failing health and desire to see him.

If you could see, my dear Father, the love and devotion of every one. To one so independent of others, it is worth while to be sick, to learn so rich a lesson from them. I look to you, my dear Father, to keep up the family tone and spirit now, as you have ever done. Shall we receive good only from God, as we have all our lives – and when the good is veiled, so that we do not see it, shall we complain? Or even bear the sorrow, like a scourged slave: My spirit rises above such abject submission, in to harmony with the Divine Will. What God wishes to do for us and with us, is hidden in the future … This Life is the gift of God; this everlasting Life, which the loss of a tired body will set free for fresh youth and zest.[47]

Eliza died on 20 December 1863, just a month after Lincoln gave his famous Gettysburg Address. She was 52. Six years later, her husband, George Lee Schuyler, married her sister, Mary.

Chapter 25

Election of 1864

After your duty to your Maker, your first and highest duty is to your government and Country.[1]

On top of war and unrest, 1864 was an election year, and Lincoln was challenged by the same General George B. McClellan that James and others had insisted he replace as commander of the Army of the Potomac. The Democrats had nominated McClellan, who promised to end the fighting. James, who had long abandoned any loyalty to Jackson's Democrats, wrote that McClellan's acceptance of the nomination was 'an act of personal as well as political dishonor.'[2]

Northern Democrats ran on a platform that opposed the war, especially in light of the Emancipation Proclamation. New York Democrat Horatio Seymour said, 'If it be true that slavery must be abolished to save this Union, then the people of the South should be allowed to withdraw themselves from the government which cannot give them the protection guaranteed by its terms.'[3] Calling abolition 'tyranny' and 'religious fanaticism,' Democrats hoped war-weary Northerners would vote Lincoln out of office.[4] However, the anti-war platform did not attract many voters among families who had sons and fathers away fighting in it. They wanted Northern victory, which Democrats appeared to oppose with their strong stance against the Emancipation Proclamation.

To demonstrate his support for the Union cause and Lincoln's presidency, James gave the commencement address to the class of 1864 at the US Naval Academy. In his speech, he repeats some of what he had written in *Constitution Vindicated*, but he also included advice as he might have received from his own father.

James began with humility, 'I am reminded by this august assemblage, the occasion, and this day that I am following the footsteps of one of the most distinguished statesman of our nation, who addressed you a year ago; his devotion to the Republic, in this hour of its utmost need cannot be surpassed, the Honorable Edward Everett.'[5] Everett was a friend of James who had run on the Constitutional Union party ticket in 1860 on a platform that attempted to avoid any stance on slavery but promote Union and adherence to the Constitution, a platform that was hopeless by that time. James continued, 'This recollection admonishes me of my incapacity, and almost compels me to withdraw from attempting to perform this duty. However, trusting to that indulgence which is due to my advanced age, I proceed.'[6]

He instructed them first on being upstanding men before addressing them as naval officers. 'Your highest ambition, of a personal and social character, should induce you to endeavor to establish the characters of Christian gentlemen.'[7] Further, 'After your duty to your Maker, your first and highest duty is to your government and Country.'[8] He warned them from 'the excessive indulgence in the use of intoxicating liquors,' which 'inevitably reduces a man to the level of the brute,'[9] and encouraged 'self-denial ... a primary virtue. It may, indeed, be said to be the only security against most of the evils incident to our unregulated nature.'[10]

James offered the young men advice on conducting and controlling their tempers. 'Kindness, forbearance, and a wise moderation, not only command respect, but induce regard for officers, and prompt obedience in emergencies.'[11] He also addressed the import of the rule of law. 'It is, I fear by some supposed to be an evidence of cleverness to be enabled to violate the regulations so cunningly as to avoid detection; and indeed there may be those who boast of such achievements, although to do so necessarily implies dishonor.' James closed with the words 'said by one of our most eminent Christian teachers, "One ray of moral and religious truth is worth all the wisdom of the schools; one lesson from Christ will carry you higher than years of study."'[12]

In a letter received from the Naval Academy following his address, James was thanked for his attendance and asked to provide a copy of his speech. 'We think that an event such as an Address from the son of a statesman second only to Washington in the history of our country, should be preserved in the records of the Academy,'[13] and so it was and remains available for us to read today.

John Church Hamilton, who compiled the biography of Alexander Hamilton that was Eliza's great mission, also gave a speech after the end of the Civil War outlining how the South's dependence upon slavery led to rebellion. It was printed as a pamphlet, *The Slave Power: Its Heresies and Injuries to the American People*. One feels that he inherited his father's passion for public issues when he says, 'And now, my friends – I mean to speak to you of things not familiar to you all – of things it interests you all to know – to state truths, which like the lightning from the heavens, are meant to clear the opening day.'[14] He continues, accusing the state of Virginia of establishing 'the permanent elevation over the heads of the American people of an oligarchic – aristocratic SLAVE POWER, professing Democracy only to make the Democracy the servile tools of its selfish, Unnational ambitions.'[15] After giving several examples of Virginians, primarily Jefferson and Madison, putting their own advantages over the benefit of the entire country, John states,

> Such are the effects of Slavery – the aristocratic owners, enjoying the fruits of involuntary labor – freed from the cares and the engaging and instructive interests of an active social life, seeking political power as their occupation, and then claiming its possession as a natural right, and the poor, uneducated, debased white seeking in the labor of the slave the indolence he covets in the toilless lives of his idle superiors.[16]

This argument is not based upon the human rights of the enslaved but upon the Southerners' economic and political power gained from them to be used against the rest of the country.

John states the 'Great Rebellion' has

> Slavery as the source – the life – the ambitious care and purpose of this war ... the arrogant independence of a few to secure and perpetuate the dependence of the many – of millions of slaves – a war sustained by poor, untaught – misled whites, regarded as a cheap sacrifice to the aspirings of those arrogant few.[17]

Thanks to Union victories on the battlefield during 1864, the anti-war platform fell flat and Lincoln was re-elected by a large margin. The Thirteenth

Amendment was passed in the House of Representatives on 31 January 1865, and Lincoln welcomed former slave and famous abolitionist Frederick Douglass to his inaugural reception.[18] Lincoln also named Salmon P. Chase, outspoken supporter of abolition and black suffrage, Chief Justice of the Supreme Court, replacing Roger Taney, who had attempted to eliminate constitutional rights for blacks through his Dred Scott decision. On 1 February 1865, Charles Sumner, who had been physically beaten within the halls of Congress for speaking out against slavery, presented John Rock to Chief Justice Chase for admission to practice before the Supreme Court. Rock became the first black man to earn this privilege.[19]

On 9 April 1865, General Robert E. Lee surrendered at Appomattox Courthouse, bringing an end to the bloodiest war in United States history. Rejoicing, however, was short-lived. Within a week, Abraham Lincoln died at the hand of an assassin, and the future of the country became hazy. Who could lead the reunification of the battered people he had worked so sacrificially to keep together? The war-ravaged land was left in confusion and sorrow.

James A. Hamilton did not record his reaction to these events. Had his family seen John Wilkes Booth perform on stage at some point before that fateful April evening at Ford's Theater? His *Reminiscences* ends abruptly, leaving one wondering about the rest of his story and his observations of the post-war years besides a few letters written to cabinet members regarding the country's finances.

In addition to public mourning, hundreds of thousands of families grieved personal losses as a result of the four years of war. The two Alexanders, James's son and nephew, survived their service, but so many families were not so fortunate. James undoubtedly rejoiced in the survival of his son even as he mourned his daughter, Eliza.

Shortly following the end of the war, James reached out to Eliza Jane Hersey Andrew, the wife of Massachusetts governor, John A. Andrew. He offered her a gift in honor of her husband's public service and support of the abolition of slavery. On a piece of writing paper, James secured a lock of hair and wrote below, 'The above is the hair of my Father Alexander Hamilton.' Further down the sheet, he attached another few strands with the note, 'The above is the Hair of "The Father of his Country" Geo. Washington.'[20] This item remained in the Andrew family until it was donated to the Massachusetts Historical Society in 1920. James also recommended John A. Andrew to President Lincoln for the post of Secretary of the Treasury after Salmon P. Chase was named to the Supreme Court.[21]

In 1866, James wrote *Malicious Falsehoods of the So-called Confederate Government and the Degrees of its Criminality* for President Johnson. In it, he encourages a thorough examination of the actions of the Confederate Congress before any consideration of pardoning them for their participation in the war. James reminds the new president that

> for the purpose of destroying the credit and circulation of the Treasury notes of this Government, immense amounts of spurious or counterfeit notes, purporting to be such Treasury notes, have been fabricated and advertised for sale in the enemy's country, and have been brought into these States, and put in circulation by persons in the employ of the enemy.[22]

According to law, punishment for this act was death by hanging, but President Johnson was not eager to harshly punish the South. Perhaps to ensure that hostilities were ceased for good, James suggested more severe treatment of those who had been in charge as the nation slowly recovered from the bloody war and grieved the slain President Lincoln.

James also experienced personal sorrow, especially at the recent loss of his daughter, Eliza, to whom he had been so close. By the end of the war, James had also lost four of his seven siblings, leaving only brothers Alexander, John, and the younger Philip. His daughter, Angelica, died during the difficult post-war years on 10 November 1868, soon followed by his wife, Mary, on 24 May 1869. They had been married for almost fifty-nine years. Yet there was also joy. Finding comfort in each other, George Lee Schuyler married his wife's sister, Mary, in 1869.

Chapter 26

A Last Defense of Alexander Hamilton

I conclude this work, which I have undertaken in obedience to a sense of duty to my father.[1]

By 1870, one might have expected James A. Hamilton to retire to his Hudson Valley home of Nevis and relax, surrounded by family. It was the year James turned 82, and he had certainly done his duty to his country, which was now a robust thirty-seven states. However, he was not quite done writing.

Martin Van Buren had died in 1862 but not before falling out with his former friend. Once confidants striving toward similar goals, by 1870 James was writing a pamphlet called *Martin Van Buren's Calumnies Repudiated and Hamilton's Conduct Vindicated*. This was written in response to *Inquiry into the Origin and Course of Political Parties in the United States*, which was edited and published by Martin Van Buren's sons after his death.

Van Buren had included negative comments about early Federalists and Alexander Hamilton in particular in his work. James especially took offense to Van Buren's accusation that 'Hamilton did more than any one – I had almost said, than all his contemporaries – to counteract the will of the people, and to subvert, by undermining, the Constitution of their choice'[2] and that he had 'been faithless to one of the most sacred trusts that can be placed in man.'[3] One can imagine what James felt when he read, 'Hamilton's course was an outrage upon liberty and a crime against free government.'[4]

James begins his response with unrestrained passion.

It is remarkable that a gentleman, who, as a Senator, Vice-President, and President of the United States, had become familiar with the legislation of the nation, the messages of its Presidents, and the published letters of Mr Jefferson, should have made such statements, when that legislation, those documents and letters, establish the fact that some, if not all, the measures referred to were sanctioned as well by Congress again and again, as by Presidents Washington, Jefferson, Madison, Monroe, and others, as he goes on to demonstrate.[5]

Since Van Buren had accused his father of 'violations of the Constitution,'[6] James promised to 'produce conclusive proof' that this assertion was untrue.[7] His evidence includes quotes from letters written by Thomas Jefferson, not known for his support of Hamilton and therefore an unbiased source. Jefferson's assertions that 'the proceedings of the new Government have given general satisfaction' and 'our affairs are proceeding in a train of unparalleled prosperity' contradict Van Buren's dire words.[8] Jefferson also recorded that Hamilton's funding system 'was passed without a dissenting voice.'[9]

By using the words of Jefferson rather than his own constitutional analysis to defend his father, James makes a solid case that cannot be dismissed as politically subjective. He goes on to do the same with the words of James Madison.

When Van Buren claimed that Hamilton's protective tariff system had been a 'bold assumption of power' which 'regarded his victory over the Constitution as complete,'[10] James quotes Madison's annual message of 5 December 1810, in which he praises, 'The just and sound policy of securing to our manufacturers the success they have attained.'[11] Monroe, too, stated that 'our manufacturers find a generous encouragement by the policy which patronizes domestic industry.'[15]

James allowed his personal feelings to show when he wrote, 'It is difficult to believe that Van Buren had not read these messages; and it is painful to believe that a man who had been a President of the United States could be guilty of such perversions.'[13]

A letter from President Washington is included to testify to Alexander Hamilton's honor. 'In every relation which you have borne to me, I have found that my confidence in your talents, exertions, and integrity has been well placed.'[14] James included quotes of almost every president from Washington to Jackson in defense of his father's work, writing sixty-six years after Alexander Hamilton's death. Van Buren wrote to prop up the Democratic party, which struggled in the years in and around the rebellion due to its support of slavery, but he must have known that James would rush to his father's defense. Perhaps this is why Van Buren had not published it before his death.

Van Buren even claimed that the Alien and Sedition Acts were 'passed upon Hamilton's suggestion,'[15] despite the well-known animosity between Hamilton and John Adams, who was president at that time. James was quick to produce a letter in which his father refers to the act and states, 'Let us not establish a tyranny.'[16]

James repeats Calhoun's accusation that Van Buren was a 'mousing politician,' in other words, one who will 'watch for or pursue in a sly or insidious manner,' before closing, 'I conclude this work, which I have undertaken in obedience to a sense of duty to my father.'[17] Finally, he included copies of several letters written by Alexander Hamilton to Thomas Jefferson and others, in which he responds to complaints and questions similar to those raised by Van Buren in his own words.

The pamphlet is one of the last items James is known to have written. He may have continued to correspond with family and those in government positions who he believed would benefit from his advice, but those letters have been lost to time.

Chapter 27

Hamilton Remembered

I had intended for some time to call your attention to the subject of this letter, but have delayed doing so by 'the sluggishness of age.'[1]

James A. Hamilton's *Reminiscences* end without recording anything more about the aftermath of America's Civil War or the assassination of Abraham Lincoln on Good Friday 1865. He had been born into a world where George Washington was unanimously elected president, witnessed the violent split of the country under Abraham Lincoln, and surely worried about the management of reunification, but James no longer tried to put his stamp on events.

It is unknown what he thought of Reconstruction, the treason indictment of Jefferson Davis, or the purchase of the Alaska Territory in 1867, often referred to at the time as Seward's Folly. Perhaps he came to agree with President Johnson's decision to issue an unconditional pardon for all participants in the Civil War on Christmas Day 1868.[2] Did James, who once warned that traitors should not be too delicately handled, agree that it was time for the nation to find healing and forgiveness rather than strive to punish the firmly beaten enemy?

Maybe James hoped, as did the much younger Henry Adams, that Grant would be a president able to rise above the swamp of politics with his 'unbounded popular confidence. He was tied to no party. He was under no pledges. He had the inestimable advantage of a military training, which unlike a political training, was calculated to encourage the moral distinction between right and wrong.'[3] Henry had served as secretary to his father, Charles Francis Adams, during the Lincoln presidency and been with him when he denounced the building of Confederate warships in England. He, like James, did not take up the political mantle of his father but became a writer of the history of which his family had played such an important part.

We can only imagine what James thought of the violence of crimes perpetrated against the newly freed Southern blacks by those passionate to enforce white supremacy against a class of people who had lost their value as property to those who had fought to own them. Once Union troops left the South and the freed people unprotected, crimes against them were rampant and usually unpunished. How disappointed James must have been in his fellow countrymen. With the three-fifths compromise finally stricken from law, black Americans fully contributed to their states' representation, but violence and intimidation often kept them from the polls, allowing the same men who had kept them as slaves to rise to power again. A long, dangerous road stretched out ahead of them.

Some, like Charles Sumner, who had been badly and publicly beaten for his abolitionist views, continued to fight for equality and prosecution for those who violated blacks' civil rights, but too many were willing to say enough had been done. The Civil Rights Bill of 1866 was vetoed by President Johnson. Although that veto was overcome in Congress – the first time legislation was passed despite presidential veto – much work was, once again, left for future generations.

As for James, age and health issues finally caused this prolific letter writer and great defender of the Constitution to grow quiet. James lived until 1878, but his final years when he resided at Nevis with his son, Alexander, who inherited the estate, remain in shadows to modern eyes.

Therefore, James was alive when the last spike of the trans-continental railroad was put into place on 10 March 1869, but he did not record his thoughts on this advance in transportation. A few decades earlier, land travel had been excruciatingly expensive when compared to ocean travel, but the railroad promised to change that. James must have been excited about the economic impact and future possibilities.

In 1872, Susan B. Anthony was arrested for voting in Rochester, New York. Did James support women's right to vote as he had enslaved people's right to be free? He was the father of four daughters, who had been educated to be quite independent, two of them not marrying until much later than normal for the time. Perhaps he was excited about what it could mean for his granddaughters, Louisa and Georgina Schuyler, who never married.

Mary Wollstonecraft had written *A Vindication of the Rights of Women* in 1792, but even in the liberty-loving land of America, people were challenged to see women in anything other than a traditional role of wife and mother. Women did increase the scope of their domestic sphere by being involved in charitable work and philanthropy, as the women in the Hamilton family often were. Some laws in the United States since the nation's founding had made it easier for a woman to obtain a divorce to flee an abusive relationship, but women's participation in politics had a long way to go.

Alexander Graham Bell made the first telephone call on 10 March 1876, shortly before James turned 88. If the telegraph had been a monumental change in how quickly information could spread, what might James have thought of Bell's invention? Or maybe he dismissed it as some did as being limited in usefulness, for how many people would have telephones in their home or business?

Also in 1876, Colorado was accepted into the Union as the thirty-eighth state with the signature of President Grant. James never traveled west of the Mississippi River, though he had seen more of Europe and Russia than most. It demonstrates the evolution in transportation over time that travel to Europe had been cheaper and safer for James than a trip to California would have been throughout most of his lifetime.

James must have remained close to his surviving children and their families, since many of them later chose to be buried near him. His son, Alexander, along with his wife, lived at Nevis with James before his death and continued there afterward. Nevis remained a home for James A. Hamilton's heirs until 1917, when it was sold to Charles Danforth. It is now Nevis Laboratories at Columbia University, which received the estate as a donation from Alice du Pont in 1935.[4]

James experienced grief in his final years, as one his age might expect he will. His brother, Alexander, died on 2 August 1875, and his daughter, Mary, who had wed his son-in-law George Lee Schuyler, died on 11 May 1877. What did James think of Mary wedding her sister's widower? We cannot know for sure, but since James had treated George as a friend and confidant for decades by that point, one might assume that he was pleased to keep him in the family.

When James died on 24 September 1878, at age 90, he was survived by his brothers, John Church and Philip Hamilton. James's son, Alexander, and daughter, Frances, as well as four grandchildren, also survived him.

John had compiled their father's papers in *The Works of Alexander Hamilton: Containing His Correspondence, and His Political and Official Writings, Exclusive of the Federalist, Civil and Military*, and, as was their mother's fervent wish, written a comprehensive biography titled *Life of Alexander Hamilton: A History of the Republic of the United States of America*. He had also been as vocal as James regarding the abolition of slavery. It is through him and his wife, Maria Eliza Van Den Heuvel, and their fourteen children that most modern-day Hamilton descendants trace their lineage. John died 25 July 1882, four years after James.

James's youngest brother, Philip, served as an attorney in New York and briefly in California during the 1851 Gold Rush. He was married to Rebecca McLane, daughter of Louis McLane, who had been a friend of James and served as Secretary of State and Treasury. Their son, Allan McLane Hamilton, wrote a family history titled *The Intimate Life of Alexander Hamilton*, in which he included some letters and observations not included in John's work. Philip, who was 2 years old when Alexander Hamilton was killed, could not have remembered their famous father, but he passed on the memories that he had inherited to his own son, nonetheless. Philip died 9 July 1884.

James's daughter Frances survived him by less than a decade, but it is through her and her husband, George Richard James Bowdoin, that this branch of Hamiltons has survived. Their son George Sullivan Bowdoin is the only one of James's grandchildren to have children of his own. With his wife, Julia Irving Grinnell, he had three children, one of which was Temple Bowdoin, one of New York society's elite Four Hundred, through whom James has surviving descendants to this day.[5]

James's son, Alexander, lost one infant son in 1848 and had no other children. After serving alongside his cousin of the same name and his brother-in-law, George Lee Schuyler, in the Civil War, Alexander practiced law in New York and served as president of the Astor Library, which became the New York Public Library in 1895. He was also a founder and served as the first president of New York's exclusive Knickerbocker Club, whose member list includes names like Adams, Astor, Roosevelt, Vanderbilt, Coolidge, Oppenheim, and many others that immediately bring to mind wealth and connections to US history. Alexander died 30 December 1889.

James also had grandchildren through his daughter, Eliza. Her three children were Philip George Schuyler, Louisa Lee Schuyler, and Georgina Schuyler.

Neither Mary nor Angelica had any children.

Philip George Schuyler had fought for the Union during the Civil War. He served as president of the New York Hospital and on the Cup Committee of the New York Yacht Club that had brought home that first cup with the *America* in 1851. He was also a member of the Knickerbocker Club and had a place on Ward McAllister's famous Four Hundred, a list of those at the peak of New York society during the Gilded Age. Philip was buried near his parents, sisters, and grandparents in Sleepy Hollow Cemetery after his death in a train accident in 1906.

Neither Louisa nor Georgina married or had children, and the sisters lived together most of their lives. Louisa, perhaps inspired by her work during the Civil War, founded the New York State Charities Aid Association and a nursing school, accomplishments of which her great-grandmother Hamilton would surely have been proud. Georgina served as trustee for the Schuyler Mansion and supported her sister's programs. Georgina died Christmas Day 1923, Louisa on 10 October 1926. They are both buried in the James A. Hamilton family plot in Sleepy Hollow.

It is, perhaps, fitting that even the obituary of James A. Hamilton includes references to his father. Published in *The New York Times* on 26 September 1878, it begins:

> James A Hamilton, son of Alexander Hamilton, Secretary of the Treasury under Washington, died on Tuesday last at 'Nevis,' the old Hamilton mansion on the Hudson, near Irvington ... James A Hamilton was born in the year 1788, while his father was engaged in the Constitutional Convention, and was 16 years of age at the date of the famous rencounter with Aaron Burr.[6]

Even when the article speaks to James's own work, his father's name sneaks in.

> The name of the deceased, James A, is familiar in the literary world, also, as the author of a work, published in 1870, entitled *Hamilton's Conduct as Secretary of the Treasury Vindicated,* in which considerable documentary evidence of importance is adduced in defense of his father's financial policy.[7]

The obituary also recognizes the family history of James's wife, Mary, who had died in 1869.

> He married a grand-daughter of Robert Morris, of Revolutionary fame … The Hamilton mansion was famous in New-York society 40 years ago, and has been the scene of many a distinguished gathering. It is now occupied by a son of the deceased, a gentleman having the strong, thick-set physique of the Morrises, rather than the tall, slender form of the Hamiltons, with the Greek nose, dashed with Gallic nervousness and decision, and the sensitive mouth of that historic family.[8]

One wonders what Alexander thought of this description.

Finally, the reader gets a peek at James's final years.

> Mr Hamilton retained the use of his intellectual faculties until within the last four or five years. His death was consequently not an unexpected stroke; but those who knew him will miss an old man's picturesque and rambling reminiscences of society and politics in old times. He remembered Jackson, and all about the great Mrs Eaton scandal, and the ins and outs and windings of Martin Van Buren's political career. He had seen President Washington, and knew all the mythology of the heroes of the Revolution by heart. He was familiar with the inner events of New-York society as it was 60 years ago.[9]

The obituary comes to an end with another nod to Alexander Hamilton. 'The funeral is announced to take place to-morrow, and carriages will be in waiting at the depot to receive friends and relatives and take them to Nevis, so named after the island where his father was born.'[10]

Notes

Chapter 1
1. Hamilton, James Alexander, *Reminiscences of James A Hamilton; or, Men and Events, at Home and Abroad, During Three Quarters of a Century*, p. 1
2. Ibid.
3. *Reminiscences*, p. 173
4. Hamilton, Allan McLane, *The Intimate Life of Alexander Hamilton*, p. 54
5. Chernow, Ron, *Alexander Hamilton*, p. 27
6. Hamilton, Allan McLane, *The Intimate Life of Alexander Hamilton*, p. 12
7. Hamilton, Allan McLane, *The Intimate Life of Alexander Hamilton*, p. 268
8. Bordewich, Fergus M., *Bound for Canaan: The Underground Railroad and the War for the Soul of America*, p. 36
9. Trinity Church Registers, https://registers.trinitywallstreet.org/registers
10. National Archives: Founders Online, Alexander Hamilton to Elizabeth Schuyler Hamilton, 2 August 1791, https://founders.archives.gov/documents/Hamilton/01-09-02-0004
11. *Reminiscences*, p. 1
12. Hamilton, Allan McLane, *The Intimate Life of Alexander Hamilton*, p. 338
13. *Reminiscences*, p. 3
14. Ibid.
15. Ibid.
16. National Archives: Founders Online, Alexander Hamilton to Benjamin Rush, 26 November 1801, https://founders.archives.gov/documents/Hamilton/01-25-02-0258
17. *Reminiscences*, p. 15
18. National Archives: Founders Online, Benjamin Rush to Alexander Hamilton, 26 November 1801, https://founders.archives.gov/documents/Hamilton/01-25-02-0258
19. *Reminiscences*, p. 64
20. Ibid., p. 57
21. Burnstein, Andrew, *The Original Knickerbocker: The Life of Washington Irving*, pp. 14–15
22. Ibid., p. 18
23. Ibid., p. 39
24. Ibid., p. 155
25. *Reminiscences*, p. 23
26. Ibid., p. 40
27. Ibid.
28. National Archives: Founders Online, Alexander Hamilton to Elizabeth Schuyler Hamilton, 4 July 1804, https://founders.archives.gov/documents/Hamilton/01-26-02-0001-0248
29. Chernow, Ron, *Alexander Hamilton*, p. 708
30. National Archives: Founders Online, The Funeral, New-York Evening Post, 17 July 1804, https://founders.archives.gov/documents/Hamilton/01-26-02-0001-0271
31. Ibid.

32. Ibid.
33. University of Michigan, Hamilton-Schuyler Family Papers
34. *Reminiscences*, p. 9

Chapter 2
1. Hamilton, James Alexander, *Reminiscences of James A Hamilton; or, Men and Events, at Home and Abroad, During Three Quarters of a Century*, p. 41
2. Biographical Directory of the United States Congress, https://bioguideretro.congress.gov/Home/MemberDetails?memIndex=P000207
3. *Reminiscences*, p. 40
4. Ibid.
5. Ibid., p. 41
6. Ibid.
7. Ibid.
8. Ibid.
9. Ibid.
10. Ibid., p. 42
11. Ibid.
12. Ibid., p. 43
13. Ibid., p. 44
14. Ibid., p. 45
15. Ibid.
16. Ibid., p. 46
17. Ibid.
18. Howe, Daniel Walker, *What Hath God Wrought: The Transformation of America, 1815–1848*, pp. 30-1
19. *Reminiscences*, p. 46
20. *What Hath God Wrought*, p. 51
21. Ibid., p. 69
22. *Reminiscences*, p. 55
23. Ibid.
24. Ibid.
25. Ibid., p. 56
26. Ibid.
27. Ibid., p. 48
28. Ibid.
29. Van Buren, Martin, *The Autobiography of Martin Van Buren*, p. 110
30. Burr, A., Charles D. Cooper, A. Hamilton, and W. P. Van Ness, 'William Van Ness's Story,' *New York History*, vol. 27, no. 4, 1946, pp. 492–499. JSTOR, www.jstor.org/stable/23148958
31. *Reminiscences*, p. 53
32. Van Ness v. Hamilton, 19 Johns 349 (1822), New York Supreme Court of Judicature, https://cite.case.law/johns/19/349
33. *Reminiscences*, p. 54
34. Ibid., p. 55
35. Ibid., p. 62
36. Ibid.
37. Ibid.
38. *What Hath God Wrought*, pp. 207–208

Chapter 3

1. Hamilton, James Alexander, *Reminiscences of James A Hamilton; or, Men and Events, at Home and Abroad, During Three Quarters of a Century*, p. 28
2. United States Senate Historical Office, 'Washington's Farewell Address to the People of the United States,' 1796, www.senate.gov/artandhistory/history/resources/pdf/Washingtons_Farewell_Address.pdf
3. Ibid.
4. Ibid.
5. Ibid.
6. *Reminiscences*, p. 24
7. Ibid.
8. University of Michigan, Hamilton-Schuyler Family Papers, James Alexander Hamilton to Timothy Pickering, 4 December 1820
9. Ibid.
10. Ibid.
11. Malanson, Jeffrey J., '"If I Had It in His Hand-Writing I Would Burn It": Federalists and the Authorship Controversy over George Washington's Farewell Address, 1808–1859,' *Journal of the Early Republic*, vol. 34, no. 2 (Summer 2014), pp. 219–242, www.jstor.org/stable/24486688
12. Ibid.
13. University of Michigan, Hamilton-Schuyler Family Papers, Elizabeth Schuyler Hamilton to Timothy Pickering, 1823
14. University of Michigan, Hamilton-Schuyler Family Papers, James Alexander Hamilton to Timothy Pickering, 4 December 1820
15. University of Michigan, Hamilton-Schuyler Family Papers, Timothy Pickering to James Alexander Hamilton, 4 January 1821
16. *Reminiscences*, p. 24
17. Ibid.
18. Ibid., p. 25
19. Ibid.
20. Ibid., p. 26
21. Malanson, Jeffrey J., '"If I Had It in His Hand-Writing I Would Burn It": Federalists and the Authorship Controversy over George Washington's Farewell Address, 1808–1859,' *Journal of the Early Republic*, vol. 34, no. 2 (Summer 2014), pp. 219–242, www.jstor.org/stable/24486688
22. *Reminiscences*, p. 26
23. Ibid., p. 27
24. Ibid., pp. 27–28
25. National Archives: Founders Online, Alexander Hamilton to George Washington, 30 July 1796, https://founders.archives.gov/documents/Hamilton/01-20-02-0181-0001
26. National Archives: Founders Online, George Washington to Alexander Hamilton, 25 August 1796, https://founders.archives.gov/documents/Hamilton/01-20-02-0197
27. Hamilton, Allan McLane, *The Intimate Life of Alexander Hamilton*, p. 111
28. Ibid., pp. 110–111
29. Malanson, Jeffrey J., '"If I Had It in His Hand-Writing I Would Burn It": Federalists and the Authorship Controversy over George Washington's Farewell Address, 1808–1859,' *Journal of the Early Republic*, vol. 34, no. 2 (Summer 2014), pp. 219–242, www.jstor.org/stable/24486688
30. *Reminiscences*, p. 28

Chapter 4
1. Hamilton, James Alexander, *Reminiscences of James A Hamilton; or, Men and Events, at Home and Abroad, During Three Quarters of a Century*, p. 70
2. *Reminiscences*, p. 62
3. Ibid.
4. Adams, John Quincy, Inaugural Address, National Archives
5. Ibid.
6. Howe, Daniel Walker, *What Hath God Wrought: The Transformation of America, 1815–1848*, p. 221
7. *Reminiscences*, p. 66
8. JQA Digital Diary, 8 January 1839, www.masshist.org/publications/jqadiaries/index.php/document/jqadiaries-v42-1839-01-08-p001#sn=302
9. *Reminiscences*, p. 64
10. Ibid., p. 67
11. Ibid., p. 68
12. Andrew Jackson's Hermitage, Guided Tour
13. *Reminiscences*, p. 68
14. Ibid., p. 69
15. Ibid., p. 70
16. Ibid.
17. New York Public Library, James A Hamilton Collection, Box1, folder 'James A Hamilton Notes'
18. Ibid.
19. *Reminiscences*, p. 71
20. Ibid., p. 72
21. Ibid.
22. Ibid.
23. Ibid.
24. Ibid., p. 74
25. Ibid., p. 79
26. Ibid., p. 80
27. Ibid.
28. Ibid., p. 81
29. Ibid., p. 87
30. Ibid., p. 98
31. Clay, Henry, 'The Speech of Henry Clay Delivered at the Public Dinner at Fowler's Garden,' 16 May 1829
32. *Reminiscences*, p. 100
33. Ibid., p. 102
34. Ibid., p. 97
35. JQA Digital Diary, 7 March 1829, www.masshist.org/publications/jqadiaries/index.php/document/jqadiaries-v36i-1829-03-07-p161
36. *Reminiscences*, p. 104
37. Ibid., p. 97
38. Ibid.
39. Ibid., p. 101
40. Ibid.
41. Ibid., p. 102
42. Ibid.

43. Ibid., p. 103
44. Ibid., p. 109
45. Ibid., p. 111
46. Ibid., p. 110
47. Ibid., p. 114
48. JQA Diary, 11 March 1829, www.masshist.org/publications/jqadiaries/index.php/document/jqadiaries-v36i-1829-03-11-p161#sn=232
49. JAW Diary, 18 March 1829, www.masshist.org/publications/jqadiaries/index.php/document/jqadiaries-v36i-1829-03-18-p161#sn=233
50. Ibid.
51. JQA Diary, 23 March 1829, www.masshist.org/publications/jqadiaries/index.php/document/jqadiaries-v36i-1829-03-23-p161#sn=237
52. *Reminiscences*, pp. 121–122
53. Ibid., p. 123
54. Van Buren, Martin, *The Autobiography of Martin Van Buren*, p. 268
55. *Reminiscences*, p. 68
56. Ibid., p. 124
57. New York Public Library, James A Hamilton Collection, Box1, Van Buren Recommendation Letter, 31 March 1828
58. Ibid.
59. *Reminiscences*, pp. 125–126
60. New York Public Library, James A Hamilton Collection, Box1, James A Hamilton Appointment to District Attorney of Southern New York, 10 April 1830
61. *Reminiscences*, p. 137
62. Ibid., p. 89
63. Ibid., p. 129
64. Ibid., p. 135
65. Ibid., p. 136
66. Ibid., p. 139
67. Ibid., p. 137
68. Ibid.
69. Ibid., p. 139
70. JQA Diary, 11 April 1829, www.masshist.org/publications/jqadiaries/index.php/document/jqadiaries-v36-1829-04-11-p151#sn=240
71. *Reminiscences*, p. 140

Chapter 5
1. Hamilton, James Alexander, *Reminiscences of James A Hamilton; or, Men and Events, at Home and Abroad, During Three Quarters of a Century*, p. 127
2. Ibid., p. 126
3. Ibid., p. 127
4. Van Buren, Martin, *The Autobiography of Martin Van Buren*, p. 250
5. Ibid., p. 339
6. *Reminiscences*, p. 135
7. Marszalek, John F., *The Petticoat Affair: Manners, Mutiny, and Sex in Andrew Jackson's White House*, p. 85
8. Wilcoxson, Samantha, 'Will the Real James Hamilton Please Stand Up?', 27 March 2023, https://samanthawilcoxson.blogspot.com/2023/03/will-real-james-hamilton-please-stand-up.html

9. *Reminiscences*, p. 136
10. Unger, Harlow Giles, *Henry Clay: America's Greatest Stateman*, p. 121
11. *Reminiscences*, p. 144
12. Ibid., p. 146
13. Ibid.
14. Ibid., p. 148
15. Howe, Daniel Walker, *What Hath God Wrought: The Transformation of America, 1815–1848*, p. 339
16. *Reminiscences*, p. 144
17. Ibid.
18. Ibid., p. 170
19. Ibid., p. 171
20. Ibid., p. 215
21. Ibid., p. 222
22. Howe, Daniel Walker, *What Hath God Wrought: The Transformation of America, 1815–1848*, p. 395
23. Marszalek, John F., *The Petticoat Affair: Manners, Mutiny, and Sex in Andrew Jackson's White House*, pp. 228–233

Chapter 6
1. Hamilton, James Alexander, *Reminiscences of James A Hamilton; or, Men and Events, at Home and Abroad, During Three Quarters of a Century*, p. 249
2. *Reminiscences*, p. 140
3. Hamilton, Allan McLane, *The Intimate Life of Alexander Hamilton*, p. 218
4. *Reminiscences*, p. 141
5. Ibid.
6. *Reminiscences*, p. 140
7. Ibid., p. 141
8. Ibid., p. 173
9. Ibid., p. 174
10. Ibid.
11. Ibid.
12. Ibid., p. 223
13. Ibid.
14. New York Public Library, James A Hamilton Collection, Box2, folder 'Polari Case,' Louis McLane to James A Hamilton
15. New York Public Library, James A Hamilton Collection, Box2, folder 'Polari Case,' Louis McLane to James A Hamilton, 6 October 1831
16. New York Public Library, James A Hamilton Collection, Box2, folder 'Polari Case,' Samuel Swartwout to James A Hamilton, 15 October 1831
17. New York Public Library, James A Hamilton Collection, Box2, folder 'Polari Case,' Louis McLane to James A Hamilton, 12 November 1831
18. New York Public Library, James A Hamilton Collection, Box2, folder 'Polari Case,' Roger B Taney to James A Hamilton
19. *Reminiscences*, p. 226
20. Ibid., p. 249
21. Ibid.
22. Ibid.
23. Ibid., pp. 266–267

Notes 179

Chapter 7
1. Hamilton, James Alexander, *Reminiscences of James A Hamilton; or, Men and Events, at Home and Abroad, During Three Quarters of a Century*, p. 149
2. Ibid.
3. Ibid., p. 150
4. Ibid.
5. Ibid.
6. Ibid., p. 243
7. Ibid., p. 252
8. Murphy, Sharon Ann, *Other People's Money: How Banking Worked in the Early American Republic*, pp. 80–82
9. Ibid., p. 84
10. *Reminiscences*, p. 150
11. Ibid., p. 151
12. Ibid.
13. Ibid., p. 154
14. Murphy, Sharon Ann, *Other People's Money: How Banking Worked in the Early American Republic*, p. 95
15. Howe, Daniel Walker, *What Hath God Wrought: The Transformation of America, 1815–1848*, p. 373
16. Murphy, Sharon Ann, *Other People's Money: How Banking Worked in the Early American Republic*, p. 96
17. *Reminiscences*, pp. 154–155
18. Ibid., p. 155
19. Howe, Daniel Walker, *What Hath God Wrought: The Transformation of America, 1815–1848*, p. 375
20. *Reminiscences*, p. 162
21. Ibid., p. 164
22. Ibid., p. 191
23. Ibid., p. 256
24. Ibid.
25. Ibid., p. 257
26. Ibid.
27. Unger, Harlow Giles, *Henry Clay: America's Greatest Stateman*, p. 174
28. *Reminiscences*, p. 258
29. Ibid., p. 260
30. Ibid., p. 261
31. Ibid., p. 263
32. Ibid., pp. 251–252
33. Ibid., p. 263
34. Ibid., p. 264
35. Howe, Daniel Walker, *What Hath God Wrought: The Transformation of America, 1815–1848*, p. 379
36. Ibid., p. 380
37. *Reminiscences*, p. 253
38. Ibid.
39. Ibid.
40. Ibid.
41. Ibid., p. 255

42. Ibid., p. 269
43. Howe, Daniel Walker, *What Hath God Wrought: The Transformation of America, 1815–1848*, p. 387
44. Ibid., p. 388
45. Ibid., p. 389
46. Ibid., p. 394
47. *Reminiscences*, p. 270
48. Ibid., pp. 279–280
49. Murphy, Sharon Ann, *Other People's Money: How Banking Worked in the Early American Republic*, p. 100

Chapter 8

1. Hamilton, James Alexander, *Reminiscences of James A Hamilton; or, Men and Events, at Home and Abroad, During Three Quarters of a Century*, p. 250
2. Van Buren, Martin, *The Autobiography of Martin Van Buren*, p. 554
3. *Reminiscences*, p. 231
4. Yale Law School: Avalon Project, South Carolina Ordinance of Nullification, 24 November 1832, https://avalon.law.yale.edu/19th_century/ordnull.asp
5. *Reminiscences*, p. 243
6. Howe, Daniel Walker, *What Hath God Wrought: The Transformation of America, 1815–1848*, p. 404
7. *Reminiscences*, p. 247
8. Ibid.
9. Ibid., p. 248
10. Ibid.
11. Yale Law School: Avalon Project, President Jackson's Proclamation Regarding Nullification, 10 December 1832, https://avalon.law.yale.edu/19th_century/jack01.asp
12. Ibid.
13. Ibid.
14. Unger, Harlow Giles, *Henry Clay: America's Greatest Statesman*, p. 170
15. Yale Law School: Avalon Project, President Jackson's Proclamation Regarding Nullification, 10 December 1832, https://avalon.law.yale.edu/19th_century/jack01.asp
16. Marszalek, John F., *The Petticoat Affair: Manners, Mutiny, and Sex in Andrew Jackson's White House*, p. 198
17. *Reminiscences*, p. 249
18. Ibid., pp. 250–251

Chapter 9

1. University of Michigan, Hamilton-Schuyler Family Papers, James A Hamilton to Elizabeth Hamilton Schuyler, 5 January 1837
2. JQA Digital Diary, 13 December 1830, www.masshist.org/publications/jqadiaries/index.php/document/jqadiaries-v38-1830-12-13-p048#sn=13
3. JQA Digital Diary, 16 December 1830, www.masshist.org/publications/jqadiaries/index.php/document/jqadiaries-v38-1830-12-16-p048
4. University of Michigan, Hamilton-Schuyler Family Papers, George Lee Schuyler to Elizabeth Hamilton, 14 March 1832
5. Hamilton, James Alexander, *Reminiscences of James A Hamilton; or, Men and Events, at Home and Abroad, During Three Quarters of a Century*, p. 243

6. Train, Russell E., *The Bowdoin Family*, p. 42
7. William & Mary Libraries, Alexander Hamilton Jr Letters, Alexander Hamilton Jr to James A Hamilton, 10 July 1832
8. William & Mary Libraries, Alexander Hamilton Jr Letters, Alexander Hamilton Jr to Elizabeth Hamilton, 11 July 1832
9. William & Mary Libraries, Alexander Hamilton Jr Letters, Alexander Hamilton Jr to James A Hamilton, 22 October 1833
10. *Reminiscences*, p. 251
11. Fielding, A. K., *Rough Diamond: The Life of Colonel William Stephen Hamilton, Alexander Hamilton's Forgotten Son*, p. 64
12. Ibid.
13. Hamilton, Allan McLane, *The Intimate Life of Alexander Hamilton*, pp. 220–221
14. Ibid.
15. University of Michigan, Hamilton-Schuyler Family Papers, 1861 Journal of Louisa Lee Schuyler
16. Andrew Jackson to James Alexander Hamilton, 17 September 1830, NYPL Coll.
17. Burnstein, Andrew, *The Original Knickerbocker: The Life of Washington Irving*, p. 299
18. Ibid., p. 302

Chapter 10

1. Scharf, J. Thomas, *History of Westchester County, New York, Including Morrisania, Kings Bridge, and West Farms*, pp. 281–283
2. Chronology of Nevis Estate, Irvington Historical Society
3. Ibid.
4. Scharf, J. Thomas, *History of Westchester County, New York, Including Morrisania, Kings Bridge, and West Farms*, pp. 281–283
5. Ibid., p. 241
6. Ibid., pp. 281–283
7. Train, Russell E., *The Bowdoin Family: Including Some Account of the Belgrave, Grinnell, Hamilton, Howland, Irving, Kingsford, Ligon, Means, Morris, and Sullivan Families*, pp. 95–96
8. Nevis Laboratories at Columbia University, A Brief History of Nevis, www.nevis.columbia.edu/brief-introduction.html
9. Burnstein, Andrew, *The Original Knickerbocker: The Life of Washington Irving*, p. 190
10. Scharf, J. Thomas, *History of Westchester County*, p. 191
11. Ibid., pp. 281–283
12. Hamilton, James Alexander, *Reminiscences of James A Hamilton; or, Men and Events, at Home and Abroad, During Three Quarters of a Century*, p. 284
13. Ibid., p. 285
14. Chronology of Nevis Estate, Irvington Historical Society
15. Ibid.
16. *The New York Times*, 26 September 1878, Obituary of James A. Hamilton
17. Scharf, J. Thomas, *History of Westchester County*, p. 187

Chapter 11

1. Hamilton, James Alexander, *Reminiscences of James A Hamilton; or, Men and Events, at Home and Abroad, During Three Quarters of a Century*, p. 286
2. Ibid., p. 285

3. Levy, Daniel S., *Manhattan Phoenix: The Great Fire of 1835 and the Emergence of Modern New York*, p. 12
4. Ibid., p. 30
5. Virtual New York City, Great Fire of 1835, https://virtualny.ashp.cuny.edu/FIRE/destruction.html
6. *Reminiscences*, p. 285
7. Ibid., pp. 287–288
8. Howe, Daniel Walker, *What Hath God Wrought: The Transformation of America, 1815–1848*, p. 529
9. *Reminiscences*, pp. 287–288
10. Ibid., p. 286
11. Ibid., p. 287
12. Ibid.
13. Ibid.
14. Ibid., p. 288
15. Ibid.
16. McNamara, Robert, 'New York's Great Fire of 1835,' ThoughtCo., 31 August 2019, www.thoughtco.com/new-yorks-great-fire-of-1835-1773780
17. Levy, Daniel S., *Manhattan Phoenix: The Great Fire of 1835 and the Emergence of Modern New York*, pp. 160–161
18. Ibid., p. 164
19. King, Charles, *A Memoir of the Construction, Cost, and Capacity of the Croton Aqueduct*, p. 137
20. Fielding, A. K., *Rough Diamond: The Life of Colonel William Stephen Hamilton, Alexander Hamilton's Forgotten Son*, p. 28
21. Levy, Daniel S., *Manhattan Phoenix: The Great Fire of 1835 and the Emergence of Modern New York*, p. xii

Chapter 12

1. Hamilton, James Alexander, *Reminiscences of James A Hamilton; or, Men and Events, at Home and Abroad, During Three Quarters of a Century*, p. 288
2. Ibid.
3. Ibid.
4. Ibid.
5. Ibid., p. 289
6. University of Michigan, Hamilton-Schuyler Family Papers, James A Hamilton to George Lee Schuyler and Elizabeth Hamilton Schuyler, 3 & 22 November 1836
7. University of Michigan, Hamilton-Schuyler Family Papers, James A Hamilton to Elizabeth Hamilton Schuyler, 5 January 1837
8. *Reminiscences*, p. 290
9. Ibid.
10. National Archives: Founders Online, Alexander Hamilton to Elizabeth Schuyler Hamilton, 7–11 May 1804, https://founders.archives.gov/documents/Hamilton/01-26-02-0001-0193
11. *Reminiscences*, p. 291
12. Ibid., p. 292
13. Library of Congress, James Alexander Hamilton to Andrew Jackson, 11 March 1837, www.loc.gov/resource/maj.01098_0192_0195

14. University of Michigan, Hamilton-Schuyler Family Papers, James A Hamilton to Elizabeth Hamilton Schuyler, 21 February 1837
15. *Reminiscences*, p. 293
16. University of Michigan, Hamilton-Schuyler Family Papers, James A Hamilton to Elizabeth Hamilton Schuyler, 7 April 1837
17. Ibid.
18. University of Michigan, Hamilton-Schuyler Family Papers, James A Hamilton to Elizabeth Hamilton Schuyler, 9 April 1837
19. University of Michigan, Hamilton-Schuyler Family Papers, James A Hamilton to Elizabeth Hamilton Schuyler, 26 June 1837
20. University of Michigan, Hamilton-Schuyler Family Papers, James A Hamilton to George Lee Schuyler, 22 April 1837
21. Ibid.
22. *Reminiscences*, p. 295
23. Ibid., p. 297
24. University of Michigan, Hamilton-Schuyler Family Papers, James A Hamilton to George Lee Schuyler, 21 June 1837
25. University of Michigan, Hamilton-Schuyler Family Papers, James A Hamilton to George Lee Schuyler, 13 July 1837
26. University of Michigan, Hamilton-Schuyler Family Papers, James A Hamilton to George Lee Schuyler, 21 June 1837
27. *Reminiscences*, p. 297
28. Ibid.
29. Ibid., p. 298
30. Ibid., p. 299
31. Ibid., p. 301
32. Ibid.
33. Ibid., p. 302
34. Ibid.
35. Ibid., p. 303
36. Ibid.
37. Ibid.
38. Ibid.
39. Ibid., p. 304
40. Ibid.
41. Ibid.
42. Ibid.
43. Howe, Daniel Walker, *What Hath God Wrought: The Transformation of America, 1815–1848*, pp. 428–429
44. Ibid., p. 429
45. Ibid., p. 430
46. Ibid.
47. Bordewich, Fergus M., *Bound for Canaan: The Underground Railroad and the War for the Soul of America*, p. 159–160
48. *Reminiscences*, p. 304
49. Ibid.
50. Ibid., p. 305
51. Ibid.

52. University of Michigan, Hamilton-Schuyler Family Papers, James A Hamilton to Elizabeth Hamilton Schuyler, 7 October 1837
53. *Reminiscences*, p. 305
54. Ibid., p. 306
55. Ibid.
56. Ibid., p. 307
57. Ibid.
58. Ibid., pp. 307–308
59. Ibid., p. 308
60. Ibid.
61. Ibid.
62. Ibid., p. 309

Chapter 13
1. Hamilton, James Alexander, *Reminiscences of James A Hamilton; or, Men and Events, at Home and Abroad, During Three Quarters of a Century*, p. 310
2. Howe, Daniel Walker, *What Hath God Wrought: The Transformation of America, 1815–1848*, p. 518
3. Ibid.
4. *Reminiscences*, p. 310
5. Ibid., p. 311
6. Ibid.
7. *What Hath God Wrought*, p. 519
8. *Reminiscences*, p. 312
9. Ibid.
10. Ibid., p. 313
11. Ibid., p. 317
12. *What Hath God Wrought*, p. 594

Chapter 14
1. Hamilton, James Alexander, *Reminiscences of James A Hamilton; or, Men and Events, at Home and Abroad, During Three Quarters of a Century*, p. 343
2. Ibid., p. 318
3. Ibid.
4. Ibid.
5. Ibid., p. 319
6. Ibid.
7. Ibid.
8. New York Public Library, James A Hamilton Collection, Box1, General Winfield Scott to James A Hamilton, 20 July 1841
9. *Reminiscences*, p. 320
10. Ibid.
11. Ibid., p. 321
12. Ibid., p. 322
13. Ibid.
14. Ibid.
15. Ibid., p. 330
16. Ibid.

17. Ibid., p. 331
18. Ibid., p. 330
19. Ibid.
20. Ibid., p. 333
21. Ibid., p. 323
22. Ibid.
23. Ibid.
24. Ibid.
25. Ibid., p. 324
26. Ibid., p. 328
27. Ibid., p. 329
28. Ibid., p. 332
29. Ibid.
30. Ibid., p. 337
31. Ibid., p. 338
32. Ibid.
33. Ibid., p. 342
34. Ibid.
35. Ibid., p. 346
36. Ibid., p. 345
37. Ibid.
38. Ibid., p. 346
39. Ibid.
40. Ibid.
41. Ibid., p. 348
42. Ibid., p. 347
43. Ibid., p. 348
44. Ibid.
45. Hamilton, Alexander Jr Collection, Historic Hudson Valley, Alexander Hamilton Jr to James A Hamilton, 29 August 1843
46. Howe, Daniel Walker, *What Hath God Wrought: The Transformation of America, 1815–1848*, p. 600
47. Ibid., p. 601
48. *Reminiscences*, p. 351–352
49. Ibid.

Chapter 15
1. Hamilton, James Alexander, *Reminiscences of James A Hamilton; or, Men and Events, at Home and Abroad, During Three Quarters of a Century*, p. 354
2. National Archives, 'Struggles over Slavery: The "Gag" Rule,' www.archives.gov/exhibits/treasures_of_congress/text/page10_text.html
3. Howe, Daniel Walker, *What Hath God Wrought: The Transformation of America, 1815–1848*, p. 611
4. Ibid., p. 680
5. Ibid., p. 684
6. Ibid., pp. 688–689
7. Ibid., p. 708
8. Ibid., p. 732

9. Ibid., p. 739
10. Ibid.
11. Ibid., p. 741
12. Ibid.
13. Ibid., p. 743
14. McPherson, James M., *Battle Cry of Freedom: The Civil War Era*, p. 47
15. *Reminiscences*, p. 354
16. Ibid., p. 355
17. Ibid.
18. Ibid.
19. Ibid.
20. Ibid., p. 356
21. census.gov

Chapter 16
1. Hamilton, James Alexander, *Reminiscences of James A Hamilton; or, Men and Events, at Home and Abroad, During Three Quarters of a Century*, p. 370
2. Ibid., p. 356
3. Ibid., p. 357
4. Ibid.
5. Ibid.
6. Ibid., p. 358
7. Ibid.
8. Ibid., pp. 365–366
9. Ibid., p. 359
10. Ibid.
11. Ibid.
12. Ibid.
13. Ibid.
14. Ibid.
15. Ibid., p. 360
16. Ibid.
17. Ibid., p. 367
18. Ibid.
19. Ibid., p. 372
20. Ibid.
21. Ibid., p. 375
22. Ibid., p. 373
23. Ibid., p. 374
24. Ibid., p. 375
25. Fielding, A. K., *Rough Diamond: The Life of Colonel William Stephen Hamilton, Alexander Hamilton's Forgotten Son*, p. 102
26. Ibid., pp. 104–107
27. *Reminiscences*, p. 361
28. Ibid., p. 362
29. Ibid., p. 376
30. Ibid., p. 377
31. Ibid.

32. Ibid.
33. Ibid., p. 378
34. Ibid., p. 379
35. Ibid., p. 382
36. Ibid., p. 383
37. Ibid., 384
38. Ibid.
39. Ibid.
40. Ibid., p. 387
41. Ibid., p. 389
42. National Park Service, Report of the Woman's Rights Convention, 19–20 July 1848, www.nps.gov/wori/learn/historyculture/report-of-the-womans-rights-convention.htm

Chapter 17
1. *Reminiscences*, p. 400.
2. Hamilton, James Alexander, *Reminiscences of James A Hamilton; or, Men and Events, at Home and Abroad, During Three Quarters of a Century*, p. 393
3. Ibid., p. 396
4. University of Michigan, Hamilton-Schuyler Family Papers, George Lee Schuyler to Elizabeth Hamilton Schuyler, 2 July 1851
5. *Reminiscences*, p. 396
6. Lawson, Thomas William, and Thompson, Winfield Martin, *The Lawson History of America's Cup: A Record of Fifty Years*, p. 2
7. Ibid., p. 1
8. Ibid., p. 4
9. Ibid., p. 6
10. Ibid., p. 3
11. Rousmaniere, John, *The Low Black Schooner: Yacht America 1851–1945*, p. 19
12. Ibid.
13. *Reminiscences*, p. 396
14. Lawson, Thomas William, and Thompson, Winfield Martin, *The Lawson History of America's Cup: A Record of Fifty Years*, p. 15
15. *Reminiscences*, p. 396
16. Lawson, Thomas William, and Thompson, Winfield Martin, *The Lawson History of America's Cup: A Record of Fifty Years*, p. 1
17. Ibid., p. 21
18. Ibid., p. 22
19. *Reminiscences*, p. 400
20. Ibid.
21. Lawson, Thomas William, and Thompson, Winfield Martin, *The Lawson History of America's Cup: A Record of Fifty Years*, p. 24
22. *Reminiscences*, p. 400
23. Lawson, Thomas William, and Thompson, Winfield Martin, *The Lawson History of America's Cup: A Record of Fifty Years*, p. 25
24. Ibid., p. 27
25. Ibid., p. 25
26. *Reminiscences*, p. 400
27. Lawson, Thomas William, and Thompson, Winfield Martin, *The Lawson History of America's Cup: A Record of Fifty Years*, p. 29

28. *Reminiscences*, pp. 400–401
29. Ibid., p. 402
30. Ibid.
31. Ibid.
32. Ibid., p. 403
33. Ibid., p. 404
34. Lawson, Thomas William, and Thompson, Winfield Martin, *The Lawson History of America's Cup: A Record of Fifty Years*, p. 26
35. Ibid.
36. Ibid.
37. McPherson, James M., *Battle Cry of Freedom: The Civil War Era*, p. 84
38. Ibid., p. 85
39. Lawson, Thomas William, and Thompson, Winfield Martin, *The Lawson History of America's Cup: A Record of Fifty Years*, p. 40
40. Rousmaniere, John, *The Low Black Schooner: Yacht America 1851–1945*, p. 61

Chapter 18
1. Greeley, Horace, Art and Industry as Represented in the Exhibition at the Crystal Palace, New York, 1853–4, https://quod.lib.umich.edu/m/moa/AGL5025.0001.001?rgn=main;view=fulltext
2. Greeley, Horace, Art and Industry as Represented in the Exhibition at the Crystal Palace, New York, 1853–4, https://quod.lib.umich.edu/m/moa/AGL5025.0001.001?rgn=main;view=fulltext
3. Museum of the City of New York, 'The Great Crystal Palace Fire of 1858,' https://blog.mcny.org/2012/12/04/the-great-crystal-palace-fire-of-1858
4. Ibid.
5. Burrows, Edwin, *The Finest Building in America: The New York Crystal Palace 1853–1858*, p. 19
6. Ibid., p. 26
7. Ibid., p. 70
8. Ibid., p. 85
9. Ibid., p. 42

Chapter 19
1. Hamilton, James Alexander, *Reminiscences of James A Hamilton; or, Men and Events, at Home and Abroad, During Three Quarters of a Century*, p. 65
2. University of Michigan, Hamilton-Schuyler Family Papers, Elizabeth Hamilton Schuyler to James A Hamilton, 12 December 1853
3. University of Michigan, Hamilton-Schuyler Family Papers, 'Nevis Portfolio'
4. Ibid.
5. Ibid.
6. Hamilton, Alexander Jr Collection, Historic Hudson Valley, Alexander Hamilton Jr to George Lee Schuyler, 23 January 1843
7. Hamilton, Alexander Jr Collection, Historic Hudson Valley, Alexander Hamilton Jr to James A Hamilton, 31 January 1843
8. Hamilton, Alexander Jr Collection, Historic Hudson Valley
9. Hamilton, Alexander Jr Collection, Historic Hudson Valley, Alexander Hamilton Jr to James A Hamilton, 10 March 1843
10. Fielding, A. K., *Rough Diamond: The Life of Colonel William Stephen Hamilton, Alexander Hamilton's Forgotten Son*, pp. 104–107

11. Hamilton, James Alexander, *Reminiscences of James A Hamilton; or, Men and Events, at Home and Abroad, During Three Quarters of a Century*, p. 64
12. Ibid.
13. Ibid., p. 65
14. Ibid.
15. Ibid.
16. Ibid.
17. Ibid.
18. Mary Morris Hamilton Schuyler (1818–1877), George Washington's Mount Vernon's Digital Encyclopedia, www.mountvernon.org/library/digitalhistory/digital-encyclopedia/article/mary-morris-hamilton-schuyler-1818-1877
19. Abraham Lincoln at the Cooper Union, 27 February 1860, https://cooper.edu/about/abraham-lincoln-cooper-union
20. McPherson, James M., *Battle Cry of Freedom: The Civil War Era*, p. 480
21. Ibid.
22. University of Michigan, Hamilton-Schuyler Family Papers, 1861 Journal of Louisa Lee Schuyler
23. Ibid.
24. Scharf, J. Thomas, *History of Westchester County, New York, Including Morrisania, Kings Bridge, and West Farms*, pp. 281–283

Chapter 20
1. Hamilton, James Alexander, *Reminiscences of James A Hamilton; or, Men and Events, at Home and Abroad, During Three Quarters of a Century*, p. 411
2. National Archives: Founders Online, Jefferson, Thomas, Notes of a Conversation with Alexander Hamilton, 13 August 1791, https://founders.archives.gov/documents/Jefferson/01-22-02-0033
3. *Reminiscences*, p. 414
4. Ibid., p. 415
5. Ibid.
6. Ibid.
7. McPherson, James M., *Battle Cry of Freedom: The Civil War Era*, p. 149
8. Sumner, Charles, *The Crime Against Kansas: Speech of Honorable Charles Sumner in the Senate of the United States, 19–20 May 1856*, www.senate.gov/artandhistory/history/resources/pdf/CrimeAgainstKSSpeech.pdf
9. Willis, Garry, *Henry Adams and the Making of America*, p. 54
10. Ibid. p. 56
11. *Reminiscences*, p. 411
12. McPherson, James M., *Battle Cry of Freedom: The Civil War Era*, p. 150
13. Ibid., p. 151
14. Hamilton, James Alexander and Hamilton Fish, *Fremont, the Conservative Candidate*, Hamilton Fish to James A Hamilton 12 September 1856
15. Ibid.
16. Hamilton, James Alexander and Hamilton Fish, *Fremont, the Conservative Candidate*, James A Hamilton to Hamilton Fish 7 March 1856
17. *Reminiscences*, pp. 412–413
18. Ibid., p. 413
19. Ibid.
20. Ibid., p. 414

21. Hamilton, James Alexander and Hamilton Fish, *Fremont, the Conservative Candidate*, Hamilton Fish to James A Hamilton 12 September 1856
22. Hamilton, James Alexander and Hamilton Fish, *Fremont, the Conservative Candidate*, James A Hamilton to Hamilton Fish 4 October 1856
23. Ibid.
24. Ibid.
25. Hamilton, James Alexander and Hamilton Fish, *Fremont, the Conservative Candidate*, Hamilton Fish to James A Hamilton 12 September 1856
26. Ibid.
27. Hamilton, James Alexander and Hamilton Fish, *Fremont, the Conservative Candidate*, James A Hamilton to Hamilton Fish 4 October 1856
28. Willis, Garry, *Henry Adams and the Making of America*, p. 114
29. Hamilton, James Alexander and Hamilton Fish, *Fremont, the Conservative Candidate*, James A Hamilton to Hamilton Fish 4 October 1856
30. Ibid.
31. Ibid.
32. Ibid.
33. McPherson, James M., *Battle Cry of Freedom: The Civil War Era*, p. 158
34. *Reminiscences*, p. 430
35. Ibid., p. 431
36. Ibid., p. 416
37. Ibid., p. 420
38. Ibid.
39. Ibid.
40. McPherson, James M., *Battle Cry of Freedom: The Civil War Era*, p. 169
41. Hamilton, James Alexander, Examination of the Powers of the President to Remove from Office during Recess of the Senate, p. 1
42. Ibid., pp. 1–2
43. Ibid., p. 5
44. Hamilton, Alexander, The Federalist Paper No. 77: The Appointing Power Continued and Other Powers of the Executive Considered, https://guides.loc.gov/federalist-papers/text-71-80#s-lg-box-wrapper-25493469
45. Hamilton, James Alexander, *Examination of the Powers of the President to Remove from Office during Recess of the Senate*, p. 11
46. Ibid., p. 9
47. *Reminiscences*, p. 436

Chapter 21

1. Hamilton, James Alexander, *Reminiscences of James A Hamilton; or, Men and Events, at Home and Abroad, During Three Quarters of a Century*, p. 422
2. Ibid.
3. Nevis Laboratories at Columbia University, visited 11 May 2023
4. Ibid.
5. Ibid.
6. *Reminiscences*, p. 423
7. Lacour-Gayet, Robert, *Everyday Life in the United States before the Civil War 1830–1860*, p. 5
8. *Reminiscences*, p. 423
9. Ibid.

10. Ibid., p. 426
11. Ibid., p. 424
12. Ibid., p. 427
13. Ibid., p. 429

Chapter 22
1. Hamilton, James Alexander, *Reminiscences of James A Hamilton; or, Men and Events, at Home and Abroad, During Three Quarters of a Century*, p. 625
2. Ibid., p. 430
3. National Archives, Dred Scott v Sandford (1857), www.archives.gov/milestone-documents/dred-scott-v-sandford
4. *Reminiscences*, p. 624
5. National Archives, Dred Scott v Sandford (1857), www.archives.gov/milestone-documents/dred-scott-v-sandford
6. Ibid.
7. McPherson, James M., *Battle Cry of Freedom: The Civil War Era*, p. 175
8. *Reminiscences*, p. 624
9. Ibid., p. 625
10. Ibid., p. 626
11. Ibid., p. 624
12. Ibid.
13. Ibid., p. 625
14. Ibid.
15. Ibid., p. 626
16. Ibid., p. 627
17. Ibid., p. 630
18. Ibid.
19. Ibid., p. 631
20. McPherson, James M., *Battle Cry of Freedom: The Civil War Era*, p. 127
21. Ibid., p. 128
22. Ibid., p. 178
23. Ibid., p. 184
24. Ibid., p. 177
25. Ibid., p. 196
26. Ibid., p. 198
27. Ibid., p. 187
28. Ibid., p. 230
29. Ibid., p. 233

Chapter 23
1. Hamilton, James Alexander, *Reminiscences of James A Hamilton; or, Men and Events, at Home and Abroad, During Three Quarters of a Century*, p. 440
2. Ibid.
3. Ibid., p. 441
4. Ibid., p. 442
5. Ibid.
6. Ibid., p. 455
7. Ibid.
8. Ibid.

9. Ibid., p. 444
10. Ibid.
11. Ibid., pp. 446–448
12. McPherson, James M., *Battle Cry of Freedom: The Civil War Era*, p. vii
13. *Reminiscences*, p. 450
14. Ibid.
15. Ibid., p. 451
16. Ibid.
17. Ibid., p. 458
18. Ibid., p. 459
19. Ibid.
20. Ibid., p. 460
21. Ibid., p. 466
22. Ibid., p. 464
23. Ibid.
24. Ibid., p. 465
25. Ibid., p. 461
26. McPherson, James M., *Battle Cry of Freedom: The Civil War Era*, p. 264
27. *Reminiscences*, p. 462
28. McPherson, James M., *Battle Cry of Freedom: The Civil War Era*, p. 265
29. Ibid.
30. University of Michigan, Hamilton-Schuyler Family Papers, 1861 Journal of Louisa Lee Schuyler
31. Ibid.
32. Ibid.
33. University of Michigan, Hamilton-Schuyler Family Papers, Diary of Elizabeth Hamilton Schuyler
34. *Reminiscences*, p. 468
35. Ibid., p. 469
36. Ibid.
37. McPherson, James M., *Battle Cry of Freedom: The Civil War Era*, p. 256
38. *Reminiscences*, p. 472
39. Ibid., p. 474
40. Ibid., p. 475
41. Ibid., p. 477
42. Ibid.
43. Ibid.
44. Ibid.
45. Ibid.
46. Ibid.
47. Ibid., p. 478
48. Ibid.
49. Ibid., p. 479
50. National Park Service: Arlington House, The Robert E Lee Memorial, Union Occupation: 1861–1865, www.nps.gov/arho/learn/historyculture/union.htm
51. Scharf, J. Thomas, *History of Westchester County, New York, Including Morrisania, Kings Bridge, and West Farms*, p. 264
52. Willis, Garry, Henry Adams and the Making of America, p. 12

53. Ibid., p. 13
54. Hamilton, James Alexander, *Rebellion Against the United States by the People of a State is Its Political Suicide*, pp. 29–30
55. *Reminiscences*, p. 479
56. Ibid., pp. 485–487
57. Ibid., p. 493
58. Ibid., p. 482
59. Ibid., p. 498
60. Ibid.
61. Ibid., p. 499
62. Ibid., p. 506
63. McPherson, James M., *Battle Cry of Freedom: The Civil War Era*, p. 274
64. *Reminiscences*, p. 501
65. Ibid., p. 537
66. Ibid., p. 503
67. Ibid., p. 504
68. Ibid., p. 505
69. Ibid.
70. Ibid., p. 510
71. Ibid., pp. 511–512
72. Ibid., p. 512
73. Ibid., p. 518

Chapter 24
1. Hamilton, James Alexander, *Reminiscences of James A Hamilton; or, Men and Events, at Home and Abroad, During Three Quarters of a Century*, p. 514
2. Ibid.
3. Ibid.
4. Ibid., p. 515
5. Ibid.
6. Thane, Elswyth, *Mount Vernon is Ours: The Story of Its Preservation*, p. 16
7. Mary Morris Hamilton Schuyler (1818–1877), George Washington's Mount Vernon's Digital Encyclopedia, www.mountvernon.org/library/digitalhistory/digital-encyclopedia/article/mary-morris-hamilton-schuyler-1818-1877
8. Thane, Elswyth, *Mount Vernon is Ours: The Story of Its Preservation*, p. 120
9. Ibid., p. 148
10. Ibid., p. 245
11. Ibid., pp. 267–268
12. *Reminiscences*, p. 521
13. Ibid.
14. Ibid., p. 522
15. Ibid., p. 525
16. Ibid., p. 526
17. Ibid., p. 529
18. Ibid.
19. Ibid., p. 530
20. Ibid.
21. Ibid.

22. Ibid., p. 531
23. Ibid., p. 532
24. Ibid.
25. Ibid., p. 533
26. Ibid.
27. National Archives: Milestone Documents, Emancipation Proclamation (1863), www.archives.gov/milestone-documents/emancipation-proclamation
28. *Reminiscences*, p. 534
29. McPherson, James M., *Battle Cry of Freedom: The Civil War Era*, p. 566
30. Ibid., p. 567
31. Ibid., p. 592
32. *Reminiscences*, pp. 527–528
33. Ibid., p. 528
34. Ibid., p. 570
35. Hamilton, James Alexander, *The Constitution Vindicated. Nationality, Secession, Slavery*, p. 3
36. Ibid., p. 4
37. Ibid., p. 7
38. Ibid.
39. Ibid., pp. 7–8
40. Ibid., p. 11
41. Ibid., p. 12
42. McPherson, James M., *Battle Cry of Freedom: The Civil War Era*, p. 510
43. *Reminiscences*, p. 563
44. Ibid., p. 564
45. Ibid., p. 566
46. Ibid., p. 567
47. University of Michigan, Hamilton-Schuyler Family Papers, Elizabeth Hamilton Schuyler to James A Hamilton, 9 October 1863

Chapter 25

1. Hamilton, James Alexander, *An Address Delivered Before the Students of the United States Naval Academy at Newport, June 1864*, p. 5
2. Hamilton, James Alexander, *Reminiscences of James A Hamilton; or, Men and Events, at Home and Abroad, During Three Quarters of a Century*, p. 574
3. McPherson, James M., *Battle Cry of Freedom: The Civil War Era*, p. 560
4. Ibid.
5. Hamilton, James Alexander, *An Address Delivered Before the Students of the United States Naval Academy at Newport, June 1864*, p. 6
6. Ibid.
7. Ibid., p. 8
8. Ibid., p. 5
9. Ibid., p. 7
10. Ibid., p. 9
11. Ibid., p. 12
12. Ibid., p. 28
13. Ibid., p. 3
14. Hamilton, John Church, *Slave Power: Its Heresies and Injuries to the American People*, p. 2
15. Ibid.

16. Ibid., p. 9
17. Ibid., p. 18
18. McPherson, James M., *Battle Cry of Freedom: The Civil War Era*, p. 840
19. Ibid., p. 841
20. Massachusetts Historical Society, Lock of hair of Alexander Hamilton and George Washington, www.masshist.org/database/viewer.php?item_id=3098&pid=38
21. *Reminiscences*, p. 576
22. Ibid., p. 584

Chapter 26

1. Hamilton, James Alexander, *Martin Van Buren's Calumnies Repudiated. Hamilton's Conduct as Secretary of the Treasury Vindicated*, p. 31
2. Van Buren, Martin, *Inquiry into the Origin and Course of Political Parties in the United States*, p. 214
3. Ibid., p. 203
4. Ibid., p. 215
5. Hamilton, James Alexander, *Martin Van Buren's Calumnies Repudiated. Hamilton's Conduct as Secretary of the Treasury Vindicated*, pp. 3–4
6. Van Buren, Martin, *Inquiry into the Origin and Course of Political Parties in the United States*, p. 171
7. Hamilton, James Alexander, *Martin Van Buren's Calumnies Repudiated. Hamilton's Conduct as Secretary of the Treasury Vindicated*, p. 4
8. Ibid.
9. Ibid., p. 5
10. Van Buren, Martin, *Inquiry into the Origin and Course of Political Parties in the United States*, p. 159
11. Hamilton, James Alexander, *Martin Van Buren's Calumnies Repudiated. Hamilton's Conduct as Secretary of the Treasury Vindicated*, p. 8
12. Ibid., p. 9
13. Ibid., p. 10
14. Ibid., p. 15
15. Van Buren, Martin, *Inquiry into the Origin and Course of Political Parties in the United States*, p. 263
16. Hamilton, James Alexander, *Martin Van Buren's Calumnies Repudiated. Hamilton's Conduct as Secretary of the Treasury Vindicated*, p. 30
17. Ibid., p. 31

Chapter 27

1. Hamilton, James Alexander, *Reminiscences of James A Hamilton; or, Men and Events, at Home and Abroad, During Three Quarters of a Century*, pp. 569–570
2. Randall, J. G., *Constitutional Problems Under Lincoln*, p. 115
3. Willis, Garry, *Henry Adams and the Making of America*, p. 76
4. Chronology of Nevis Estate, Irvington Historical Society
5. Hamilton Family Tree at Hamilton Grange National Memorial
6. *The New York Times*, 26 September 1878, Obituary of James A. Hamilton
7. Ibid.
8. Ibid.
9. Ibid.
10. Ibid.

Bibliography

Adams, John Quincy, JQA Digital Diary, Massachusetts Historical Society, www.masshist.org/publications/jqadiaries

Bordewich, Fergus M., *Bound for Canaan: The Underground Railroad and the War for the Soul of America* (HarperCollins, New York, 2005)

Burrows, Edwin, *The Finest Building in America: The New York Crystal Palace 1853–1858* (Oxford University Press, New York, 2018)

Burnstein, Andrew, *The Original Knickerbocker: The Life of Washington Irving* (Basic Books, New York, 2007)

Chernow, Ron, *Alexander Hamilton* (Penguin Books, New York, 2004)

Chronology of Nevis Estate, Irvington Historical Society

Curtis, James C., 'In the Shadow of Old Hickory: The Political Travail of Martin Van Buren,' *Journal of the Early Republic*, vol. 1, no. 3, pp. 249–267, 1981

Fielding, A. K., *Rough Diamond: The Life of Colonel William Stephen Hamilton, Alexander Hamilton's Forgotten Son* (Indiana University Press, Bloomington, 2021)

Hamilton, Alexander Jr Collection, Historic Hudson Valley

Hamilton, Alexander Jr, Letters Collection, William & Mary Libraries

Hamilton, Allan McLane, *The Intimate Life of Alexander Hamilton* (Charles Scribner's Sons, New York, 1910)

Hamilton, James Alexander, *An Address Delivered Before the Students of the United States Naval Academy at Newport, June 1864* (Ticknor and Fields, Boston, 1864)

Hamilton, James Alexander, *The Constitution Vindicated. Nationality, Secession, Slavery* (Loyal Publication Society, New York, 1864)

Hamilton, James Alexander, *Examination of the Powers of the President to Remove from Office during Recess of the Senate* (Wynkoop, Hallenbeck, & Thomas Printers, New York, 1861)

Hamilton, James Alexander and Hamilton Fish, *Fremont, the Conservative Candidate* (Northern Illinois University Digital Library), https://digital.lib.niu.edu/islandora/object/niu-lincoln:38334

Hamilton, James Alexander Collection, New York Public Library

Hamilton, James Alexander, *Martin Van Buren's Calumnies Repudiated. Hamilton's Conduct as Secretary of the Treasury Vindicated* (Charles Scribner & Co, New York, 1870)

Hamilton, James Alexander, *Rebellion Against the United States by the People of a State is Its Political Suicide* (Baker & Godwin, New York, 1862)

Hamilton, James Alexander, *Reminiscences of James A Hamilton; or, Men and Events, at Home and Abroad, During Three Quarters of a Century* (Charles Scribner & Co., New York, 1869)

Hamilton, John Church, *Slave Power: Its Heresies and Injuries to the American People* (Loyal Publication Society, New York, 1864)

Hamilton-Schuyler Family Papers, William L Clements Library at University of Michigan

Howard, Hugh, *Mr and Mrs Madison's War: America's First Couple and the Second War of Independence* (Bloomsbury Press, New York, 2012)

Howe, Daniel Walker, *What Hath God Wrought: The Transformation of America, 1815–1848* (Oxford University Press, New York, 2007)

King, Charles, *A Memoir of the Construction, Cost, and Capacity of the Croton Aqueduct* (Charles King, New York, 1843)

Lacour-Gayet, Robert, *Everyday Life in the United States before the Civil War 1830–1860* (Frederick Ungar Publishing, New York, 1969)

Lawson, Thomas William, and Thompson, Winfield Martin, *The Lawson History of America's Cup: A Record of Fifty Years* (Thomas W Lawson, Boston, 1902)

Levy, Daniel S., *Manhattan Phoenix: The Great Fire of 1835 and the Emergence of Modern New York* (Oxford University Press, New York, 2022)

Marszalek, John F., *The Petticoat Affair: Manners, Mutiny, and Sex in Andrew Jackson's White House* (The Free Press, New York, 1997)

McPherson, James M, *Battle Cry of Freedom: The Civil War Era* (Oxford University Press, New York, 1988)

Murphy, Sharon Ann, *Other People's Money: How Banking Worked in the Early American Republic* (Johns Hopkins University Press, Baltimore, 2017)

National Archives, Founders Online (founders.archives.gov)

Randall, J. G., *Constitutional Problems Under Lincoln* (University of Illinois Press, Urbana, 1951)

Rousmaniere, John, *The Low Black Schooner: Yacht America 1851–1945* (Mystic Seaport Museum Stores, Connecticut, 1986)

Scharf, J. Thomas, *History of Westchester County, New York, Including Morrisania, Kings Bridge, and West Farms* (L.E. Preston & Co., Philadelphia, 1886)

Smith, David A., *Presidents from Adams through Polk, 1825–1849: Debating the Issues in Pro and Con Primary Documents* (Greenwood Press, Westport, Connecticut, 2005)

Thane, Elswyth, *Mount Vernon is Ours: The Story of Its Preservation* (Duell, Sloan and Pearce, New York, 1966)

Train, Russell E., *The Bowdoin Family: Including Some Account of the Belgrave, Grinnell, Hamilton, Howland, Irving, Kingsford, Ligon, Means, Morris, and Sullivan Families* (Privately Published, Washington DC, 2000)

Unger, Harlow Giles, *Henry Clay: America's Greatest Statesman* (Da Capo Press, Boston, 2015)

Van Buren, Martin, *Inquiry into the Origin and Course of Political Parties in the United States* (Hurd and Houghton, New York, 1867)

Van Buren, Martin, *The Autobiography of Martin Van Buren* (Government Printing Office, Washington, 1920)

White, Richard, *The Republic for Which It Stands: The United States During Reconstruction and the Gilded Age, 1865–1896* (Oxford University Press, New York, 2017)

Wills, Garry, *Henry Adams and the Making of America* (Houghton Mifflin Company, New York, 2005)

Wood, Gordon S., *Empire of Liberty: A History of the Early Republic, 1789–1815* (Oxford University Press, New York, 2009)

Index

Adams, Charles Francis 98, 113, 135, 167
Adams, Henry 4, 120, 123, 143, 167
Adams, John 4, 16, 20, 123, 166
Adams, John Quincy 2, 14, 18, 25–28, 31, 33, 35–37, 39, 51, 63, 81, 95–98, 102, 113, 120, 122, 143, 147, 155
America (schooner) 106–110, 111, 171
Andrew, John A. 162–163
Antil, Frances see Tappan, Frances Antil

Biddle, Nicholas 52
Blatchford, Angelica Hamilton (daughter) 16, 64, 66, 69, 70, 74, 101, 134, 163, 171
Blatchford, Richard Milford (son-in-law) 66, 69, 134
Bowdoin, Frances Hamilton (daughter) 14, 64, 70, 170
Bowdoin, George Richard James (son-in-law) 64, 70, 170
Brown, John 125
Buchanan, James 121, 124, 138–140, 144
Burr, Aaron 7–8, 16–17, 74, 83, 171

Calhoon, John C. 2, 18, 34, 40–41, 43–44, 51, 59–62, 95, 123, 126, 166
Cass, Lewis 57, 74, 97, 98, 121
Chase, Salmon P. 2, 55, 86, 119, 142–147, 162–163
Clay, Henry 2, 18, 25–27, 32–33, 36, 42, 43, 51, 54, 61, 86, 95, 97, 106, 133, 148
Constitution of the United States 1, 4, 19, 25, 27, 34, 45, 61, 80, 82, 119, 126, 130–132, 137–141, 145, 146, 149, 154–155, 160, 165
Constitutional Convention 1, 5, 118, 130, 155, 171
Crawford, William 18, 25–26, 35

Davis, Jefferson 153, 167
Donelson, Andrew Jackson 41, 122

Donelson, Emily 41
Dorr Rebellion 93
Douglas, Stephen 120, 133, 135, 145
Douglass, Frederick 93, 103
Duane, William 57

Eaton, John 40–44, 52
Eaton, Margaret O'Neal Timberlake 40–44, 172
Emancipation Proclamation 152–154, 156, 159

Fillmore, Millard 106, 110, 122
Fish, Nicholas 22, 120–122
Fremont, John Charles 120–123

Gallatin, Albert 7–8, 36, 50, 53, 56
Garrison, William Lloyd 49, 65, 80
Grant, Ulysses S. 167, 169

Hamilton, Alexander (father) 1–9, 11, 12, 14, 19–24, 32, 34, 35, 45, 50, 53, 69, 74, 75, 82–83, 92, 117, 118, 136, 141, 146–147, 157, 162, 164–166, 171
Hamilton, Alexander (brother) 4, 10, 11, 70, 74, 111, 114, 116, 134, 161, 163, 169
Hamilton, Alexander (son) 15, 36, 63, 64, 66, 68–70, 82, 92–93, 111, 114, 127, 140, 157, 162, 168, 169, 170–172
Hamilton, Alexander (nephew) 15, 67, 69, 117, 143, 157, 162
Hamilton, Angelica (sister) 4, 6, 9, 128
Hamilton, Angelica (daughter) see Blatchford, Angelica Hamilton
Hamilton, Angelica Livingston (daughter-in-law) 66, 70, 93, 169
Hamilton, Elizabeth Schuyler (mother) 1–6, 8–10, 12, 16, 20–24, 28, 63–65, 74, 75, 105, 115–116, 150, 161

Index 199

Hamilton, Elizabeth (daughter) see Schuyler, Elizabeth Hamilton
Hamilton, Frances (daughter) see Bowdoin, Frances Hamilton
Hamilton Grange (New York) 5–6, 9, 10, 28, 67, 75
Hamilton, James of Scotland (grandfather) 4, 78
Hamilton, John Church (brother) 3, 4, 11, 16, 67, 73, 114, 134, 143, 161, 163, 170
Hamilton, John Cornelius (nephew) 73
Hamilton, Mary (daughter) see Schuyler, Mary Hamilton
Hamilton, Philip (brother) 4, 6–7, 83
Hamilton, Philip the Younger (brother) 8, 45, 134, 163, 170
Hamilton, Mary Morris (wife) 11–12, 64, 74, 88, 163, 172
Hamilton, William Stephen (brother) 65, 73, 115
Harrison, William Henry 86, 88
Holly, Elizabeth Hamilton (sister) 115–116, 134

Irving, Washington 7, 10, 36, 66, 67–68, 70, 92, 109, 114

Jackson, Andrew 2, 11, 14, 18, 25–26, 28–34, 37–39, 40–44, 46–48, 50–58, 59–62, 65–66, 69, 74, 76, 77, 80, 86, 92, 95, 124, 139, 159, 172
Jackson, Rachel 29, 38, 40
Jefferson, Thomas 3, 7–8, 10, 16, 35, 36, 50, 118, 161, 164–166
Johnson, Andrew 163, 167, 168

King, Charles 17, 22, 71, 73, 109, 146
King, John A. 124–125
King, Rufus 4, 20, 22, 136
King, Samuel 92–93

Lafayette, George Washington 103–104
Lee, Robert E. 143, 162
Lincoln, Abraham 2, 117, 133, 135, 141–145, 152–153, 156, 158, 159, 162, 163, 167
Livingston, Brockholst 7
Livingston, Edward 45–46, 48, 52, 57

Madison, Dolley Payne Todd 5, 14, 65, 105
Madison, James 4, 5, 10, 13–14, 26, 50, 155, 161, 165
Marshall, John 2, 20–22
Marszalek, John F. 41–42
McClellan, George B. 152, 159
McLane, Louis 43, 47–48, 54–57, 170
Monroe, James 25, 26, 165
Morris, Gouverneur 9, 11, 15
Morris, Richard 11
Morris, Robert 4, 34, 172
Mount Vernon 16, 21, 150–151

Nevis (Caribbean) 3, 68, 172
Nevis (Hamilton estate) 67–70, 127–128, 168, 169, 172
New York American (publication) 17, 22, 71

Pendleton, Nathaniel 11, 20
Polk, James K. 94–96, 99

Reynolds, Maria 5
Rush, Benjamin 6

Schuyler, Elizabeth Hamilton (daughter) 12, 63–65, 69, 70, 74–77, 106, 113, 116, 141, 157–158, 162, 163, 171
Schuyler, George Lee (son-in-law) 12, 63–66, 69, 70, 74–77, 86–93, 106–108, 111, 114, 158, 163, 169, 170–171
Schuyler, Georgina (granddaughter) 168, 171
Schuyler, Louisa Lee (granddaughter) 116–117, 141, 168, 171
Schuyler, Mary Hamilton (daughter) 16, 64, 66, 70, 116, 150–151, 158, 163, 169, 171
Schuyler, Philip (grandfather) 4, 6
Schuyler, Philip George (grandson) 171
Scott, Dred 81, 129, 130, 133, 162
Scott, Winfield 85, 88, 140, 142–143, 145
Stanton, Edwin 157
Sumner, Charles 113, 119–120, 162, 168
Swartwout, Samuel 46–47, 86

Tallmadge, Benjamin 4
Talleyrand, Charles-Maurice 74, 82–83
Taney, Roger B. 57, 81, 130–132, 162

Tappan, Arthur 14, 49
Tappan, Benjamin 14
Tappan, Frances Antil 14, 49
Tappan, Lewis 14
Taylor, Zachary 96, 98, 106
Thirteenth Amendment 141, 156, 161–162
Three-Fifths Compromise 4, 16, 18, 49, 137, 141, 146, 168
Trinity Church (New York) 4
Tyler, John 86, 87–88, 95, 123

Van Buren, Martin 2, 7, 12, 17, 25, 27, 31, 32, 33, 37–39, 41–43, 46, 48, 49, 52, 54–55, 59, 62, 76, 77, 81, 84–86, 98, 164–166, 172
Van Ness, William 17
Ver Planck, Johnston 17
Victoria, Queen of England 78, 104, 108–109

War of 1812 13
Washington, Bushrod 21–22
Washington, George 1, 3, 4, 7, 13, 16, 19–24, 25, 68, 83, 105, 112, 118, 139, 162, 165, 172
Webster, Daniel 2, 85–86, 87–88, 97, 126

Dear Reader,

We hope you have enjoyed this book, but why not share your views on social media? You can also follow our pages to see more about our other products: facebook.com/penandswordbooks or follow us on X @penswordbooks

You can also view our products at www.pen-and-sword.co.uk (UK and ROW) or www.penandswordbooks.com (North America).

To keep up to date with our latest releases and online catalogues, please sign up to our newsletter at: www.pen-and-sword.co.uk/newsletter

If you would like a printed catalogue with our latest books, then please email: enquiries@pen-and-sword.co.uk or telephone: 01226 734555 (UK and ROW) or email: uspen-and-sword@casematepublishers.com or telephone: (610) 853-9131 (North America).

We respect your privacy and we will only use personal information to send you information about our products.

Thank you!